as has, so let

Tom Eagle

WHITE LIGHT

THE LOST VISION OF MONTANA

anabasis

Tom Eagle, **WHITE LIGHT**
The Lost Vision of Montana
Copyright, Thomas Lowe Taylor, 1978, 2000
isbn 1-930259-12-3

my left hand to Vincent Ferrini
who has seen this through

Published by
anabasis Oysterville Wa 98641-0216
anabasis@willapabay.org
distributed by amazon.com

The Alleye Trilogy:
White Light, the lost vision of Montana
The One, The Same and The Other,
  Spectacular Diseases/Texture Press, 1992
Mandala, for her of the earth's whole place & name
  www.willapabay.org/~anabasis

Book One
RETURN OF EAGLE

Chapter 1   KUNG FU

"I sat there on the coast of Marseilles. . ."   Mr. Jimmy.

The point is to remember.

Light comes slowly through the narrow slot in the curtains, gray light makes the room somewhat larger than it really is, or softer, it makes the air in the room thicker.

"You...make it so hard to forget...." His stomach made no resistance to the coffee. He thought that after he had felt the first, perfect taste of the fresh-ground French Roast, that his stomach would knot up against the acids, but, no, it just tasted good, he was awake in the gray light, in the quiet of beginning thoughts and the imperfect reasoning of his life magnified by what he was into an opening in the wall, and the fervor of leaning forward into acts & seasons.

"No, I still did not get over you. . . ."

But beginnings of projects are simple enough: a resolute description of energy, the flux of presence at the start of a description. He watched his face before he spoke: a singular twisting of muscles around the limits of his face, the foot taps once or twice, his hands did a compulsive number, shoulders thrown left and then right, exploding *word word word*.

Speech is explosive, but remembering is ingestive, digestive, precursor to thought, the cool drift past feelings hopscotch into mental spaces identified as a range of action; remember what and for & both.

A story is simple enough to tell; there is the impulse to speech in conversation, "I know!" and the rest proceeds fitfully out of rest and energy.

Well, let's see, the first poem. . . really, the love poems to Sea in college, revolved, exploded like a beginning, could be fifteen, no sixteen years ago.

2

So yesterday he put them away for awhile, all the poems; no, he put them away. He finished the Ghost poem of return and release yesterday morning.

He and Tom went to the Xerox at 8:40, they were just open. Black hair, coffee, nothing is going on. . . . "Someone should be documenting this," Tom says.

"Go ahead, run it yourself," the guy says, and leaves us alone to watch the green light slide back and forth, pages popping out, two and two. . . .Two copies, hot off the press the day it's completed. Facsimile notepages from accordion infinite Jap notebook ricepaper feltpen blots review the craft now perfect, studied acts of balance and synchronicity; but finished, now, the lines expand to fill the space they have, twenty-six pages in doubled sevens followed him page by page the three weeks of the quest-adventure-journey, this one, that is.

So somehow the completion of the poem and the stomach protest, a poison passing through, are related. Sharon says it's Mcdonald's, and really, he agreed. And Jack-in-the-Box for lunch, it's no wonder you fell apart, you've been going, yeh, three weeks full speed ahead and then crash and burn.

It's mailed to Sea, his original home, the imprint of his life, unseen unthought for years away his whole life went zooming by at full throttle into its two marriages, a specific turn and glimmer at the avant-garde of poetics, superhip, top-of-the-line, crash and burn, and painting houses, or rather *house*, house after house, for three years, almost to the point of talking, mumbling to himself, poetry as suppressed speech.

Top corner, edge of brush thrust or stuck, hand-eye, pulls the line across, a straight and perfect freehand edge of color against bare wood. The latex stuff sinks into the wood slightly, runs along the surface, all the bones in his hands moved independently, muscles pull puppet-wires, the mind commands, "Work!" it says. You speak and I listen.

Slap of brush against inside of bucket, hit the wall and pull fast, the radio playing or yelling at the forest, "Bounce back!" it says. The day is moving ten o'clock and half way across the front cutting in. The fastest painter in Mazola, Montana, the forty year old dynamic demon, flailing furious leaves across the wind, his families loved and scattered, the roller sleeve jammed into the five gallon bucket, rubbed or pulled or scraped across the screen and thrown up onto the wall, splat, and pulling down and bending over the music the joints the beer the hustle and sweat makes your body breathe as fast as this the speed of light is how you see, can the body go that fast. . . .

A welcome change from teaching, ten years was long enough to be enclosed, and anyway, when the war is over, and you've won, you should re-tire, it says.

"I. . .haven't stopped loving you yet. . . ."

Tom left the article out for him about the man who was a woman, a single-parent father trying to boogie with two kids in the other room: which was familiar enough

3

to him, Laurie and him on the back porch, the third time around, three faces in the window, really, watching my three sons skate the past few years back and forth, the ladies, turning over every rock in Mazola, they squint up into the sunlight, "What do you want. . .with me. . ." He drops the rocks back.

Alone three years, wedged into an old used-up hippie slot, watching the familiar faces become older men tied into their anxieties, lightly hoping, scared to move an inch, witnesses of failure, they held onto their jobs and lost their minds, stopped eating, grew beards of sadness, left their families, bought new houses. Sought new lives and slightly missed.

He lived on the air.

So they mailed the poem off to New York, his stomach collapsed, they talked about novels after dinner, again, about voice and stance and passion, and left-over television at ten o'clock. He took his stomach to bed and watched dirty movies in his mind to fall asleep, again.

Santa Barbara sun-signs, after three years of no beach or being, he really thought he had disappeared into the hole in the sunset, after the years of professional baseball Poetics, slip-sliding through the packs of losers and imitators, brief encounters with art super-hustlers, the image of new words and languages hung like a carrot, "the antennae of the race." Which was OK as far as it went, but no bucks. A fine and happy life, one says, a good hobby. Get a job. Whew.

There is that distance between meditation and success, he supposed, where the poem lies to hand in spasmic intensity, aptly said. The cosmic masturbator in his realm.

All that, and running mad-dog crazy twenty years they never caught him, he was always careful to go to the woods to howl at the moon. You wouldn't want them to see you frothing at the soul, would you? Those are private moods and griefs and the whole motive to be crazy and public deprives poetry of its romance and the poet of his power. The old ways are used up. There are words and the states of being alive: the words. . .

Only just healed over, only a year ago, at point nine of the second nervous breakdown he said "Help!" and go for it, the lady sends him to her shrink, or captor he said; and then over to Dean who sewed him up in six hours of intense recall the pain, the pain is gone, the neurotic motive built into syntax and style, another transformation has taken place, he was a man at last. He was still sighing over it.

A simple enough story is simple enough. But it's not simple, either, and simply the events do not describe the ambience, the melange of the totality of the career, the madness, the release into the mundane return. It is dramatic enough, and when you finish with all that, suddenly, in the dead center middle of your life, why, what a release to your seeing, even, even the colors renew the intensity of their power, even the size of things diminishes, part of consciousness recedes to its proper distance.

The cosmic adventure of poet super-hero is a captivating dream-world: the quest for the Beloved, the secret garden, symbolic energy states correspond to mystical diagrams. But it is exhausting and, perhaps, not quite real. There is the art business to consider, and the potential for bucks, and where we are now, he'd said, the whole thing turns on just that.

But an attitude toward what was happening right now would be different.

Buzzword cha-cha, total chatterflap, psychobabble. The distance of Montana unreal distance, end of the line, in 1970 you dig a hole and crawl in, which he did, and only now, on Easter Sunday 1978 did the miracle reoccur in him, they pushed the rock away and stroll about, revived, renewed, returned from solitude. Those poor monks, man, he sits there and spends a year or two designing his own mandala, and then they sit him in front of a wall and he paints the sign in front of him, his own, while they wall him in. For twelve years he meditates on his own mandala, and then they let him out.

Well, he put that away, too. He insisted on being ordinary, otherwise, where's the world? His genius, friends. . .his genius-friends. . ."Oh, yes, that's him up there, a crazy lonely genius poet with his cosmic diagrams blocked out on the floor, he just walks around in them. . . ."

It's all true, every word of this, and everything they say. Only the innocence has been maintained to protect the names. So you sit in the laundromat, two inches away from some immense anxiety ghost, "drilled out on loco weed," and the fat lady comes in and talks and talks; you relax after awhile and then it's over, and you fold up your laundry and go home to nothing and no-one, your perfect note-books are still set around importantly. It's a good depth to resort to, to spend time there, but the whole vision of the whole life has got to have inclusion at its end. They're all there, for instance, from Faulkner to Olson, stoned out, boozed out at the end, down with the boys or the ladies, freaks and parasites, strung out, pushed down, Nobel-ed or other. Top of the line lonely, or sailing streams aside for love, for love would the macho give up his life. The husband-man returns and calls the world a healing place. He wrote that.

Then who was he, Eagle flown, seed-sown son of the sun-son, a species of light returned from the soul's darkness, is that who he was? Names resound too loosely, they go by too fast. What did you say, the intense irregular other sings his song against the tides.

Slow now, says the voice, don't run away with it, ah, the telephone rings and the business of varnishing cabinets intervenes and the music from the other room returns the rest of the day from the remembering that took place.

"You've got it, you've got the voice," Sharon says.

"A novelist, is there a novelist in the room," she says.

He went through the light to the place on the other side. There is a bridge there, and men can cross it safely. This is a poet's book. Anyway, in your mind, in your experiencing of dreams of power, there are places to cross, and none of it is done without seeing, just as we have been told, and none of it is without seeing.

And the friends are there, and they have names, too, Buffalo and Eagle and Bear and Owl and the rest are all spoken names which only the heart hears, there are no other words in the place across the light for it is only the place before the Great Light of which nothing is spoken.

Well, the time before the crossing is generally the Great Fear. That is only feeling and it is not expressed. But only thought itself is unrecognized as something which passes.

Two small bowls recede in thought to piercing arrows.

The names are gone.

* *

The Sea is my home, from the Sea I came, to the Sea, my return.

Picture this. Ordinary sunny late January day the thin air of Mazola clear, it's cold, sort of, no snow on the ground, an indication in the air that the year is new. '77 is done, at last, we all say, a dead space following the great bicentennial hype, but empty. '78 we all say, is the year to break out, break on through to the other side; really, it is in the air.

Now Mazola is my town, and I control my behavior as much as possible, careful to exactness that my new, squared-away self be recognizable. I drink too much, but then it's a little bit hip to be a little bit alcoholic in this part of the world. Ex-prof painting contractor hippie Tom who writes every day, lives alone with impressive and beautiful eleven year old Alex. Dumpy Isla Vista pink house.

So diddley-bop, I come up the sidewalk for lunch and hit the front door into clean well-lighted place, the white kitchen shines through the doorway of the living room, two long steps. . . .

"Hi, Kathy, what's happening." Long dark hair, thin, large breasts carried halter-high, clean open face personality being, good near-husband Dan. Twenty-four-year olds, he an ex dealer from Japan, stories of a quarter in bills in a cardboard box under his bed, ran from it, stashed it, can't get it. . .going straight, full energy Aquarian brother, and Joshua, the two-year-old, "Erdo?" living in my basement all winter, really.

"Oh, nothing much. There's a letter for you on the stereo; my tickets for Japan came. . ." she says songly. On my heel, "on the record player...."

Into the living room a beige square envelope. It's my own handwriting! Amazing, who is this fr. . . .

And from about two light years away, my long eye traverse the darker space, slow telephoto shot of infinite depths, slow trajectory of stars and planets and satellites, the green earth subsides pleasant acres shower light upon my house, the postman blue uniformed turning away from the mailbox, days after the big four, running hard at forty, my nets and fathoms cast around the town, the beige letter envelope in my hand, slowly turning slow, the very impatience of my life, no love around the bend, eye, eyes focus slowly form the recognition, the word, "Sea". . . .

The rush. My stomach sinks, my temples throb, I gasp aloud "My God. . ." I am not given to gasping. My feet and fingertips sweat, my heart pounds briefly, and at the millisecond of light, I black out.

"Do you know what this is. . . ."

"What, what!" Kathy says. For three months, like brother and sister, we have talked about love and loneliness, about poetry and life, about fathers and families, my three, no, four children, ah, the four.

"This, this is, uh, from, my God, fifteen years; this is all the way back."

Happy face, she says, I give her eyes, the recall of the smell of classrooms, of her flesh, the head swarming ecstasies, the stairway up from somewhere to the cloud heights.

"This is the original blonde." I look at the letter with my handwriting on it, carefully jam it open, the pages, two! And opening to, the photograph.

The thousand words describe her face unchanged, the cleft nose-tip, immense features perfect mouth, and the hair held by windblown studio-shot and the eyes which speak and reach out: receded, thought-full, unfulfilled and seeking, speaking my name, an immediate recognition flows the loop is now unbroken return the long snake lazily grabs his tale begins to turn, return.

"Tom," she says, 19 Jan the day before my birthday; I am stumbling into my room, the chair at the old rolltop halfdesk. I read ". . .An enormous intake of breath, all the wonderings and wanderings of how to write you - - a space signed with love?" I am crying. "All the events of these quick years - - all the growing up."

And more, "Ernie sent. . . a striking picture," All right! And more. "Tried to reach you last summer," did she get the book? "The first really concentrated effort. . .write me a letter or a tap dance," crazy life, an "actress", poems, journeys of the spirit, an animal of the earth.

She speaks, she is completed! "...you gave me nourishment. . .too foolish to really understand how one worked with such elements / All this time that is really a firefly. . . .Sea."

The sea of Sea: diving return of light around the heart, the sea breaking on my shore, the sea of light in which we live together man and woman sung alive and well, no dream has broken open here I am, here I am again among the sea.

I sit back, astounded, thinking. I tried to send her my first, self-made book; a prose poem to love in my private language, about the love affair with Michelle, a Pisces lady who was also a copy of the original as well as being herself. In July, just after it was finished, I sent a copy to her via her brother, who lived ironically in a town called Freedom.

No, my God, it was old Ernie, wa hoo, I remember the sequence of events, calling cousin Mike in December to check on a rumor of her existence from a letter from my mother.

More than that, I am surprised to see my life returning, and to its roots: I ran from graduate school the tunnels of the poet's career in the battles of the sixties, a hard, hit-and-run career of ten years in the front lines, teaching jobs and writing, a strange cowboy life in almost modern dress. I thought when I crash-landed on a final personal retreat, near divorce already two children and one in the oven, that I had evaded my past, a pioneer, the first hippie to build in Ah-lee.

"Well, they should leave them alone here," the guys said, when they delivered the truckload of 2 x 4's and particleboard with which I built my house.

The long letter resumes, my own response, I mean, my own.   I summarize to four pages of delight, unexpressed sentences run around my solitary room: desk, bed, stereo with one speaker, table I built for Jody, double 16 x 20 prints of abstracted snow forms photograph on the wall, an old oriental rug, the strange queen birdwhistle from a pottery in Mexicali, my "corpse-box" of papers and three more cardboard boxes stashed by the heat vent. They were mildewing in the closet.

"You are the original imprint of my life. . .yr Eagle."

And the poem, from somewhere past the middle of "The Solitudes," a list of erotic midwinter fantasies.

"Light's power arrived at calmer signs collected, hours repeat, the years do not exist, sweet lady, yr eyes reach out from deep within a perfect face, feathers flying forward scan the air between yr arms, my heart encompass sailing arcs of light, and love redeems us parted somewhere past the corner of the wall, returns again, implicit in our lives this term and sign renews the time against yr body, warmer, present, expressed, the final arrival, year and room, white light bending slowly from around you, walking slowly forward, hearing my name." The next day, more. . . with ". . .hands across the light, you are, the moment, sailing."

Amazing. "I have totally dismantled my life," I write, "Standing here absolutely free, almost self supporting, I have cast off the old neurotic life, of pain and art, I am a man first and a poet after. For a long time I had it quite the other way around. I learned about the pain, it's been almost a year since my healing and five since the vision. . ."

What can I say: the I Ching is shouting at me for the last and the next month, Chen, the arousing, in fear and trembling he sets his life in order. Tell me about it. Treading, he steps upon the tiger's tale, it does not bite him! Success! I mean, really.

I borrow twelve cents from Kathy and head for the post office.

* *

The days follow: late night phone calls, the deep musical rumble of the sea, dirty jokes, cosmic cackle, "I'm all right!" Humping the bed and laughing. "Alex, that was the lady from New York, in the picture."

"I thought so," he says. He thought so, he's great.

Then my mother calls and plans for me to visit them in Oakland in their new condo. Three hundred old people, getting it on. I call Sharon in Santa Barbara, my sister-in-law, Sue's brother Tom and Sharon; they hid out smoking dope at our Detroit house the year before the whole city blew, harbinger year; yes, I'll visit. "But you said that last year. I'll never see you again." "Give me a month." Sea and I have our rendezvous.

So I pack and unpack about thirty times. Wally calls with a quick hundred dollar day painting at the duplex Wally's building for himself on spec. A twenty-six year old maniac speed freak beautiful guy coke head careful woodbutcher builder, solid son of the only farmer in Ah-lee to give me work. Dan and Kathy split, she and the kid to Japan and he to some sunny rooms in Bonner. Steve and I paint the soffit on the duplex and Alex packs his cello and skateboard and goes to stay with Frannie my exfriend good friend who runs the Gilded Lily New York tea room lunches dinners the only espresso machine in the northwest, I think, hustled off of old Pete Yegen. The only coffee in Mazola, Montana and I buy my $55.00 ticket on the Dog.

Wally rolls me some joints while I read Penthouse the day before I go.

* *

We join the community without any separate aims of our own. Wilhelm

The Dog.

The alarm at 5:30. Frannie loaned me her clock after dinner last night, I tucked Alex in and a good hug, strong voice, "OK, yeh, see you later, I'm off on my adventure." Walked home with the alarm clock under my arm.

Wow, dark, coffee's on I'm ready to call a cab, and Steve's up from the basement, shy-sly smile on his face overruns. . . . I mean, we have a rendezvous in San Francisco, just before Easter, coexistent fables: for a true story, my heart is pounding, for real.

I must have smoked that half ounce in two weeks, the hot little brass bowl, copper tube jammed in, sealed with window glazing from the job.

I'm going down to see my beloved old parents, seventy-five is not yet eighty or ninety or a hundred is a good target. . . . and my Beloved, face to face: a shock for the poet in me. The release of tension and energy parallel each other, I'm soaring, loose, the romantic heart meets reality, it is too much!

And Easter Sunday, my personal holiday: walking up the perfect canyon at Big Sur Hot Springs in 1960 pre pre Esalen days, with Mary, the original redhead, first near-mother, ah, Tiajuana, my grief, tears and shock. . . Harvey in the little house by the big house; making love with The Mare in gray light of huge front room, Harvey in the dark, burning tics off his arm with matches. Croquet on the lawn. Lighting Chumley on fire and throwing him off the cliff, a dog. Piloting the fleet out of Miami for L. Ron, his PR man. . . .

So when the cab comes, I am out the door, all to easily to be believed, a dark exit from three years' stasis and patience, and something in mind. I'm so exhausted from the two weeks prior tension and hard work hustling the last few bucks to be hustled, scamming the Dog, I sleep about half way, except for some snapshots: At Biggs Junction, on the Columbia River, the Dog turns left, down to Bend and the long run to Klamath Falls, wha, two hundred and fifty miles. A windy roadstop freeway zooming on to Portland. The big trucks lined up, the fucking wind: I'm out by the rocks, three matches to light a joint, toke, toke, the wind blows the tip off. I go around the corner to get out of the wind and there's three or four People there, a fat lady and her young daughter both drunk, the daughter wants a joint, both of them ugly and human and loud. I roll the roach into some tobacco and stand there anyway smoke up and head in for dinner. I finally get a double Blackjack on the rocks, a Michelob and order roast beef and. . .

It's a slim gray pile of strange thin flat things, with dark brown thick paste set around, oozed, the soft mound of white, and little green globes, the foxy waitress unconcerned, I am hungry enough to eat this. . .stuff, and do and get on the bus, a young driver from Trailways, and we get a good rap up for the hours into Bend, a nice sunset ride down the line, my thoughts have not left the center of the double drama I'm into, into.

First day in a new notebook, The California Ghost Fly-by, which it certainly is, which I certainly am. Information, like pools, and feeling. I mean, what am I doing? I'm another guy, housepainter on vacation, coming back to the state of California, after, really, seven years up in the sticks, in the Montana of the world, two divorces, a house, another sedentary life overturned.

And the poet's life, strangely off key: I never doubted in the least the direction my writing took, those lyrics and long lines sweeping out, twelve pagers, intense strange codes unwinding through the various descriptions of consciousness, never once doubted that I was right. And the strange total disregard I encountered: at first anger and despair, and finally a retreat and indifference, ah, my own fame, and suddenly, a new tack on the matter, a release from any attitude at all about "The Poems." Well, it's what I do, and what I do, I do well. . . authentic.

And that magnifies in both directions. But the mundane life, ah, so welcome. How do I tell Bill Cummings, if not here, that he saved my life by teaching me how to paint houses: when he yelled on the phone to me, in Berkeley 1967 "You think that if a guy has to go out and work for his money, that he's a sucker. . . ." And I had to admit yes, to him, I remember that one, in a payphone on Telegraph Ave, just up from the house, our scrungy hippie pad, across the street from the Genius, Art Lives.

But the bus rolls on, the faithful Dog that stops at every stick and post along the way, and these are the meditations that go along the way, you are, there, in your seat, and bobbing up and down, exhausted, stoned, in transition from one life and into another, your own, both, it is all just what is happening, and that serves to pin a name on it, there, you are.

Crossing the bridge, light to light, back from where I was into where I am, here, returned from the cloud heights, those are the delusions, and love, the calm center of my life, named in the Sea to which I return, ah, the carrot, I bob and weave along the trail, man-man nude, the dogs around me, ahead, Ed's dog Gabriel runs ahead and stops to turn once in awhile,"He's a good trip-dog," he said, "He'll take care of you," and how he did! Fifteen miles in and five back to the truck.

Long ago in another time, and all that. . . .

The Dog rolls on. Out of Spokane, earlier that day, after a quick breakfast and throwing the coins, I sit up by the front door. Blue sky makes a hemisphere, some white puff-clouds stretch across the light. The rains have come, and probably saved the day, the summer windstorms won't blow us off. Edge of green among gray stubble weed, there are pools of water here and there, blue sky and clouds in the. The flat earth rolls and sounds, the soft flesh of Eastern Washington.

And Mazola looming in my background, a prison-place, a chrysalis place, up in the woods, living the poet's dream of greatness and isolation and solitude, "fronting the essential life;" reading the myths of the shaman and thinking that I'm a god, and cut off so far away from ordinary human life, ah, then, this Return which is so storybook and which is nonetheless happening, to me, I don't ask, and drift back asleep, coming up to the light, the pools along the road, and ducks in them, pieces of sky with birds floating in them, diving down. Or up.

There is still paint on my hands, from Wally's soffit. Walking around it, roller on the end of a twenty foot pole, absolutely leaning on it, pressing around in one day, Steve up and down the ladder on the windows, or coming down the roof hanging onto the rope with one hand, it is tied to a tree on the other side, bucket and brush in the other, for $5 an hour. I mean, really!

But if you're surviving, we say, that's the point. A little Welfare and food stamps, a little dealing here and there, living the good life, they call it. Strange acceptance of lesser lives; the bus rolls across Eastern Washington, down to the wide Columbia, my God it's a big river all along the dry bare hills, and in the summer, whew! how much longer is this transit?

The cool winds scatter harmlessly, it's been an easy winter, plenty of water, houses going up left and right, the boom is coming and everybody rubs his hands together, they're coming, up from California, they sell their houses for a hundred and fifty, buy up here for sixty, and live on the rest. I've seen them at K-Mart, pointed boots, mouton collar down jackets, sleek gray, doin nothin, just hangin around. For awhile, maybe even ten tears, we parasitize off each other, but without jobs, we're only postponing a confrontation between work and workers.

So the rap goes, the bus is only a small projectile floating smooth across the photograph on the wall. Bus trips I have taken, up and back twice in two weeks from Palo Alto to Mazola on a hundred dollar pass, I packed my boxes quickly in Gerard's driveway, Patrick didn't understand why his closest of all possible playmates, his twin, perhaps, Alex, had moved back to Montana, indeed, why he had wanted to. . . but that's life and family and lives intertwined, and even singing Country Roads together, and crying, man, let's get out of here. Calling Ann, another time, from the Palo Alto Dog Station, smoking dope all fternoon at Tom's apartment, Big Tom, mysto-macho, and touching her big breasts, she's seventeen, head spinning firming of flesh nipples, eyes go soft at touches, the lines around the floor are smooth and crystal clear. We rode bikes all afternoon around the green-tree city, watched the tennis players in the park; I gave her a hoot, she went around the corner, turned, eyes on eyes at fifty yards, smile, pop! she's gone. The Dog.

From Klamath Falls, where the Trailways guy gives me a little sensimilla bud and tells me how to smoke in the bathroom at the back of the bus, down into Weed, into Red Bluff, first sign of California body types, nation-state consciousness, actor styles, psycho-types, the fox with child, the Mexican parents, the fat lady and daughter, and the loud, modern young guy, San Francisco and the world about him. Out of Red Bluff, we talk all the way into Oakland about schizophrenic fantasy events, weird work scenes, carrying bags of manure all day, and the strange story of Sister Something and her Morphine Habit in TIME.

Somewhere north of Woodland we make a quick stop at the roadside rest. We get out for a joint; "Are you guys smoking pot?" the old guy asks. He'd throw us off. "Not on the bus," I say.

"Well, you can call me J.J., or you can call me Junior, You can call me Johnnie or you can call me Just Jack. . ." It's John Jackson, fresh from three months at an apiary, working for $1.85 an hour, headed back to his North Beach hotel. . . there's a writer in Mazola by that name. Are you a writer, yeh I'll call you from Oakland. I'm going up to Napa for a forty dollar bag on Thursday morning. I'm going to see my folks for the weekend. . . I go on.

The green hills of California, saved by rain, a reprieve. Washed clean, it looks great down the line and into the green green hills of Contra Costa County, where have I been? I watch the traffic line up at Bay Meadows at 7:30. We roll into the Oakland terminal and I sit in the coffee shop over the I Ching and my poem. I throw the coins three times. Eagle has landed.

* *

4.8.78

Eastside Branch Library, Santa Barbara Public Library System. Martin Luther King Jr. Memorial Wing. Montecito Street. Buzz of BMW eases left. Rock n roll car radio chamois over wet bronze painted ma-chine. Old guy at the drive-up book drop, cars easing up. It opens at ten.

About nine I give a buzz. "Oh, you should have called when you got in," my mother crackles with excitement.

"Oh,I had to write," I say.

"Well, I'll be down in a minute."

In front, the black guys running cabs and numbers and each other; jive talk and serious, different colored cars roll by, the street is slow for Monday morning. I'm loose against the wall, stuffed-up zipper bag and tight leather briefcase, no handles, "Pure Juice" sticker on the side. Really; long hair blows around, the green Mercedes and my mother, a little spaced, roll by.

A few minutes and I'm waving her down at the second pass.

"Well hi, my but you look great."

"Really," cool flush of yes, and she's older and smaller and I am older and larger. "I'm just great, really, different, changed. . .and Sea, I can't believe it."

"Well, I heard from Mike that she was in LA last summer looking for Willie, and I wrote it to you."

"Yeh," laugh, "I called him immediately. We must have decided, finally, to look for each other.

At the turn, many brick floors, a tall building, for my folks whom I remember in houses. I press the button on the Star Trek goodie and the steel grate slides up, we roll down into a cold dark garage, Mercedes, a battered VW Ghia, low concrete sprayed cream. Up the elevator. "They take forever."

Pete the soft old security guard. A process of signing in and out I don't really understand. I'm still stoned, exhausted. There is more to do here than wait for Sea's phone call Wednesday night. An acknowledgement, an endorsement, a passage from my old expired self into this new thing I see thrusting forward from my inner being, and it all revolves around my healing and Pisces, and the Pisces lady, Michelle.

Ah, the summer of '76, we all played "Together" together at the coffee house, the only show in town. In my old '56 Chevy red truck, ladders, paint, behind the coffee bar, chattering speedfreak long brown hair, the perfect ex-prof. The few guys I knew still teaching looked tired and strange and different, from the five years previous, but then none of them had been really crazy, let go into the full flaming jump of the it. Thank God they threw me out of that monastery. . . .

A blonde with White Shoulders, Well, say what you will, but it was a definite re-run of Sea. And, painting Val's place in mid-summer, had coaxed her over to my place, Michelle, to check the soup, and jumped into her mouth, and the next day, we had a nicely said talk about relationship and love and intenseness and how good it was,

But love's intenseness, from between the legs, the heart exploding, the release of wanting, expressions of all the rush from adolescence. We fell into dream fucks, the longer days repeated touch and song we lined the hours, rolled on top and underneath, in view of the freeway in the bushes, we played the same, still, poet and lady, housepainter and student. . . .

We rode the season down to fall. The hours broke open, pain white light rushed the darkness swallowed up my heart, her mother died, she went away, and the poem-book started only after the model had fled, I pushed through into December.

The Oakland skies are clear, the weather is amazing. I meet the old people in the elevator, everywhere, it's like what a friend said about being in Japan, you feel like Superman, they're all short, and they have our money. But the apartment is perfect, tasteful, like what my homes had evolved into, browns into greens, pale into chinese plates, eskimo sculpture into jade plants. I can see the evolution of the furniture even to where the couch has been recovered.

And the terrifying balcony, the Eagle afraid of ladders. But we sit down, I drop my bag and light a Sherman and then get up and get a glass of Old Crow, and we chatter, and. . . .

"But you look so well. . . John and Mike, both, heavy."

14

"Defeated, I think, by life in the civilized world. The hard cheap work of the last three years, wrestling with my failures, trying to get going, why I'm on top, really, and something's happening, I don't know what, but it's exciting and it's about the writing. . . .

And another glass and a long nap, and my father comes home from his work at the Conciliation Court, dealing with the children, one would hope, of broken situations. He comes in the door, we embrace a huge hug, I'm taller now and eyes across each other, I am calm at last, to be here, the pain of unknowing knots mended, at last the seas are parting, on my wing, return, at home.

At point nine of the second nervous breakdown, I finally cried for help. Michelle herself, hip to help and helping, turned a name my way. But first I set it up, a little magic of my own to throw me in, but not like 1973, I put my finger down my throat there, and here I was only making appointments and doing what I knew how to do, getting stoned.

I booked a bed in the psych ward and made an appointment with the only psychiatrist per se in town. It was the language I had studied. David and I went up to Jerry Johnson Hot Springs. About half way up I dropped some acid. We parked at the side of the long road that snakes along from Lolo Pass into Lewiston, Idaho, along the Lochsa. Across the wooden suspension bridge and up the trail between tall Ponderosa, the stream is white and frothy, it is December.

We drop our clothes and step into the first pool. It is only a bunch of rocks at the streambed, cold water runs around them and leaves us isolated in the heat. Gentle David knows a lot, a solid stock of physical body, a firm mind, a brother of the doobie, once we finished a roach clamped into his fly-tyer. We like each other, we painted houses and smoked our beers all summer. . . .

He dances from one pool to another and the acid begins to pull me in. We are lying in a perfect pool, head and toe, and talking about the light which plays around us in the heat. He leaves. I am floating in the pool. The clouds are reflected. In the peak of the rush, my cock floating through the clouds, the unconscious pops out one, two, three images all at the same time: I hear a voice a song an image of a face I do not know, the finger flicking at my penis "What a cute little thing." And the isolation, pain and dark hallway floating through that, into the intensity of my feelings is suddenly real I feel forever the first time the pit, the anger, the rejection, all the textbook shots are there and I take my photos.

Slowly, though, I imagine the moments in her body, I am not wanted.

I get up at six from the couch. I smoked my last joint out on the balcony last night and we sat in front of the tube. I had a Lowenbrau and it was all right, cruisin home over M*A*S*H and a mellow Alan Alda. I didn't care about anything and took the portable radio to bed with me.

At six the air is clean, the radio is on, traffic reports; I gaze down at the joggers circumventing Lake Merritt. Tall buildings have replaced Mazola. Strange figures with different sorts of minds flog about down there. There is no woods here, no solitary state; it is gone.

I get the Chronicle and make some coffee. I find the horoscope, but alas, it is not Omar. It's not the same at all. My father goes down first to breakfast. We check out the Chronicle and head down later, my mother and I trail the lighted hallway, aboard ship.

And the old people, one on one, couples, singles, companions, the lady like that, a spread of gray and white and friendliness, quite mellow, constant chatter of how do you do and. . . .

"My son, from Montana."

"Oh, really, it's nice of you to visit."   Few do.
"Your parents, just, fit in so well here."   Ultimate.
"Well, I want to know," my father says, eyes up from gray crewcut hair, "when are we going to visit the grand-daughter?" My heart leaps. I had thought there wouldn't be time. "How about today?"

We settle on after breakfast, and my father and I trek out to the freeway, across the Richmond San-Rafael Bridge and up to Sonoma State Hospital. The sun calls the birds around us, driven before a light wind, they hover close and stand in the bright air over green fields, water stands in close ditches, we turn up a dark back road, and follow signs among concrete state buildings past the switchboard, over to the parking lot, to the concrete steps up and into the nursery. How can I stand this?

I am near tears. . . .

Down the slick hall to the first left and into the large room, up to the crib, three feet off the floor, I find my daughter. She's got thin short brown hair and good color to her skin. Three years old, past the statistics against her survival. The spirit which emanates from her, a bright small light inside the body, and where parts are perhaps missing, the opening above the mouth which seems to go all the way in, and sleep where eyes should see, I pick her up, like a baby, my hand goes underneath and I bend over close, pull her to my chest and pick her up, and her absolute joy of sudden snarfling curiosity.

"Hello, little Mischa, it's your father," I choke out, eyes tearful, heartburst and proud.

My father and I go down the hall to the playroom, and I father around with this bumbly squiggly excited being from my life. She sees with the end of her tongue, and the palm of my hand does for a conversation.

We have some visitors A short Chicano lady, obviously one of the people who does much of the touching in this child's life, comes in.

"We are so happy you're here."

"My heart is full," I say, "She's obviously surrounded with love,"

"She's so responsive," she puts it out. And a young woman, serious, her life-teacher.

"Well, I finally realized that if she couldn't see, then how could she learn about eating, so after a lot of trying, we finally got her so she could eat by herself, and so she's now a priority for corrective surgery, and we think that will make her life a little better."

I get her to the couch, she has gotten quiet, and we sit there, my father and I, while I stroke her small back into sleep. All this time he is silent, watching me, I think.

"Really, it's almost corny," I continue. "When we put it together, me and the shrink, why it was so textbook. The daddy goes away to war, and mommy throws attention to the baby, some of it erotic, her last baby, she smothers it, was the word he used ,and daddy comes back and kicks the kid out and he hates them both, she rejects him for a total stranger."

"Yes," my father says from his ten year's practice at psychotherapy, "I always thought that when I was away, those years from three to five are the most important...."

"Really, that's what took Alex and me back to Montana. I thought that for better or worse, they'd have me there, Yar and Robin; there, still making up for my own father's 'failure', I would return."

"But then," he says slowly and thoughtfully, "You were Kate's and John was mine," he drops it in over lunch of crab louis and Wente's Gray Reisling, great! But it is the bombshell I had not anticipated, I had not included that in my re-run script, I am in fact doing the very same number with my own kids right now, his and hers. And I give it this shot: I put my head back, strike it with the heel of my right hand and say "Holy Tomato!" It is that relief.

And punishing my parents by failing out of job after job. Maybe that's the spirit of the sixties, like the monster movies from Japan, an attempt I from the cultural unconscious to explain the atom bomb, to make a myth of it. . .maybe the sixties is a legion of kids punishing their parents for World War II, led, in part, by one of them.

"I can understand that," I say, "but what I don't is this. Given my seriousness about my self. . ."

"To cover up your feelings of worthlessness and rejection," he says. We are driving through Vallejo. Self service gas. "And given the pain, why did I internalize it so totally? Why did I hold it in?" And we go on. Raveling out the soup of failed love affairs, this summary and sharing, a father and son finally coming around, a parable, a fable, a look like any other. And my brother, split apart from his family after twenty years of marriage; all this current of life and flow is sending shock waves of new growth through my senses. My very being is extracted from itself, it has flown separately into the light. After all the work and preparation, I see this moment as a summary of my life as a being from my family. It has fallen away entirely, and this visiting of my parents becomes a celebration of our separate lives, a passage.

* *

Wednesday night we are going out to dinner. In fact we drive up a few blocks and into a tight pewter named redwood and ivy place, ah, with a bar. We are all pretty loose together, at this point, and whatever went down went down pretty well unnoticed. It is a tight place where our words are framed close in by other people. Dinner in public, deranged poet and father harangue, share the wealth, over Jack Daniels and white table wine. It is hardly a moment to hold back. How can forty years of distance go by in this immediacy of eating, but it does.

"I can understand all that," I'm saying, "that either by pain or conscious will, the energy bypasses the heart, a Kundalini of pain. I mean, in all this time, I was never able to give myself, I was spiritually frigid. . . a sort of celibate, and now it seems as though, I don't know, like I'm living my life backwards, old Indian contrary, the cool reflective thought of an old man, and then erupted into madness, the passage, back into the calm, mundane, ordinary world of simply being myself. But alone. But well."

The Sea breaking on my shore; and literary history.

"It's different, you know," he says of Pisces. "It doesn't work like other writing, it's new, and you'll have to account for that."

"Yeh, it doesn't go by images," I say, ready to go, "it provokes the dreamer by its rhythms, direct transmission, it's trance-fiction. . . ."

"OK, but you must know what happened before to anyone who had something new to say," he's hunched over the table, 73, dynamic. My mother drove home, and, loose as we are, we'll have to walk back.

"Well, Gertrude said that in a time of war, the artist is the foremost of all tacticians, and that everybody looks around, suddenly, for new tactics, because they're afraid. Well, where are we now?"

"But it doesn't happen because it's right," he says very slowly and right on. "It happens because of getting your message to the right people in the right places...."

Years of unreturned manuscripts. Special fourth class book rate. "If they only knew," she said. Dropped into the memory hole. I mean, I went specially down to see Arguelles in Oakland three years ago, with the first Vision of Eagle and he got it through to what's his face in New Mexico of Shambala, I thought they were best for it, and he wrote me, Arguelles, something like ". . .most dramatic account of male initiation I have ever read." I mean I was stoked; and met with silence. Xerox copy

18

shitcanned, I suppose. And Bly's "The mind has enslaved you," for a signoff. I mean, really, what a trip!"

But the conversation on literary history goes on to the origins of consciousness, the split brained man, the reason for art, I mean we're sailing, and these poor people next to us, chatter away trying to cover us up, loose and rambling we finally get off the table and think about heading back to the apartment.

Up we get, he heads off to the men's room. There's some singles on the plate. He's feeling so good, he throws a ten on and goes off. I grab the ten and stuff it in my pocket and go out into the patio, to wait for my father so I can walk him home. What a rout.

"Sea called;" my mother says cutely, when we stumble in, "One o'clock tomorrow afternoon."

The night has turned wild inside my heart. Anticipation of voice over telephone. The second call she made to Mazola, we rambled on long distance late at night for about an hour. We are the same. She lives with a him, I find, and that there are problems. The easy surfer life has turned to booze, and this season of the sea, she is so smart.

The words go so well by my ear, they strike my mind as good, I find no holding back inside our speech, the same rooms are described, the same lines have been drawn by different hands, we slide along each other, letters criss-cross this rendezvous point like buried treasure, directions on the wall, you have to read them closely to see anything at all, and we turn the lines over and over, both of us pushing buttons, waiting for a few days in space to say the very best.

What is the original impulse to hold so long, my heart a prisoner of choice, intense longing not for ecstasy, the body's prisoner says, escape and fly, the souls mix after lovemaking, we wander through the light.

It was the specific capacity that love energy created in us both, we find, years ago, the very years that have suddenly ceased existing, that made a poetic tension for the beloved in us both. Is it that? Are we both that mystical artist arose from pain or distance from the other father?

I don't remember. There are snapshots of feelings stapled to my body, tatoos and scars, stated purposes of ignorance and the learning of the ways of love's times and seasons from the flat run across space and time together yielding nothing, ever, for this spirit of return that comes so suddenly, why, you wrote me? Why, I was all but buried up there, why bring me back? How could I not? she says. Unarguable. We decide to check it out.

From a letter. "Yearning, mind creating all bliss all patterns of bliss for the absolution. . .for those of us mad like this. . . . So then the need to move in on the pattern, fill out the dream with flesh and bone - - only to see it dissolve, too."

In the morning my mother takes me to her beauty shop, which, actually, I don't mind at all. A better cut than the Barber Shop, after all. A big guy, Mike, three hundred pounds at least, taking care of the ladies. and three Chinese-Americans, clip clip clip. ("They're going to quit..")

All Oakland cool, and the guy and I talk about his new Porsche. Really, he races. "If they knew what I do it'd be worse for their macho," he says. His kid is new. He's a family man and likes it. "Yeh, everybody's havin kids again," and we go down the list of things to do.

Steam Beer

Do yr laundry

Catch tube at noon

We get back and Sea calls from New York. The goddam plane!!

"I can't stand it!" she's yelling. We could almost stroke the wires, sudden hands at the very distance, long release of light throughout the distance, a terminal against the moon.

"Really, Sea, it's been this long. . ." I don't believe it.

"I can't stand it."

"Don't worry, I'll get a hotel and I'll be there for you."

"My dear," she coos.

"Really."

I give farewell to my parents. It's the best visit we've ever had, in spite of the fact that, in general, my life is at ground zero. The spirit, though, the immanence of it is so overwhelmingly good, that this ceremony with one's parents is complete, final, it is like growing up over dinner.

I am down the elevator, out the door and on the street. Bags in hand, gifts in heart, erect within my being, the plane won't be there until four o'clock, so impatient am I that I decide to kill time at the airport. I have been off the dope for four days and that's great. The unwinding excitement of the poem and the I Ching are all running quite along together, we are finally tied into each other, into self, life and work, a synchronicity of art and life, no separation, though I think that the man is leading them all, and that really, I am the man in question, I am watching my own movie.

I hang around a mob of school kids, waiting for the bus. Up the stairs and drop my bags, a perfect sunny day, and hot, for just before Easter. What a rush. Just a few bucks in my pocket, a hundred for the weekend, and my ticket back to Montana on the Dog. I have totally dropped out of my own life, I am here to meet my destiny, totally loose with a lady who isn't.

But that's the way it always is. Are there two beautiful people happily together in this war-torn land we seem to call our own? The very intensity of the cultural explosion, the very numbers of us, blown open by birth, the very millions of us, here in this state of California, lotusland, dreamscape without heroes or examples, all stumbling our way toward love, I won't be a cliche.

The meeting. Well, I can see that it's intense. "I want all of it," she said. And so do I, the moment of absolution in the ceremony of our lives, the meeting.

I get to the tube, people tell me how to operate it, I am such a rube now, and happy to play cowboy, they love to tell you how to survive in the city. I mean it looks OK, this old Oakland, I don't belong here, maybe I belong back in Montana. . . . I mean I pioneered that land all by myself. " A wild and intractable people," the I Ching said once or twice, not that they noticed. I am I, nonetheless, and spoken out.

Afterword. I mean, when what happens to you is real, then there is no "fiction" to speak of, there is only what is happening to you. And when what is happening to you is real, really happening, well, then, you are, and that's all there is to it, and you can put that in the bank, as he says. Stop, a sound.

And the art to it, well, that's just feelings and remembering. Well, so what; if what you're feeling is always a bummer, I mean, Sea, I said, "I'm not going to see any art, dammit, no more bad feelings. If it doesn't get me off, then the hell with it." "Well, you've got to go through all the phases of it, all the stages." And I have and I know what makes me feel good, and I like to feel good, all right!

"Man falls 29 stories," spread-eagled, survives, splat, I WAS SENT FROM GOD, he's yelling as they carry him out, "I want to see the boss," Trans-America pyramid power, really. Probably a thousand mics of clear light burning through his eyes, loose, all right. But survived, I'll buy it, he did, cosmic enough intersection of media and truth, but you have to look closely, "Leakage." And the nine-hundred pound man. Look out!

But is it time? And the dream? Cosmic trance-dance, the slow turn out into the open, lightning flashing around my house right now, a message enough, the rains, the rains, no dream but what is really there, and what is really there is real enough, and that's the art to it, hitting hard and splashing. Yellow daffodils out next door. Messages and readings, then, you are.

The mixture of times, the beauty of the words, directness of feeling, you might begin to learn that you are being sung to, in common speech, in the admixture of styles, a common message, really it's all the same, it's all the same, and a passage is also a return, and a return always involves a death. Ah yes, death and the new age, when will we get around to that, and who are the teachers, are they all from other cultures, other lands, or victims of our own organized practice? Is there no voice to speak out of solitude and quiet but my own poetic snapshots, a craft of times and seasons, swimming through the arrows in my heart, any ordinary Tom, "Interchangeable Toms" we called the paint crew. . . .

* * * * * * * * * * * * * * * * * *

Recall permits reflection.

I mean I'll have a dinner party with Alex and Yar tonight, something personal, pork chops in the wok two days with pineapple and orange and mushrooms and Wente Gray Reisling, a Heineken's for Sea and a Sherman for Sharon, my vacation my life in motion, clearing out of here in a month or so, is that what we need, some personal snapshots? The day goes on, rainfalling,

Mazola, the left hand wins again, the Beegees, on around the day and tuning up for the last paintjob, two story victorian, two days scraping, spray it wheat color with coffee brown and royal blue pinstriping on the trip and windows, a five hundred dollar job for Wally, split it with Steve and cover May's rent. It is usually that close.

A voice says "listen", I have something to say, I'll sing you to sleep, and you say What ya goin to do, over and over Bill Cosby voice, and Voice says, Listen, it's your own thoughts, I speak and you listen, and that's your story, you open your mouth and you tell your story, and if you listen to what you're saying, well, then, that's your story, and you believe it, and it's what you are, because that's what happened to you.

Ah, the solitude, the solitary wanderer, moved within his own space entirely, the risk immeasurable. . . . I learned of it from Herbie the same time I fell in love with Sea. It is your own space, if you can fill it, if you can stand it.

And love, immeasurable energy from within, the light around the body. A poet's view, and seeing, seeing the lines along the ground, running up the trail, almost on all fours, reading the hieroglyphs of the patterns of the sticks on the ground, reading the natural handwriting. A slow trail out and a slow trail back. . . .

CHAPTER 2   JUST THE WAY YOU ARE

"Eagle, wings expanding as air nourishes the lungs, up and out, growing, stretching, simple and clear beyond self a way of getting there, to self. Which is both beyond and right here - - " Sea, 28 Mar 78 Barbados.

Billy Joel, Just the way you are.

Love is largely, I think, two people, man and woman, each coaxing the other to give.

I am out. The long ride through Disney color coded tube-stops, each station consciously different. You couldn't have them all the same, really, they wouldn't know where to get off. Clang! Two subway cops get on, one young-tough, one old-fat. Indian eyes, staring out at nothing, trusting to semi-conscious peripheral vision to pinpoint them. It is not New York, yet, it is only San Francisco, and the years do not exist, you are the sea, rolling at my feet at East Beach sea-time, foot-wet and sprinting, the feet pad and splash the ocean's roar is not no mother drawn against her sons, but the lady in the waters, Sophia named as wise and beautiful, both.

It stops, Click. Color green and yellow stripes across your eye, the tube is cars alight the space design a flower on the wall. She sings inside my head. The plane was scrubbed, there is another. I am looking at two hours in the fucking airport bar, the dream a step away, long yellow hair from yesterday. Barely remembered photographs in my heart's gallery, white light calls the air a passage.

Where is it, South City. . . .

Dusk light afternoon haze has gone, the air is March perfect, the earth is gift enough; California rains have called the drought off. Mudslides, sure, but the earth is radiant, a reprieve, the rains have said, don't ever let it happen again. The lady busdriver is official.

"Well, ya know, I only been driving for three months, round robin, and so I know all the fare changes, in the zones, ya know, and when I get on a route from one of the old guys, to cover it, ya know, well the regulars get on and give me their quarter and I say, well, that's thirty-five, and they say, well, he never charged me that."

A horny Indian guy, the overseas variety, and the cool Nicaraguan lady, hustling, he says, "Those buildings, yes, I built them, I am the contractor, there," at crow and flying. "But they went bankrupt and now I am not getting my money. But are you staying here?"

"Well, no, seven years is a long time," she says.

"But my daughter likes it here, and so I think we'll stay."

"How long do you stop here," the fat guy riding shotgun says.

"Only for those other two connections, 3:53 and 4:00, and then we go right on to the airport, on the freeway."

* * * * * * * * *

The Airport.

Spaceport lines of folks on journeys. In through sliding doors past trip-faces, blank eyes set more on destinations than presence. But seen, at least, they do not bump into each other.

Held by love, the voice is speaking.

All right, you just be cool, drag yr bags up there, the escalator isn't working. Line of people, ask for re-routed flight. Too many people. The place looks smaller than I remember, I remember her presence, rush of heart, my mind is aching, rush, peeling from my skin; deep breathing stills anxiety. Stand up straight.

Song voice from the telephone after long silence. Indian eyes, watching everything all at once, they live without thought, just seeing. All this is pressed dirt, rolled flat, heated, compressed expressed, breath of machine drawn process-like from the earth, the airplane is really a fancy lump of dirt.

The Bar, dirty, smudged bamboo poles bolted not tied together," Luau Room." With bunnies in short skirts red crotch-panties visible when they bend over which they do. The foxy, huge breasted 47 year old lady and her balding, wasted old man, they are without the heat of their bodies between them, a second Michelob on the table.

Smoking Camels.   The hour.   And a half.   Another Bud.

The pretty classy lady and her equally classy man. Soft black polka dot blouse, a spot of turquoise. His clean white suit, intense and public, at kissing close, eyes open to each other over his artbook gift.

I watch them, since they're sitting next to me, I like it, they're cool, absorbed, personal. I head for the flight.

The long tube down the stairs around the crowded places left by people on the mark and spinning left and right to push around machines, the freak against the wall has fallen into silence again, my heart is pounding her's own no doubt the same pretending time still has no meaning but the life between your legs is rising up the spine, no sexual excitement, the heart, diaphragm a pulsating membrane of light, the center of my forehead ripe with space and light. My own life loop-tail rendezvous with self, no other bothers to describe the day's delivery, eyes across the day would

24

still revive me once again the seed, the seed, and spill my waters calm against your names at sea and season flying home.

Impatience called no more would turn my life around. I stash my bags on a nearby chair. I get ready. It is really the third plane. I checked the passenger list, I can't stand it.

A guy who is young and truly beautiful, feet up against the window ledge, waiting for someone, totally absorbed in a book. Nice but not really pretty wife and five year old mellow kid, they're all mellow. But he is ignoring her. What's the book, I stroll by and look over his shoulder. "The Various Positions of Love. . ." A manual, but not for dreams or love, or even events, but the lesser catalog of choices, Sit on my face.

But I'm calling her in.   Land, Sea, Land, Sea, land-sea. We'll meet.

Four people at the entrance to the exit-tube. Brown jacket, two mamas, and an old body-guard with no one to protect, he must be retired. Everyone lives with someone except me, I said to her. I'm going to hide behind this guy and grab her the minute I see her seeing something in the air, joy. A touch before thought.

Like oranges coming off the grader in the cannery. Pop. Pop-pop. Pop, pop-pop-pop, they come out of the tube. Blank seeing New York faces called west for light, for meetings and reunions, for business. Coats and hats, Montana on my mind, the Eagle calling forward, mates for life and flies alone.

The faces are all the same and stranger.

. . . two shoulders slowly slip left, intense slow motion almost stopped entirely, says, remember this moment as the best in your life, when dream and reality met, a foot is slowly swinging down in mid-stride, the seeing is so slow. Gray cloth meets to polka dots. The shimmer of size, the head, large, featured, prominent, eyes are straight ahead and brave, I'm propped behind the brown jacket. I see a reverse rerun of Ruby shooting Oswald in the stomach. I'll step outside and touch her heart with joy before I'm seen, I'll make the other unexpected light remind the day ahead, Return!

Slowly forward comes the wave. Slowly, lines around the planet burst. Slowly, dream dance says you are! And dream-time turns on life time. I leap without moving. I brush two people. "Jesus," he says. My arms around the world. Heart's brake calls "Surprise!" She's open to the moment.

"Gotcha!" "OH!" "OH!" 'Yes!" "It's you!" "It is" Sea. Sea. Sea.

A dance, a spin, noise of them recedes, the same strong body, you are taller, your body. . . . my body. The souls mix.

She touches my face, willingly. The eyes are still my own eyes, green, the expression in the iris where it lies just below the gloss glaze of fluid, it is the same! I am looking into my own eyes!

25

My feet sweat, heart exploded.

Dazed. We are far from speechless, wandering dangling through the halls and passages of the underground terminal, the bus to the city.

"You're so beautiful!"

Deep throated musical laugh. The dark bus driving crowded, unseen channel into the city. Enthusiasm, touching lightly: having covered the distance, having grown up separately. We meet to make the future.

"Where have you. . ." "What did you. .." Laughing a lot aloud along the way.

"My dear. . ." I lean across the space between us, I touch her arm, at her ear, "I have carried you here, Sea, all along the way, you were always in my heart, you know, and I found you everywhere, but you were not with me. Perhaps those years were really a waiting for just this moment."

"Oh yes. . ." she breathes, my eyes look back. "It was. .. so difficult," she pauses, "just not knowing, I mean, where you were. Ernie and Don and I, we all sat down last summer, really the first concentrated effort."

"That's just when I started looking for you. . ." Amazed. Stumbling out of the mountains, looking for nourishment. I am fed.

But really, it is the immediacy of the meeting which is so intense. Relaxed, open, the Now of what we want to do, be together. The clarity of the moment, two flames rising brightly upward call the day, love's.

Suddenly, we are traveling together. We are very together. We get our bags off the bus, the exchanges of money and you pay this and I'll pay that are immediately shared. The nose, the lips, her large features grown more beautiful, seasons: I am calm in love to this presence of myself, lady-woman-dream-other, dream upon the wall, yr eyes aflame and present, red-gold and streaming fire, wings beating old drums to carry music home where it belongs. . . .

The strange downtown dumpy hotel. COLUMBIA. Brown veneer paneling. Double bed, shower and toilet. Fifteen bucks. No bugs, no nothin a window on the street, we drop our bags, we look out the window. We face each other, reach out long arms across the years, and, like the guy in the show who falls without bending his knees, Splat! onto the floor, we slow motion onto the bed, laughing.

Satie, Socrate. Angel S 36846, side 2, par Mady Mesple

I enter the secret room.

Slowly, I enter the secret room, your fingers on the cup, at edge and sign. First the middle finger of the left hand, the center of your body gasping forward.

There is a light essence covering the top of my head, a tingling sensation, also in the pit of my stomach, my balls are glowing. I move my hand, my arm, I am inside the secret room. My time is my own, longly, the white pole the center of my body glowing arc across my heart. A slow roll beyond the eye, Sea seeing me with my own eyes, sister, twin and other.

But, I am inside the room altogether the nude body strung and alert. I touch the dimensions of the dark soft walls, ah, your eyes soften and glow inside my name.

She walks slowly forward, a song escapes her lips, it is this music I am listening to, again, it seems. You are this song, lady, Sophia, sea-sung and wet. The sensation of quivering to life, motive from beneath me holds my heart's stomach, it is like that, both ends gasping for life and made against the moon, Easter's miracle this year to be full and one the same, the same day of 1978 in California, where the beach will shimmer the giant ring, she weaves me down and through the light, to the other side of the world, I enter the secret room. . . .

The last image of Sea that I have, with utmost clarity, the reality of it pressed into my life like life itself. It is 1962, and I look like *that*, and she, the same and younger, really. I mean, by the end of the recall, I can see neither she nor myself. It is the drama of the even which I remember and the intensity with which I felt it. It was neither "romantic" nor "cinematic" nor anything else. It was what was happening.

I mean, really, just where do you live?

She was up the tall stairway, to the cloud heights, at the corner, where she could see down into the driveway between the two buildings. There was a ten foot high board fence and a door. I had walked through the doorway and I had turned around. I was going away, the next day, to Michigan on my first teaching job.

"I love you," I shouted. Sure, it was raining.

"Good-bye"

We repeated it, even.

Sea-song and wet. I am at the inner secret of the return. The hermetic room, where the formulas have been written down over the years. It is the mystic's chamber, white walls, desk, the pen moving across the pages one by one, it is me, here, now, telling the story the way it was, my life a song against the wind, wheeling, pinwheeling surf against the shore, the bird, the bird. The room is the retort. And in the room, the seed-child growing in the fires of this ecstasy, formed from the vapors of energy, pin-point of first light dawning. And of that homunculus, the Eagle flown, sudden against the sun, and mated, meeting the final absolution.

She is arced back over me. I am lying on my back, pale pole rising, how we have learned, as free, this motive to be together, in the secret room, there are no signs

27

left. When we left, there was nothing there, three days worth of Chronicles, the article on memory drugs and another on sales of faith books. Already we see the drama more than poem, neither self conscious nor furtive, simply, what we are doing, a meeting in the present state of things.

Her brown body patched with light, brown masonite siding against white ceiling, well, certainly we are human. We are not talking about it' we are making love. It is not urgent, it is complete, it is love. Well, we are smiling, we are laughing like crazy. . . .

The bottle of cognac on the table, my Sherman's, her Merits. I remember White Shoulders and Salems; ah, Patchouli, I am mad, incensed, the curtains have sent the world aside, day before St Patrick's Day, Downtown center Garage, Columbia Hotel, 304, or 401, or 403, I don't remember! Up the stairs, one more flight than you'd like, second door on the right, the key, a knock, "It's me," and laughing, dancing, spilling out sentences, poems, lines apart and sending, sending out.

A moment that enlarges into all of its contexts.

This music. High turning, sailing forward climb and turn, the joints quiver expectantly, bird-tossed and pluming down the valleys, overturned and overheard, her knees, horse and rider underneath the sun, signing light around your body, said like this calm beginning at the center of life, calm designations of the physical realm, "the sweet steam of well working bodies," she said.

And saw the world turned around, the center of the day within your forehead's lining, inseen and eye, you pushed aside the lighter poles upraised with flags and pennants waving colored armies blue and green and yellow. Daisies by the cup, your hands are large at stroke and center cooled the lines between us stretched tight exploding wires caught the angles on your face with light and dancing hours repeat the dreamer's sleep no nodding out or falling forward in specific songs, Miles Davis in my head from long ago, Aranjuez.

Pictures from the older days are spread around the oak and pewter sentences: you held me through designing hours were made along these other lands where strange faces seemed to be the name of light, strange faces peering quite intent, ah the energy of life's sensuality, this Tantra of hours, the body's perfect dance and perfect mating meeting slow rooms the center of the world and spun.

I am Eagle. Bird turned, named at sign and story, solitary soaring wing and frame, eye from distant regions focussed down at pinpoints pinwheeling favors from the sun and motive of the air's breathing light, a cool swim through gasses, sighting far below the nest and center, pinnacle proud, roof and pole survived, the far leap from distant airs reviewed, the woods with calling sounds at flood and pattern.

You call my name aloud, lady, sea-sung and wet, we pull apart the coiling arms and lets, feathers fill the room and say the walls have slipped away and mountains rise around us. Clear Montana light the clouds are huge and wall along the sky with solemn refuge scored among the natives, restless, subdued, imperfect centers of developing strides and gaits, birdsong, shriek-chatter, semaphore unwinding through her hair, brown and gold and gold and wheat-white, the soft hills of California throwing pale yellow wands and figures through the time beyond the mountains.

We call the room a poem in the air, it is the moment of our parting waves returned to be the same. It is this capsule from the heart's wars left beyond the gate, the city called a haven for these others in the night, shades, shadows, others, the moon's children sailing lines beyond the air, you are, you are. . . .

Or are these tributes undelivered less profound? These hours have no time, the top of the line and moving. The pale pole rising in her body says these simple sensations have lingered at the edges of the sea. In our youth, a perfect time: late at night we are somehow coming into my little condemned house in Daly City. Books, armloads of them, boxes of them, piles of them. Harvey is in Berkeley seeing Nan, I think. We make a kind of love and fall asleep. In the middle of the night I am awake, aroused, erect, alert. She is asleep. I get up vibrating inside my being with more than wanting. It is a poem. I go into the other room and write.

Sleep-presence calls across my shoulder to the white page. I let go. We move across the rooms to the darker, inner space. The horse is falling into her, wild and moving, my arms around the body of the sea and driving forward, sharp acres call profound distance sweating names are called aloud. . . . and from the center of my body, bare bulb, root of, up the line, focus of light, the hot line focused forward and rushing out, deep within explosions of light.

And in the sunlight the next morning, a photograph with my shadow in it even then: seated on a wooden box, the face is calm, empty, the body perfect, this deep climax a moment in life's conjunction where sense and energy are the same, the joyous union of perfect and simultaneous explosions going deeper than bodies and pleasure, the deeper rush of energy from within me made the world my own.

And when we drove back to the cloud heights we stopped along the sea, and stood at the cliff for a long time silent before donuts and coffee. Absolution from the pain, a review of the origins of life, a speech delivered before the gods, for we are set among them, this reviving of Amor and Psyche which blurs our individualities, which makes us more than Eagle and Sea, but calls us the center of the moment explaining gift and season for the world's benefit, we have saved the world, and not alone, but in the secret room, final alchemies are real , and spoke, and carried forward, a banner.

Six o'clock gray light calls me to work, my early routine of the last six years. Coffee! Where's the god damn coffee. Hot water and instant, yuk! She coils silent motive said asleep and cools her head my noise awakens.

"Coffee. . .mmmmmmmmmmmm. . ."

"I'll go for coffee and read the paper. I suppose you have your own morning routines. You are so beautiful, my face between your legs, drinking from the fountain of light."

"Oh my, you're wonderful," she opens the smile and birds fly out.

My eyes, or I have hers.

The street, calm at early hours. Downtown city I would not leave the woods for this, but there is the work, what we have all been doing. White walls, a counterfull of regulars, ladies chattering behind the counter. It is small, they seem small, different, the return of the mole people. Where have I been?

At coffee, my heart rushes through the window. I go back up the too-many stairs hop and run, she is around me, in the secret room, awake.

Now we are looking at bodies. "Yes, there is time in them." "Do you remember what I was like, then." You were more compact, or fleshier, different, a girl, I suppose.

It's the acrobatics, I feel stretched out. She bends over backwards from the waist, I am amazed. I do yoga every morning and vitamins, lots of B-Complex and champagne. A laugh at that, ah, yes, the food-free diet. Coffee beer and dope. Straight run of energy, the body digests itself.

She is hanging from the closet door by her hands, like a bat. I photograph.

We like that.

Your back, that was the picture from Kalamazoozoo, I sent it from there, you are sitting in the bedroom at Santa Cruz, at the farm. Oh yes, what a nice gray-dawn shot, the lady at her table, soft back of flesh and light. What is it now?

Longer, vertical, upreaching. Her arms high over head. You are different.

Well, I'm a man. The body changes, we see that. And the children, and Montana, and being poor saved my life, made it. Hard work and being crazy. The desperate edge, nearly losing everything, at the point of choice and loss, deep within the madness was the opportunity to stay there, it is all high energy and cosmic : I AM THE CENTER OF THE DRAMA, it says, I AM!

The desperate struggle of the ego to dominate the unconscious. I mean, I was going soft and fat in El Centro. Hands in pockets. Wildman fat and not doing enough work. Genius static and wired. But really the slow accumulation of facts is my freedom.

And you went away? We all loved you so much. I didn't believe it, all the years of rejection, reliving it, making those early incidents happen over and over. Still, it saved my life, it made my life.

And now? We are standing in front of the hotel. Left or right in this pre-Easter city we thought we knew. Up a block, hands touching, holding her arm, stopping to gaze in mutual disbelief at this calm beauty we have grown into.

"I don't know, Sea. We have all grown up together." We are naming names. Don; and Ernie, who expects to see us this weekend. And Willie in LA, you must see him, it's important. Ten year relationships breaking up, sudden review of lives and art careers all around us. It comes to this. The essential boredom of the old, dying, used-up culture has thrown us into the present. We are looking around at our world, hmmm, how to take it back? We made art our life, Sea, me, all of us. Now we want what's ours. To speak, to teach, to share.

Somehow we are totally lost. Van Ness is, yeah, over there. And the Beach, that way. One block up and one block down and one block over to the sea. The air is crisp, warm, clean, bright, rare San Francisco day.

It is light, speaking of the hours after breakfast and coming down the hill, corner of Union Street, in front of the bank.

"Oh, Ernie lives somewhere, right near, up the. . . ."

"Sea, Sea, hey, jesus christ, Hey!"

Black tree bush bristling natural balding some, the head up, eyes burning dance a dance, I turn slowly to my right, has grabbed her arms around her turning on the sidewalk in front of the bank, it's Ernie from, where, or when, or after what, unchanged older, thin and wiry, intense aloud, tapping feet and shaking body wired-out on creative juice but yes, mellow. . .

"You look GREAT Tom, jesus christ you look great!"

"All Right!" I give a hoot, heads are turned.

We are all three hugging for this reunion before the sunny skies.

"Where have you been? Montana. What, and. . . ."

Sea goes off to see Chiarra and Lucia-baby, Cia-Lucia, and Ernie and I go off for espresso, but no it's closed, Heineken's in the corner.

"Your book, Tom, it's beautiful, really, I mean, the style, but it'll never sell. . . ."

"I know that, man, I knew that all along. . . ." The private, secret, hermetic, coded language, maybe from the seventeenth century, Sir Thomas Browne syntaxes, "Brownian Movement," I call it.

Quick chatter at hot words, recall of beaches and epithets, careers and travel, sharp shots. . . .

"My novel? I was hungry in Paris, I mean we had no money, nothing, none! I had a teaching job in Hawaii and I bagged it and Chiarra said, she's a writer, said, for christ's sake you're a writer, go and write! So I did! I knocked out three chapters and wrote a synopsis and sent it to my agent and he said Yeh! go ahead. . . ."

"Yeah, an agent, I don't know where to. . . ."

"He's here! In San Francisco, and we're having a party for him, Sunday, to meet some San Francisco writers. You and Sea will have to come, really."

My head disembodies itself. Synchronicity of life moments. I stumble out of the mountains looking for something to do with my life and talent, and here it is, a meeting, anyway. . . . "But not as a poet, no, I'm not ready to say that, poetry's dead-hat, man, and I ought to know. Really." It's OK, but not business.

"Well, you come and meet him, he's a nice guy, the best in the business," Ernie says, and gives me a list of accounts. At Ernie's and moving right along. The stairway is dark, wood paneled. There is a purple curtain on the window downstairs glass door and no name scribbled on the wall by the buzzer. Wood walls, railroad flat, and into his kitchen, home-space, and beautiful Chiarra, Sea, signing, a bottle of champagne. Chiarra comes out of her eyes, across the waves, hand to hand a gentle lady laughing hello, another novelist! What life. We drink together over Cia bambino.

Soon, my old Leica, exchanged one winter in Mazola with Frank for Jung-lessons, it is snapping away. Two winters ago, after Jody had piled up my things in the middle of the living room, ah, January of 1975. Anyway one day he snuck this old M-3 into my hand, collapsible lens, the spy-shot.

We are all taking pictures like crazy, hipshots, quick shots, standing or running, ah the champagne, the Sea running through my veins, eyes across the meeting, we are headed for lunch and outrageous stories.

"Montana! For seven years! Whew." I tell them of the collapsible mountains, spacecraft sightings, the immense mountains and puff-skies, the thirteen year old virgin queen of my transformation. "You've got a story!" Ernie's shouting.

"I was down in Palo Alto for two winters, the first after I was crazy, in two rooms with Alex, on welfare, exhausted, shot-down. I ate and slept and wrote the first Vision. The second year with Jody. When the baby was born." I tell them of my visit with Mischa.

"But you stayed here." America.

"There was a time, in Greece, when there was a sixty dollar a month job and another, the same sort of a deal, in Turkey. It was enough, really, to support us in an expatriate life, but I decided against, in '66, I thought it was important to stay around here and be an American writer. I was an expatriate in Montana."

"Well, I wrote my novel, and I made some money. . . ."

"I've never made a nickel on poems."

"Whew, time to change."

"Yeh, really. I don't know where to go."

We've made a center on the table, everyone is listening undercover to our chatter. Amaretto, Heinekens, the chicken curry cold salad white sauce so unbelievably good.

The words go on, cameras watch each other, down the street, lone lines flutter up. The years do not exist. I paint houses in Mazola, Montana. A visit to the sea. I run my number, I play that tape, just to remind recall, the flavor of the distance. I mean, the street.

Pop-talk, punk rockers, shits and spleens. Jive talkers slow walkers.

Rooms around the bend, and bending over white socks rolled up blue belles, platform songs, a punk, really. Sex styles, intense not personal, hip downgrade of whores, shots, loops, distant stations, teeth at the ends of fingers. Freaks and frauds and losers; hippies queers niggers and redheads, muffs in muffins, tinned around the hand. Buttfuckers and queens, space shots and hitmen carry fashion from the cookie shop. Twenty-seven flavors of chocolate chip. Peanut butter. A snapshot of Sea with the cookie bag. Ernie wheeling the baby through the seedless grapes. This world, this, without the child. Only sensations and fucking, where has love fled, to what retreat, and here among friends, the invisible community of friends leavens the air, earth-bred and fat.

"What a luxury to have so many recent images in blood and bone to linger over. Sweet. Sweet. So right. Cappuccino Monday morning. Blue and white," she writes.

We are walking up the steep alley behind Carol Doda's workshop.

Snap snap. Him and the kid, me. Procession, a small parade, Sea and C. Ernie rolls the kid down down, I run almost fall, wild mountain hoot, hooray.

"I didn't know about how much I'd love Lucia. Loo-cheea, chia, cheeah. . . . It was after about three months, after she was born, and what a rush, from somewhere deep, wow!!"

"It made a man out of you."

"Really."

For coffee after our feast of lunch. At Enrico's around the corner. Grouped at the street around a table. Ernie on Punk.

"It's the total downer. The final style."

"Waiting for a new one, the rebirth."

"Well that'd be great, but how."

"Ah, live it first in your own life, and then the world's transformed."

"As easy as that?"

"Easy?" The bare plain meadow, the hot Montana August dry dry wind, blowing dry pain-dust through the absence in my being, 1973, stuffed stoned in the chair, in my house and children, she's gone: sighting through the window on a group of trees a quarter of a mile away. There are three dark spots, shadows in the group, and I choose the one on the far right. I confine vision to the contour of the darkness. There is a hump on the upper right side of the whole. I focus attention on the softness of the curvature of the vague hump on the edge of the corner of a shadow on the landscape a quarter of a mile away, lost, gone, point- less, seeing, seeing the eye that sees.

There's a six foot white punk with rouge and dark mirror glasses, stoned-out across the street. A black guy and a hassle ensue. A quick shot from the black guy, swinging in tight and up, punk head shakes back. A white something or piece of wetness flies from punk head trajectory back flown head snapped back, turns and runs two steps, shakes his head, says something and cooled out strolls across the street.

A minute later, a black chick, chasing a guy, hard-assed, fast, both of them, flying, she's pissed, a car stops her, he slows immediately and strolls away, the scene dissolves.

The stroke of her perfect hands along my hair, my heart stops present reeling future mixed remembering how I am new now made alive by love. Winding down the day, we take the bus back to the hotel, exhausted.

Later, at Ernie's for dinner, and telling stories around the floor.

I run ten blocks up and ten blocks back on Market Street. We pick up Saturday Night Fever and a bottle of Port and make a visit, after all, to talk about it, where have you been, man, to look so good, and here with her, man it's storybook, Ernie says. Well, isn't that the point?

"Burning Karma. It's the burning, water turns to steam, messages from the radio, playing Billy Joel over and over, "Just the way you are", I keep thinking you're singing it to me. "And so I am."

I enter the pain. I said I would never go back, even through numbness, but I see that I must, and re-enter cautiously, moving through the yards of seaweed. There was the day it took six hours to get from the hotel to Fisherman's Wharf, talking at the bus about the general plan for life, talking at the Buena Vista over Steam Beer and her gin fizz.

Well, yes, it is storybook, but it is the handle on the line that beats the shore. The sun conspiracy has melted, the waves are melted, sand-point and healing waves, she has her distance, which suits the day, and lets the words have their own content.

"I mean, is it all that, out there, in its difference that amounts to what I am, or the calm point from which I am seen," we say. Lying on the grass, rolling the empty beer bottle around, thinking of crab louis at Number Nine. Making love is exchanging charges, lighting each other.

It is spring, and we have been charged with light, exchanges on the bridge. Specific details on the wall and sounding forward. A dark point sounding at the bottom of the hole. I am the man who has gone through to the other side, into the white light at the beginning of time.

You are the same there, I am alone, and well enough to wear it out. The voice of self, of the self that speaks has your liners down, days drop doorways down the tides are broken on your shore of faults revived.

But there is the part to be heard. We speak our lines around the day's discoveries, they make us new. I am signed in to the group again, a pole of youth revived. We play with the baby, I take some snaps, at light and sentence, she holds this other child, and I remember my own. And it is our child she is holding, no, really, it is me she is holding, I am the child of the year. . . Ernie and Chiarra return with the goodies for the table. At 4:00 I go out to let them all have their time, the phenomenal scene.   I scan the street "Vibrator sale, $12.95." Really, a special on dildos. Alcoves at City Lights. For a book. There are none. It is the Darkness, it is the Great Fear.   I hide out at a bar down the street for an hour. I must empty my head of this party and just go to it, it is part of the story. Two double Blackjack on the rocks and two Heineken's and I fade to Jimmy Buffet on the box. I'm ready for the party, and up to the door with the purple curtain, and buzz, and in the door, Sea is coming down the stairs,"Who is. . .Tom,where.. ." And Chiarra says from above, "Oh, it's family," my heart soars.   The slow mood prevails. I'm wired, restrained by the Jack Daniels and a week with no dope, but alert, feeling fine. Sea in black, Ernie and Chiarra lovely, Lucia asleep, by miracle.   The door and the stairway, comes, blond hair mustache, another, white shirt, a lady, three impressions.

"What's that," blond says, Gary, an engaging Brownie from Sacramento.   "An elk button with crushed coral, gold wire," around my neck. Danny's piece, from this winter's work.   Hands around the way, we move around the corner, around the time my eyes descending.   "John Hawkins," Ernie says, he sizes me, I rap it out immediately.   It's his party. Why can't I hold back. . . .

"Well, yeah, I've been doing avant garde poetry for fifteen years, and no bucks."
"Really," he says, "It's a good life but nobody buys it."

The Hawk and the Robin, his wife. He swivels headset eyes, rocks back in his self, talks with thrusts and senses, the air around him seems the same as anyone's. She listens, at intuitions made receptive, to call the mood professional, all right, and clear the air, not so competitive, but the way it works. You'd think to see knives flashing, it is hardly so. The Hawk flies a loose match. Everyone gets touched as they come into the room, filling it, gathering around the food, talking, the air grows wild. . . . The dancers, the dancers.

"Well, poetry has its content, I suppose. I'm starting a piece about it and about being lost in Montana and coming back, something between Pirsig and Exley, I suppose, scenes along the road. This is part of it."

We spin off to Montana writers, Chuck Kindor and Diane Cecily and Max Crawford. Other people coming in. I get Chuck and talk about it.

"Where's Keester and Jackie," and he says, "We'll call them." And we do, five or ten times. I say, "Really, Mazola's OK for writing, but it's no place to be a writer."

"Why do you call it Mazola?"
"Well, it's a cheap cooking oil. Keester knows all about it."

And the famous horny writer, gray, different, sociable, around the time and spending light hours. Teachers of creative writing.

Semi circular hours rotate, professional intent gathered on the topic of bucks, market, easy chatter on the price of acreage. Movement flowing easy conversations make the hours lighter marks along the way. "I'm finding out something." The way it is, perhaps. Well, we're all pros, I'd say, perhaps my expertise is obsolete, obscure. But in translation might the thing pursue itself.

The air and smoke and people in the room. The cold point of consciousness sees the event, meeting from deep within the woods, Eagle, seen.

Wine bottles move around.

She draws a joint from somewhere and turns around. Delighted. Home grown sensimilla, a fine taste draws my dry head sharper songs pursue. I put on Saturday Night Fever, get the volume slowly from 5 to 7 and cool out.

I am talking to Gery, about condominiums in Aspen, house painting. . . .
"Is Brown running for President?" I pop.
"Well, we don't want him to, California's enough. . . ."
"Really, California's the world, man, after seven years in Montana, whew. . . ." At a rap and slipping through party hands.
"Let Carter fool around. The fifth largest country in the world."

"Are you from Montana?"

"No, man, nobody's from Montana. I'm from San Diego, third generation, not too many of them. My grandmother had stories of riding her horse across downtown LA for her violin lesson; corny but true." So it goes.

Well, I am spaced out, by the wall: I must recede, head is spinning with the sound of the sentences. I retire, fold my arms against myself and breathe. Eyes go flat, or numb. Escape and the alcohol. The air of the mood is high. I like the atmosphere; it is light and serious, everybody hustling for the carrot, Hawkins, too, it is his party.

Poetry lives in the secret room, a forgotten wisdom but for the people it passes through. Inaccessible to media, obscured in lives lived for art rather than the communion of the marketplace, which is also the real.

Too long the poet lives his pure and solemn silence, *"...Stayin alive, stayin alive...."*

Criss cross bridge of light. The poet walks across the line, this line exists. The market, he says, is changing. . . .

"TV audience off two percent last year and two percent the year before."

"So," the lady says, "that's more readers." And "And that's bucks, too, lost on advertising revenues. You don't advertise in a book, not yet."

"Better for writers."

"Not for agencies, necessarily, we're in competition, too."

"It's the audience, bored with TV's sameness, the huge bunch of people, getting into thirty, I mean, I was one of the teachers. . . Now they can read. And they're reading, too, thinking. Demanding a quality product, complex, amazing. . . ."

It is the event itself, maybe a millennium to some and the end of the world to the others, the "them" of artists. The audience is so huge that it demands multiples, doubles, copies, facsimiles. And the poem, really, is a unique and private thing, there, a thing. Media is flow, and for poetry to transform itself into media it has to stop competing with images, mental things, really, and just flow, the word, pure juice all over the walls, the "blood and bone" of it; and fading out, I loose myself, and go down the hall to boogie jive a little bit, I shake it loose, my gray hair shortly short. High flyin visions of the cosmic satellite, reading a poem to the world, soft, Eagle, settle loose your hero's wings. Make a nest.

We are dancing, Ernie and Sea and me. We are high flyin birds. Everyone has gone but Hawkins and Robin and Gery and two others. They are seated on the rug in the other room, watching us disco twirl and spin, Tom on Sea and Sea on Ernie on Tom on Sea on Time and dancing lines around the room spin and turn the day is singing songs. . . .

"The years do not exist."

". . . you don't have to show it. . ."

"I just love that falsetto," Ernie shouts, clap hands, spin.

All right! Turn and kick your hips around at turn the day and touch her hair her line blows past, *"More than a woman to me. . . ."*

We slow, stop and sign around the dance is going slow and singing my song's voice, I go long low I hear your name against the seas, more than a woman to me, more than a woman. My heart speaks to myself at large and turning. Let history repeat itself. I am high flying, love, my heart is full, a bird among my seasons falling through the darker side backwards flip-flop over and back and back and down, cross turning turned along the air's currents, the Eagle smoothing out at three old friends doing their dance from fifteen years ago, three old friends doing their dance and turn and turn and leave them sighing far below, free birds flying home. . . .

They leave. "What a nice party."

Sea and I are dancing at two in the morning, before sleep. *"I'm goin to take care of everything, I'm goin to take care of you, . . ."*

I'm not asleep, I say, five times rolling over all night long *non tocare*, the lady from the ocean restless beside me our last night together. High tide breaks the shore apart. No seed calls the spring's season left unsaid, but joy.

I call the light at six AM, again. The California Ghost Fly-by. Toss the coins and read my name, a song against the wind.

The corncob hangs in the corner of my room from a cup hook screwed into the ceiling, hairy yellow twine around the base, looped, a slip knot. The only yellow kernels on the tip, go back about three inches from the tip, which is bare, rust-red. Up the string is the owl-feather Jerry gave me, "for yr kitchen," he said. The Vanderberg kid shot the owl up behind Jerry's cabin, up behind my house in Ah-lee. An Indian kid on some kind of trip, and he gave Jerry the feather to atone for it, I guess, or for the power.

Alex found the cob when we were in Ohio with Jody. Ah, serpent mound, pointing south, the deep broad vista from the cliff beneath the tail. . . .

In the LA Dog station, April 9, 1978. Going home. I breeze in from Santa Barbara on the Dog, 45 minutes to kill. A raunchy chili verde and a San Miguel, across the street for a joint. Up the stairs to door number six, bags down, and up walks a pretty lady, really, forehead bristles, stomach turns, cock alert. "Salt Lake City, really." "Yes," she says, "I'm Ahn,"a name,a musical voice from New Zealander throatsong, and brown skirt lady on the road from London yesterday on the plane, skiing in Utah for a month. Voice music lilting up from throaty laugh, the dream continues without speaking, "Gentle Tom", we're walking up the blacktop alley in Barstow smoking a joint, I touch her face, we walk along the alley, playing soccer with a pebble. At coffee laughing, looking out at mountains, sun behind her windy hair, really I'd like to take pictures of you, have you model for me, snapping pictures with my hands in-frame. Riding out of Barstow into darkening light, where long slow looping ridge-slides ten miles covered covered with yellow yellow flowers waves against the light against the hills. Coming into Las Vegas, my fingers in her mouth, laughing song-voice, you said those words all night long we sang that song. . . .

Touched small breasts came yr nipples harder, hairs around the bend, we had a beer in Las Vegas, half a joint, the man goes by, I freeze. Diving into yr lips, tongue on tongue, arrived, my finger in between yr legs, lady, flyin high, she started bouncing, at last, blue light from a fading sunset, the black guy across the aisle sleeping, I get her mouth, and shot light stars along the ceiling bright lights pushed her head, the cars going by and by and by and by. . . .

Eagle at cloud height, the terms for union and ecstasy, the lady in my arms and singing songs all night into Salt Lake, of New Zealand fame and stature, gentler breasts to touch. At dawn, my right hand in between her folds, and wet, she goes again, and gives, her legs open white brief butterfly flower, I fill my hand with light, the guy across the aisle, bill of his cap pulled over left side of his head, arms folded over his chest, nobody cares, ah, far flame flying home to work. Addresses, words.

I sleep on the Dog for the thirteen hours into Mazola. Three hundred and fifty dollars in my pocket from the stucco repaint: peeling, scraping, spraying, talking, rolling, walking, smoking, moving, caulking, dancing, singing, thinking, soaring, flying, being the same, and brothers, long along the way to be the same, and moved....

CHAPTER 3

NO MATERIAL THING IS BEAUTIFUL

Robert Henri, *The Art Spirit*

We creep out the stairs go down the street, return. The dream recedes, how to disengage. It is pure grace, San Francisco Union Street parade of no-one, 6:30 Monday morning Easter a week away. The planetary plunge.

"Sh. . ." and down around the corner, to find a coffee at time's beginning moments.

"All right, here. . ." My old English teacher corduroy jacket, Jim Webster left it at my house in 1974. The scarf, her hair, we pause over the glass wall behind the window inside the tiny coffee house where four people, regulars, hassle over the new week.

We look at bear claws and giant frosty sugar things, the lady pulls the handle of the espresso machine.

"This is very special to me, you know. "

"Really, Sea, our absolution, rebirth to a higher form, we're on the bridge, together, now."

"And what continues, dear, is just what continues."

"I knew that, before I came downstairs."

"Oh, but you mean so much to me. . . ."

"And you to me, Sea, and we're permanent."

Blue and white of coffee cups, my eyes sparkle in both our heads.

Light goes bright Monday morning outside.

We are standing by a pay phone. I try to call the Dog about the time for Santa Barbara. Getting businesslike.

"Listen, Sea, in a while, well, we'll just be standing there or getting out of a car, and I'll turn and wave and say 'OK, see ya!' and you say 'OK, see ya,' and off we go, just like last week or something."

"Really," she says, and holds my hand, "I'd like that, too."

We go back to Ernie's, where we spent our night on the huge four poster in the front room. At the door with the purple curtain, "This is comfortable, Tom," a quiet voice at the foot of the stairs.

I turn back to her eyes, "My old lady." Smiles. Up we go.

At our second breakfast, Ernie and Chiarra both ebullient.

"What a party," his voice goes up into enthusiasm on the last syllable. "Everyone got dealt with, everyone." And he looks at me. "Do your first three chapters and send it in with a synopsis. . . ." I'm stoked.

"What about me," Sea says, "nobody asked me 'And what do you write?'" Her closet full of poems. And mine, too.

The strawberries, espresso, and time to get to work, the conception of my return, my madness, and my history begin to form a work, a story, my own *eclat*, voice from the mountains.

"And you guys," Ernie says again," this is really storybook."

"You know," Chiarra says softly, "it's what you need, you know, and what you have to say that's delicate. . . ."

Duration, the book says, and my stanza of doubled sevens rolls out: changing to Grace, we are all that, and life's songs pursue me, even here, to speak my lines along your face and pleasure seeming seen, again, we move to go.

I mean, I must pack it up, she does the same. Ernie is driving Sea out to her noon flight, where I'm to get off at the freeway entrance and walk the blocks down Market Street, my heavy shoulder bag and my leather bag of papers and an immense box of super-goodies from the party the night before.

I go down the stairs for an Anchor Beer and a pack of Virginia Slim Menthol. We sweep the floors. I smoke a joint.

"Here, Sea, for you. . ."

I put on Lay, Lady, Lay, and we dance this morning's new light together, wedding dance of times and times again. we have this turn and turning I catch her head against the room with the Leica. We dance together and I'm taking pictures. I give her the camera and she shoots me and we put our heads together and I hold the camera out for a selfless portrait, our own.

The ceremonies of leaving are without mercy.

And Chiarra at the top of the stairs, flash cube and warm smile, Sea is holding Cia.

"Now the two of you together," she says. "Me, too," Ernie says.

"No, just the two of them."

It is Sea and Eagle and the infante Cia, as light, so is. FLASH.

"The holy family," she says. I break up.

And my god, we hug and dance.

"It's your book, old T," Ernie from the beach. "Sock it to 'em baby."

The Sea in my arms.

The car runs madly downward through San Francisco noon-time streets, we are all yelling and chattering, and we turn to stop, double chatter of singsong presence.

"OK, T, we'll see ya around," from two mouths, jumble, and my own.

"All right!" Brave chatter, "see ya around, All Right!"

I reach for the door handle. It is not there. "I'm not meant to get out!" Ernie produces it, the door pops open, I'm on the street, faces through the glass, Sea oh Sea, and away.

Somewhere in the financial District, I feel like an old vagrant cosmonaut mushroom which has been suddenly teleported, dropped in time, left on the shore of the strange land. Pack-a-back. Super-hip. Top of the line.

I head for Market Street, which seems so far away. I stride strongly wired, through the crowd, I take long steps forward. At the light I stop and sweat. I hoof it across, packages. A beer, I'll stop for a beer, I have forty-five minutes.

On the street and walking, faces in the crowd are floating past, and the mask, the mask is on them. Where does the primitive life mix with our own presence, our post-modern life. Have the gods returned? I mean, she's smooth, a fox, high and high-strung, saucy, a sharp shot and moving, clicked-out in high heels, a lavender leg or two, in motion, would go off angry between the legs, but let go large volts of light, ah, if she would only give. I see her fifty feet off, I give her Indian eyes, to see within in no-thought, but hold a clear intense fantasy thrust, one knows when he is being checked out. No-eyes bounce along the street, the mask is straight ahead, tight breasts would be hard along my arm, pink-knit sweater close to, the face, is painted out, worse than whiteface. Plastic lips shine a little, the general ambience of a snarl, a snarl of pseudo-punk attraction, this do-with-me-what-you-will, and lets me in not to see, not to be seen. She'd bite yr cock off. Punk queen. Whew. Vision on Market Street.

I stop for music and not a beer. Rest, panting, from half a block away, it's a re-run of "My Favorite Things" down by the cable car stop. I mean, a soprano sax, and good, clean sound, not a copy of the original Coltrane at the Workshop '62 before I split; a black guy with his case open, running a little music history past the numbered tourists of post St. Patrick's Day. I stop and drop my bags. Perhaps I do look like a space cowboy. Anyway, my approval, sir, I bend in front of him, to be seen, and drop a buck down. Step back. Ah. He lets loose with appreciation, he sings for me, hot shot of love, driving to the airport, will they make it, my heart's song just beginning.

And across the street, a few blocks up, the waves part in front of me, no in front of something, anomalous people move smooth around what's coming forward, slowly, shuffle and thump, the demon on his rounds. It is a guy with super-wild, windblown, kinky, dirty hair. It should be filled with blood, or spittle, to connect with the image, and he pulls at it, the image and the reality. But he is stumbling, shambling in agony and unconsciousness, in a stupor of ignorance, one foot in front of the other, slowly, slowly.

His face is red with zits and sunburn. His teeth are crooked, a scrungy beard. Ah, I think, far out, the *real* Frankenstein, no not really a real Frankenstein. . . .we find that the gods are real, and not that we are gods but that we are real. It's what he's into, being the schizophrenic hero. Well, perhaps he is that. But no, nobody cares, nobody sees him, shambling down Market Street. Is this my self?

At the bus station, waiting for the Dog south, I go across the way for a Heineken's and one to go in my pocket. They are talking about John Travolta.

"No, I didn't like it at all." Means he did.

"Yea om abitger beer," mumbles the other.

"When's the Academy Awards, next Monday?"

"Yeah, he's up for it, too," another guy puts in.

"For the dancing; well, yeah."

"For dancing alone; you know, you never see anybody at a disco dance alone."

Winter nights, Mazola, two years ago. I had to dance. It was Pisces time. I'd go down to the Top Hat and jump into the middle of things. And once when Kostas was playing loud and Lewis was having his fifteen minutes of being famous. It was good, so good Kostas fired him. Nobody cared, I danced around by myself, turn and turn and try to get the concentration of nothing out of my brain, I started singing, hooting, going right between the notes in the amplifier, filling in the cracks with my own song. He didn't like it. Solo artists, whew. . . .

And on the bus, doped, smoked, eaten out, my head unscrewed, I collapse, I fall out, I open the box of food and graze, I start crying and I fall asleep. Oh, Santa Barbara, let me finish my last poem and put it away, this place I seem to have come from, southern land by the sea, California is Greece and Santa Barbara is its Athens, and now, after fifteen years, more like nineteen, I'm sneaking back, greasing in, a house painter on his spring vacation, looking for a miracle. And just as the sun shines forth in redoubled beauty after rain, or as a forest grows more freshly green from charred ruins after a fire, so the new era appears all the more glorious by contrast with the misery of the old. Wilhelm.

Hippie days are over, it says. Time to put away the L.L. Bean catalog and go to Penney's. Rock and roll radio from every lamp- post, wired, hooked up together, communicating, the laws present themselves, to be discovered in the watching. Perfect admixture of styles: all voices, thoughts, motives, times, all pass by the eye of the instant. One survives, then, one comes home after the long run on the road.

The Dog rolls up Carillo St. at 9:30 Monday night. Easter is next Sunday. I've always thought of Easter as my personal Christmas, it you can figure that one out. I mean, it is green. From Santa Maria to Gaviota. The beaches watched and washed. Poppies over San Marcos Pass. Crossing the light into my arrival, there must be five big buses coughing us out all over the place. On the ground, I pass through feet and clusters, around the corner, my eye scans the windows of the bus station, there's Tom my brother. My brother-in-law. Brother-in-ex-law. Six-two or something, beanpole hard, leaning backed against the pin-ball machine arms folded over black sweater chest, folded flow of red-hair cascaded back the red beard pulled in over the chin by the stroke of his own thoughtful hand. I stick out my tongue in the gesture of hello by a man with both hands full.

"Really," he says. "Howdy, brother. It's been awhile," I respond. No gratuitous claps on the shoulder. Contrary style demands that the greater the feeling the less the show.

"You're here." "Yeah, I could use a beer. Immediate need."

We get out of there. "The weather, man, what a gift."

And up two blocks to the new invisible bourgeois brown Pinto wagon. The Sportsman, a dark cowboy bar, ah, where the alcoholic slow loser sings and drives us out, later. We fall in and start to jabber.

Straight ten dollars an hour, better to be a painter than an *ahtiste*. We speak the same dialogue. Been here four years, quality jobs in Montecito. I sprayed it out in three hours, give the job its due, it's the quality not the price, what a rap. Colors, striping rooms, the craft and the job and the professionalism. Painting: carrying the portfolio of shots from job to job, passing by the gallery business with its fifty percent rakeoff, whew. The book I'm writing the adventure. Well, there's work here, start tomorrow, they've never seen such speed, roll a house out in four hours, two-coat it in six. Slow hands, a slow talk over dos Equis, a pretty lady down the bar, looking our way with no-eyes, an odd mixture ensues, the time of the rap and the time of my seeing mean the same. Tom, my brother, my double, my twin, my son, my clone I bounced him off the garage door in Detroit shooting baskets in the driveway in '63, in between him and his dad, Bill, who taught us both how to paint. Sue's dad. Patriarch of small hours, the house in Detroit, rooms, white light. . . .brush and roller. Cleaning up after your-self, something I forgot in the atmosphere of Mazola speed jobs, giving a cheap price, half a price, really, doing it in half the time, coming up at twenty dollars an hour and exhausted. Whew, the long hot run, the speed, the rage, the hunger. "Gimme the money, I'm done." "I got the money, I got the money," I chanted to Danny in Ronan just before Christmas, we knocked it out, outside two duplexes in three days, pasting the snowflakes down on the sills as we rushed to get out of there, cut the heavy bodied stain with clear stain to improve the flow to one coat, it was fifteen degrees and snowing. Four hundred dollars in two days.

The space of the air, Tom's personalism and power come through the beers. It's kinship and family at the same time. He talks about the family reunion in Colorado last summer. When I called after six years incommunicado, to thank Bill for teaching me how to paint. Sue too beginning to end our hippie exile in the mountains, the kids grown up enough to think of moving on into life's writings. . . . I am moving. Tom and I, Aries redhead left hander. Speeder, dynamo or organization, clear shot at the art business. Business.

"I don't mix with your so called cohorts. . ." Old friends, *ahtiste* from the old days, college, twenty years ago, who stayed. "I called George to give him some work; I mean if you're a painter I figure you can cut a sash, for straight across ten dollars, and he didn't show up for work!"

"I don't want to see them, they're losers. I want to come down here and paint and make some money and get my book started, get back to Mazola for awhile, come back down here when Alex's out of school. Besides, I want to see Bette. . . . But I always show up for work, I mean, it's bucks; hungover, crazed, dazed, lunatic or other, I show up for work. That's my problem. Tom who does anything in any weather for money. Stayin alive." Another beer. "I mean, really, they're living art lives, out of formula, all of them. Bummed out obsolete hippie beatnik loser styles. Living the styles of famous artists before they're famous. Why not go for it, full out, flat out and screaming, if anybody gets in my way I'll kill him. . . ."

"Easy, Tom." "Really."

"Ya know, we tried at a different style in Detroit and California, and look at you! I mean I sent you to Dick for some teaching and he turned you down. I can't forget that."

"Well, maybe he's not a teacher."

"Well, that'll be hard to say, but it's true, they're living the lives of geniuses, like I did. But that's what being crazy and having a vision will do to you, it puts the man before the art, and not the other way around, I had it that way. . . ."

He's tuning up. A drunk in a leather jacket, and too close too intimate voice, edging into a dirty joke. A cowboy and a sweet young thing in tight enough clothes to be for hire.

"Whew, it must be his birthday." We split.

Dark hiss of tires back streets of trees, the warm, moist air smells like Santa Barbara. The earth is pungent, alive, reborn erotic by the winter's rains. Down Milpas, past Jack in the Box. "My tongue's getting hard." JACK WILL SPEAK TO YOU. Barf-dog. Really, be a nerd. A total nerd, finally, relax. Familiar look of stucco and clean, fresh, yards and flowers. . . . The only place I ever was for more than a year or two my whole Navy-brat childhood and school and teaching life, except Mazola. And there I was in and out, a year in Sacramento for the second, pirate MA, my own job, really.

And two winters in Palo Alto. Welfare and gloom. Two years resting up from the Jump of '73 and three years learning to stay alive at the shangri-la outpost of civilization, tucked away in the mountains, reasoning, writing every day: piss on it, I'll paint houses.

Up the driveway to the white house with flowers all around it. Rustle at the window, beautiful Sharon. Scott's asleep. I'm landed, home, among family. Somewhere. Long red-brown hair, slim gentle presence, the eyes, leans forward to say hello.

"I'll never see you again, hello," I jive, reading back what she said two years ago. "Calls for both of you." The wild goose has landed in New York.

We're at the round table of the Detroit kitchen transposed to Santa Barbara. The message center by the phone. My box of goodies from Ernie and Chiarra, red-wine, the colombian. . . .

Tom's throwing paintings around. Images, pic-toors, scenes remembered with emotion in the lines and colors. "I've pushed just about every button there is for feelings, personal snapshots, say, here, feel this, and I sell them. . . out of the garage, you don't know who you're talking to in Santa Barbara, I can't say that enough, you don't know who the fuck it is, a Mercedes pulls up and some cool dude comes up the driveway and says I'll take that and that and lays six hundred on you."

"Man, you're really good. . . ." He cackles a laugh and hugs me tight—"But Tom," I say, "they're all different, there's no style."

"That's the style," he pops up and down, he waves and weaves, energy rushes. Sharon, cool-eye, warm smile, watches us both, loving us both, kinship.

And midway through a longer rap about it, about paint jobs and the airless and his business, just starting to be a survival which frees his productivity, Elvis on the easel, a fifteen color silkscreen. The house is stacked with paintings from Tujunga '73 to the print of his hand and broken finger, the two foot by four foot silkscreen of his driver's license, an edition of one, his identity piece. . . .

"Why are you two talking about painting jobs?" Sharon says.

"You're both artists, why aren't you talking about that."

We're out in the garage, looking at media pieces, silkscreens, was pieces ready for casting. They are all   multiples, not at all in the direction of 'genius', but based on feeling and presence. They have their genius.

"Well, you grew up with Leo in the family, they didn't I mean, you tend to live art history if your craft isn't personal."

"And you got a good shot from your dad. You're not fighting with your mother the same way. . . if art is feminine, which it is, then most of these guys are stuck thinking that they're women, fag art. But not really, anybody is two halves, and if you're limp it's not because you're an artistic person; that hasn't been there for a long time, you know, that art is full of energy, energized moments, and that it is the man's way of making a child. He has to have his birth, or go unseeded, really."

"You lost me."

"Well, look at us. You can be a man and be ordinary and make art and make bucks, and that's not art lives, either, it's business. Oh well, I feel bad about not making a living of any sort out of writing, for my kids. Just living my crazy poet's life and for what? Why? Sure the content is there, the mysteries and all that, the transformation, even, but no bucks, just a whole line of speed jobs and stayin alive."

"Really," we're saying, "we should go into business, get the silk-screen shop together; do T-shirts, four color silkscreens of land-scapes. . . poems. . . I could restore my photography again. You know, I've never showed the shadow pictures."

"Well, that's where we're at, by-passing the galleries and going straight to the customer, hustling is   what it's called." The glassworks, the pottery. He's tuning up on me. "I mean, there's us and them. And we don't have much to do with them because they're not doing anything and we're selling." All right! "It's better to sell five hundred at twenty than one at ten thousand, more people have the product."

"And the audience, it's huge. Seventeen million people in LA!" And we're into megabucks again, rapping it cool off the line, running with it, we get the calculator out. Surely, it is a new situation, and what I started out with in 1960 is gone, to be a writer in 1960 was a waste of time. Neo-Lawrence, the biggest seller, maybe, 1966, Jacqueline's Valley of the Dolls, nine million, whew, that's not much, and off we go, trailing fantasies of the art factory left and right.

We drive around the city, up to Goleta, back down by East Beach. "I'll have to write there Sunday. Drop some mescaline and see what the Easter vision is. I'll finish my last poem and start my book on Easter, what a criss-cross. Synchronicity of year and act, I'm stoked. I'll put away art lives, which is true, we lived them out to the final flip-flop." The best minds of my generation and all that. No, we didn't go mad, we went sane.

Sharon and I are at the table. I don't know her. "And you live alone?" "Me and Alex; Yarin and Robin are with Sue and that seems OK, I'm changing custody over." I get started on the history, she is the archivist, Alone, since Jody. Michelle and Frannie: brief intense outposts. Alone and poet, not loneliness and poetry. And leaving the old used up life.

"Yeah, I can feel some changes."

"How do you write?" "Do you write?" "I want to, but school." "You can't write and go to school. I didn't start writing, really until Kalamazoozoo."

I describe my morning routine. Up at six, coffee, the horoscope, coffee, the I Ching and a joint and then write a page, every day for the last three years. Eight hundred and seventy five pages of unrhymed couplets, among other things, my Homages of Anabasis. "I was going for 1001, and the model left, again. My life changed."

"Maybe you'll finish it." She stares long deep eyes deep into me. I try to give, to show myself to get into the same personal distance I have with Tom, personal and intimate and *non tocare*. Perhaps. This meeting of art spirits; for, suddenly, it is here that Robert Henri comes in, the master-teacher and painter from just before the time that modernism taught us schizophrenic part-styles, or styles of partly seeing.

We flail, we charge, we run at it full bore, words, visits. Scott is moving through the rooms, ten year old long red hair her deep Watchful eyes. Sammy the immortal white rat smoothing around his shoulders. On the table munching a kidney bean. Getting honey from the bottom of the cup. Scott is sly, he watches with Capricorn eyes, he pushes buttons. Kiss and the demons from Hell on his wall. Skateboarding. The tube.

He snuffles twelve times in a row. "I should be on the Gong Show."

M-Marty calls, Tom's painting partner. There's some more work at Harmony House, on Thursday, and they're going to try me out on the crew. Where? Oh, it's psycho-energetics, or something, moaning in the hallway, you know. A scam. Bucks and healing, a walk-in private outpatient clinic, or something. Quality painting for good bucks. In the skateboard factory. The shipping room, nudes and hotshots from skateboard magazines, "Ultimate Equipment!" Piles of wooden slats, drilled to take the trucks and wheels, megabucks. Tom and me, picking up Sharon from work. Yeah, I'll help her move, on

Wednesday, from the little apartment she had for three months over on Santa Barbara Street. We can talk some more, I'll take your picture, I'm trying to find a model. We are walking out the door, over to the car Tom and Sharon in front of me. "If you look carefully, you'll see Dick Fitz' white van coming down the street." Not exactly unannounced, five seconds, the white van, handsome, smiling face. Old Dick from college and 48B Fairview, Ivy in the bathroom. Friend of fifteen years, the only person I've visited here over all that time.

Painter of light and color, painter of experience and moods. Some-one I have something to tell; I am a little afraid, I tense up. I wanted to see Bette first, to ask her how she is, I sent her a note this morning, I love her, but here's Dick first.

"Tom, hey, how are you, what, three years?" We embrace.

"I thought you might get down this winter."

Over my shoulder. "I'll call you later." Tom and Sharon run off.

Kidnapped. Steely Dan, really.

He's tall: big and strong. Snapshot: wine glass, big smile, just great. There are those memories. I admired his genius, and it was from me that he learned the attitude, although we all were shown that attitude in college, in the late fifties. The art super-hero was not yet born as an ideal, we were meant to expose the genius in man with our lives, that was the line in fifty nine. Radical. We didn't any of us know the gauntlet was down. Some-what like the pitched warfare between man and woman right now, full epidemic breakdown of the love ideal, check the stats on incidence of rape, wife beating and worse going on per minute. So. Dick and I were roommates when I was a senior in '59. Bette came up from SC one weekend. They'd been together since they were both nine or something. It was love at first sight with her and me, and they're still together, kids, lives. . . she's like that.

He's chattering a friendly rap of the old days. I'm cold, afraid of changes and saying goodbye, being as cool as possible. We come up to the house and studio, tucked into Montecito by the creek. Around the bend, into the driveway, everything overgrown too much lost to be seen. The chocolate brown brown stucco house, the studio, bricks, patio, blacktop. A lot of work and a strange neglect. An isolation. A genius.

I should talk! My Montana front yard with beercans everywhere, dirty hippie kids, beautiful and dirty. Dead trees, a half finished house, I moved back in March of '73, burned piles for three days, a lot of stuff Sue bitched about, but the fires. . . throwing objects with thoughts attached to them into the flame, the ceremonies of the flame, all night seeing under the calm mescaline glow of the mad Montana moon big big sky, voicing strange songs there squatted by the glow, songs from nowhere voice deep within me, losing my mind in the fire . . . .

The inside of the house is a dismay. The pure watercolors on the wall, some small pieces, mostly, the visual-mental flip-flops. The bed, for some reason, in the living room on top of what looks like two old desks. A strange painted lady in the bed, kids running around. Bette's college room mate, coincidentally, visiting, trying out the license on make-up and masking.

The kitchen, which is familiar with brown bags, piles of, no room to, looking for, the absence of, and so forth. I know it well, everything but flies.

"Where's Macho?" The big fat cat. "He exploded."

Dick draws out the Bushmills, for two big glasses on ice and I grab a dos Equis from the box. Two horses. I down half the whiskey. "Come on, I'll show you the hot tub."

A nice job, really, it's going to work.

"I have two hundred slides of the construction," he says, like a shrine, to having done something.

"But is it a prototype, could you go into production?'

"No, it's for Bette."

"Come on, she said that, I don't believe it, it's for you, man, come on. . ."

He won't.

So we go down to get Bette, in her friend's $8,000 Ford something or other. She talks about getting back together with her old man, why?

Dick talks about his gig at Adult Ed with the old ladies, he isn't happy about it.

Maybe you don't belong there any more, he doesn't want to hear it.

Slow outside a Santa Barbara house, some fence, some stone, clapboard. Small, an artist's rental. There she is, after working out in Goleta, supporting her family, good Spanish lady that she is, Guatemala and old LA in her bloodlines.

She is out on the pavement, long black hair, body presence of woman, a depth that is real and feminine, she won't speak of it. Bob Todd, wrote a whole bunch of love poems on her. I hold her close. "I came to see you," to the ear.

Back to the house, the dishes escape, and a crab salad appears, and wine and dinner and a topic of conversation from Dick to Bette's friend.

"Yeah, Tom comes around every other year, to check on my wife, to take her away."

"I told you it was love at first sight," thrown back.

"Well, let's talk about sexual jealousy," he turns.

"Well, how about non-sexual jealousy," she and I both.

But he goes off to teach his night class and we have a couple of hours. Pretty lady from long ago and myself, as usual, doing the dishes.

"You mean, what I need is a better dishwasher?" She laughs like hell.

"No, I mean you're supporting a parasite."

"But he's beginning to know that, Tom, really. . . ."

So I drop it.

But we sit down at the table and I put my chair in front of hers, I touch her face and tell her this.

"Really, Bette, I'm bailing out of Montana, finally, and going for it' Something, The Big Scoop. I'm through with the phony vow of poverty. And now, really, I'm all alone, and well. Me and Alex. I'm looking for my ladies. I don't know how people do it, really, multiple lives, but everyone is with someone but me, it seems, I'm the loner."

"Well, you always were, you know, and here we are again 'will she or won't she'."

We have Keith Jarrett on, Lausanne, side six, slow sign fills the air remembering the attraction, the distance of the dance, the years across the light. Yeah, I am alone, and surprised by it, this land of promiscuous lemmings, down in the last edges of decay, the love ideal almost devoured by the sex ideal, from heart throb to masturbation, the Penthouse ladies on the Redd Foxx show, whew.

And we talk about the job, the life. There is growth, I see, but slow and steady doesn't always win the race, I remember my father's descriptions of being passed over, in the Navy, it sounded a little like a Cat D-9, moving through the woods, leaving immeasurable snail trails, towing out the big corpses with orange paint at the base, stacking them up, on the truck and into the mill, the tree cemetaries. . . .

Late at night, they call me on the phone, yeah, I'm thinking of yew, tew.

When Dick comes back, there is a disintegration between us. Bette drops from view, Dick and I get down over some Pastoso and Bush-mill's and his own outrageous home grown, the dizzy confrontation, he drinks too much and I'm too drunk, stoned out. It follows.

We're down by the creek he transformed. The pools, built over five or six years, constant risk of painter's hands, barring boulders around. Better carrying cement. We talk about Tom.

"Maybe, now that he's making some money he'll be a little less aggressive." A portrait. "I mean, he'll make it OK, he's good. . ."

"But you're not going for it, man, what's the top price now in the major leagues? Isn't that what you're playing in. . .?"

"Well, a good Diebenkorn goes for thirty seven five. . . ."

"Don't you ever imagine doing multiples?" The audience. Hungry.

Quality silkscreens at Penney's for twenty five dollars. . . .

"No , I'm still doing prototype experiences."

"Come on, Dick, let's go into business."

We're down at the studio. I'm cold and I have to piss. Big canvases, turned to the wall. Eight by twelve feet and such. Two hundred of them, at least. Patches of color, light that turns to object. Mental equivalents for speech, motives of light and color combined, grace of silent airs in refuge from the present, swirls of air that take time to grow from the frosty blind silence of thought. The air reels. Large episodes in rarified separation. Not communal, not famous. The play. For all of it. Top of the line and holding out. It was Dick who taught me to see paintings.

"Really, I think that if I'm in the studio, here, doing my work, I don't care how long it takes, someone, some time, will come up to the studio. . . ."

"And you'll be discovered."

"Well, yeah. . . ."

"I'm the only one who knows you." Not fair.

I remember my pre-sexual fantasy, in the back yard at Lemon Grove, when I wasn't blowing up the tomatoes with cherry bombs or shooting cans thirty feet up into the air. I figured that up in the sky, far overhead, a silent Gary Powers' sort of airplane, silently winging the atmosphere. The door slides open. A black foot nudges a package over the side, into the light, pop! A package, a white parachute, echoing slowly downward, toward the aerial map below. I am standing in the yard, a chubby twelve, looking up at the pendulum of, of, well something arcing back and forth, coming down, or growing larger, down, down, a little brown attache case, in a white parachute, landing, smack! on the grass in the middle of the yard, it pops open. Bright sunlight on fluttering paper, Dollars, a light wind breezy blowing them around the yard, a million dollars! I faint with pseudo orgasm, my pre adolescent fantasy of rescue.

Somewhere, we fall aside, and unroll some foam on the living room floor. I pass out.

And light at six. Bette is stirring, going to work. They sleep on the platform. She pulls her pants on, I catch a ride, oh, my head, hangover gaze of self conscious anxiety trembling, the nature of alcohol. Something happened. The slow ride back over gray-light hill to Milpas Street. Bette talks about Sharon, she likes her. In front of the house.

"Isn't it nice that all he has to do is paint? He doesn't ever have to do anything but paint." My heart sinks. I stand in the van, her head goes back, I press myself to her stomach and stroke her breasts and kiss her mouth goodbye.

I go up the stairs to Tom and Sharon's. She's ready. I stumble around, 6:30, coffee, out the door, riding to the university for her last final and we're going to have more coffee and move some things home. I grab the Leica and snap her freehand while we're driving to Goleta. Gray air the uniform apartments there were none before. A campus of fifteen hundred, grown up.

A quarter for a paper to stick to the window, for parking. We find the slot and say we'll meet at ten. I go for breakfast at the student center, across blocks of buildings where I remember none. And it's not nostalgia as I understand it, when you see change and feel sadness for, for something, for not having changed, probably. Nostalgia seems to me to be feeling as though you weren't really a part of it, that what grew like a mushroom had nothing to do with who you are. No, I remember fields now filled.

Space where there is none, objects where there were none before. It's like seeing the evidence. When you build you soon forget what was there, so involved is your attention with what's happening that you miss the space. Yeah, a building, there, a thing, a cube, a rock, a space, there, and sidewalks, it's made like that, wow, and I go to look for coffee, I need it. I have to wait half an hour.

So I sit around and throw the coins and think about my page, the lagoon outside the window and the guy sitting over there, turns out to be a 45 year old Yale economist, out for interviews. I tell him about the I Ching and that I'm researching a book, my own story and we fall to about Charlie Reich and Eric Segal.

"A lot of guys like you," she says with some respect for different lives. "Intelligent men around forty, with nothing to do, ex-teachers, they'd like to hear from you."

It's peculiar, though, the empty walls, the dead university during finals week, barely populated. The wave has certainly crested. Old Mudhen over there, in his office, I won't even bother, he'd just give me some shit about Pisces; I sent him one, of course. And Herbie.

It's time to meet Sharon, and I sit in the sun, with more coffee and load my camera. It's a beautiful day.

It is a slow dance we do, this life emergent, the tread and toss of the bare foot, a hand in the air, a voice which calls from deep within, as speech, as word and energy uprushed from the center, a celebration, the grace of it. Feelings accumulated over the years, constituting a memory, and choice which takes what's good and discards the rest, images, thoughts, feelings, burns them, removes them. Edit. Recall is selective.

"Je parle le francais, tous les jours," she speaks a low music over and over, the freeway hum, the ride to town.

"I moved here in January," the voice goes up at the end of the sentence, not in question but in emphasis. It makes you listen. A nice moment, a meeting and a confidence, and we turn, and turn, and slide between hedges, a big old victorian house in good shape, the gatehouse apartment, we park the car. Through the hedge into the next yard, a gleam of white plastic roundness, large. Peer-ing through, a donut shaped sphere with no hole in the middle. A cute little spaceship has landed. On a pod, hinged window-ports. A playhouse, a smoking room. . . .

In the height of the ceiling, the space enlarges, light from between the blinds, I raise them turn and snap a line, her eyes see and then another line. She puts the coffee on.

"I like it percolated, no?" Luziane, with chicory and a Sherman for each of us, and we sit at the small table, in chairs, across from, each other, and, really, chatter.

"Awkward and flamboyant and distant, all mixed together," she said on the phone yesterday. "A first day."

"I respected you so much, but I was afraid of you."

"I didn't want you to know me. . . ." The old days. "Asking for closeness from everyone and pushing it off quickly because it hurt too much to feel. Anything."

"And what happened?" Upvoice.

"Ah, then, I gave it up. I went in for help. I resolved to wind it up, the pain. So I did my work and we finished it in about six hours, really."

She has done counseling and submitted to some. "Whew." Eyes.

I snap a line. "Is that comfortable? I mean the artist and the model should talk."

"Of course." She smiles. "My father, yes, that's the photo on the bookshelves, at the house. He's pretty loose at fifty."

We'll meet, I guess."

"And you, what are you doing, coming back into a new life, what can you see to make you do it?"

"Oh, Sharon, it's the end of the road up there. A place to be, Perhaps; and the woods, of course; but I got lonely. Suddenly, my heart's here, it's time to come back and share a little, some-how. I like it, being a man, myself."

Glittering, we snap back and forth, the camera passes both ways.

"I mean, the picture, the picture is, really, a gift, and what you're showing is your message, that's what looking back means."

It is easy conversation.

At the dishes, later, the crystal   and the lady, image of speech voice, and music. I see it.

And we play around certain postures, at the mirror, the lady in the kitchen, I am learning and shooting. "Better than the Penthouse Pets, much as I love them; we should have other images of the feminine. I'm always seeing a version of my own woman, and, as Sea said, "Sometimes it's a raincoat and sometimes it's an old raccoon." All right.

"I'm knowing you better," she says.

Some boxes are packed.   She has *Pisces*, and asks me to read from it.

"Will you read?" I unwind four or five pages of the cosmic trance dance, of the words I fall with grace the erotic flow of syntax and rhythm, I run my number, I play my tape. A moment of the present disappears into the ear's reading of the text.

"I see, you have to hear it."

"No, you have to listen."

She wants to write a book. "Sometime, I'm only twenty-eight," is old enough to write every day. I remember the years of horse and rider, the rage and terror with which the battle for self discipline was fought, with the erotic flow which is the creative play of acts. The silver surfer, gliding through the years, watching for pitfalls and cataclysms, caught by one gigantic storm and swept through the valleys of the spirit, at a fresh shore grounded, here, Santa Barbara parachute drop.

Really, I'd like to find a lady to work with, for a long time, years, and coax these images out, like, the foxy lady, the wise and sensual lady, all the versions. . . it's a project, you know, and my learning."

"Well, we do have to move some boxes," takes another hour, it seems, the film run through my eyes, "Mental Floss," Tom says, reaming an invisible pipe cleaner through his ears. . . .

Reluctantly, we drive across town, the secret room a meeting, and simple, or plain, as they say, just that.

* * * * * * * * * *

Mozart Clarinet Quintet, K 581, Benny Goodman.

In the time after completion, one might radiate in the crossing itself, in the feeling that you have survived, ah, and let deep sighs out; but not really, there is a danger, in falling back into a new hole. Rather, in contemplating the forms of the world, is the world changed. Sun through window, light on the page, the pen sliding on. . . .

At work, the next day, I paint trim at Harmony House, a slick spot on the map. They are healing the wounded downstairs. They come in and drop their shoes at the front door, ten or so, gathered in the front room, bent over, hands on knees, swivel hipping. I mean if you never boogie, never dance, and spend the gray light of morning with only your left hand for company, the body goes numb.

"It's sort of a waggle," frizzy red hair says, an MA in Psych, probably, doing his thing.

Upstairs, we are striping the rooms, a two inch royal blue stripe around the lower perimeter of the bathroom, it floats away into design and green plants, orange and green and dark green in the bedroom, false wainscotting. Tom and I smoke a joint and off we go, running drops and sentences, and exploring the art spirit. "Robert Henri says it's the writers first, who make the breakthrough, because people listen to them; the painters come later." "I don't know, you can see a hell of a lot faster than you can think, but you never have to think a little to see something you've never seen before. . . ." AM radio, Jackson Browne, Runnin' on Empty.

They are moaning, oh God, the pain, this chorus of agony from downstairs, alfalfa sprouts in the shower. Oh, God, they are moaning. Marty stumbles in, his arms outstretched, Frankenstein gaze pasted onto his being. Soundless mimic. Equally soundless, we collapse on the drop cloths, slapping holding rolling back and forth with no sound permitted. Oh, the paintners are here, scum of the trades, high on fumes, hiding out upstairs. . . . I'm on the crew.

"Oh, it's looking good," a sweet young thing says.

"Oh, yes," I say, "escellent, escellent."

"Escellent?" she laughs and walks away. I see her later, by the picket fence, painting it. "Yes, I'm a universalist," I say, wiseacre.

"We practice all practices, we practice the universal diet, we eat everything. For trances, go to coffee, beer and dope. You'll be insane in three days."

"Yes, I guess if you're happy, your system can take anything. I used to smoke dope all the time," she says, a little wistful over her loss of evenings at hippie's delight, listening to the stereo with the silent tube glowing a nonstop abstract film. The cinema of the future!

And at dinner that night, at the Plaka, a long harangue from the greek owner, about how great his show is. We are all packed in to table, Retsina and Mousakka, and only OK, too. I mean, it's packed with people, doing the great Greek dance, even a hang-in-there old grandma; the surly Greek with the microphone: "And NBC was here, with their cameras, and they filmed us, and I finally saw it" You know, I have never seen myself on film, and I said, pretty good, I said." Every night, I guess. Well, pretty soon he's got the fucking table in his teeth, the leg running down the front of him, and he's up and spinning around, twirling with the table, around around mad clapping! "All right!" Hoots. And then two tables, really, not bad, and we fall apart. Intense cautious Margie talking about Hiam Ginott, and kids. Alex who twisted the grape-fruit into a strange, smiling, pink mouth. "Jemmy Cartuh..." Ha. Ha.

Good Friday I'm up at six, I throw the coins and put the last poem away. "Dispersion," the book calls, changing to "the taming power of the small." Really.

The light around yr body, perfect, unrestrained as passage calms attention turned throughout the day's beginning in the heart you come to see as forward lines become the time you are to me, a life returned to being in and of, the light, the day. The spoken moments aroused and singing, at larger turns begun. . . ."

My stomach collapses, my body is seized with an immense pain.   I collapse, go down for a cycle of sleep. A final poem and a final passage, I am freed, then, to go on with it, I sleep without dreaming. Inside, development continues, ". . .the day of the expanding man. . ." Flying homeward bound, a lady on my mind and letters waiting to be read. Astounding!

Ah, to prose, at last. I must only find the voice. Sunday, mescaline, the vision on the beach. I am ready.

Chapter 4   EASTER EASES

Saturday morning, Tom and Marty and I go up the hill to stain some cabinets. Four hours, rags with brown fluid, I'm squatting in the sun, with the garage door open, knocking out shelves for an hour and a half. Ten dollars an hour and I'm broke. Top, flip, edges, wipe it back, stacked up against the wall, fifty shelves with birch veneer, walnut stain, looking good.

"Is this demeaning," Tom jives from the door. "Huh? Is this demeaning, ten dollars an hour?" "Yeah, man, it's the shits, work is pain, work is agony, work is bucks." "Really." "Yeah, good ol' Workus Bux, organizer for the scabs. . . ." We develop the mythology of Workus Bux, leader, follower, teacher of hard labor.

Cousin Mike, my own, driving up from LA, this afternoon, for a little family, jesus, all redheads. "Commies, punks, freaks, hippies and redheads," we chant; and pick up Pastoso, Lowenbrau Dark and Sherman's for lunch. I'm going shopping for Easter Dinner with my $50.00 in food stamps. The day, the day the day.

We pull up from Mrs. Sweeney's shelves, Tom and me, and there's redhead Mike, cousin from years, who lived with us all along, on and off, with grandmother Hazel, followed me down to Santa Barbara, and went to the museum at UCLA for ten years, installing shows with Willie. He sees. Collages: tight drawing, a wing-poster from his Mythical World Show. Isn't that it?

"Hey, old buddy, really, three no four years, far out, yah, Palo Alto, here I am, wow!"

A little dance, and we have Tom and Mike, two red hair left handed Aries artists, hard at it, "You're good, really," Mike keeps saying; Tom is ecstatic, he starts throwing stuff around the room again, the wine bottle shares our words fillingly spoke, and family fills the air. And the day goes like that, goes and goes, through Bimmy Juffet and Steely Dan and Abbey Road and the Starship's Miracles, our Easter morning song from Sharon. As has, so let.

Sharon and I go to Von's for our food-run, a basketful of goodies, a fresh leg of lamb. "It's the menstrual beast, the beast that bleeds, the blood of the lamb, for Easter dinner," "Oh, traditional, yes?" She speaks along the aisles we're after artichokes and biscuits and a special mint sauce. I'll cook the meal tomorrow, I love to cook.

And in the car," You should have a family conference with Sue, you know, have you ever done that?" "No," and ". . .of course you can't feel guilty, you know, they'll be all right." We settle on the banquet and drive the short space, light across the wheat field of my mind, really, the soft green flow of the golf course. Steam against the rocky mountains, a sharp relief, the palm trees against the background of the purple horizon, the Channel Islands out there, yes, a seaweed cutter gobbling organic mountains. Mopeds.

Up Mason to the curve, we call around the spaces left by love and kinship, the art kinship which illuminates the most ordinary meals and seasons, we arrive at large and singing out.

It is the Saturday night before Easter. We are stranded in front of Miratti's, stalled, out of beer. Tom grabs a six-pack of Lite half quarts and throws me a dark San Miguel, "He popped the top." Really. A Sherman goes between the joints and we head up into the hills, Mike and Tom and Tom and Scott. Dark hours call the moon nearly full, it is not yet risen.

Somehow, the Pinto climbs the hill, we turn on switchbacks in the darkness above Santa Barbara, with pinpoint curve of the lighted coast clear clear below, damp air surrounds this growth, and the moon pops.

We stop against the mountain, slowly stopping, sliding into an opening beside the cliff. We're high on it. The beginning of the year, spring's rush of ceremonial thoughts, a joint.

Mike hesitates, years ago doubled over in paranoia, carried back to San Francisco, almost, from Mazatlan, he's never smoked since. "Really, Mike, it's circumstances as much as anything else that brings you down, and look where we are. . . ."

The full round pendant of ice, hanging in the blue dark, we're stacked along the side of the car, bathing in our pale luminescence, growing light with the light of it, the immanence of the hour and the meaning of tomorrow. And where we are is here among our presence, the globe-glow at full and resurrected, a rare concurrence of myths and hours, of years and visions.

"Really, man, this is the place, welcome to Athens. Let's get together and pool reports, let's make this thing go." It's what we're all saying, the full moon fuller, centered on the harbor, centered on our selves, and now a huge ring fills the sky around the moon, fills the entire sky, mandala pin-point, celestial target, diagram of use, message from the year of the great rains. Renewal. It is our year, at last. The circle of the moon, repeated lines, the huge circle in which we are caught. Mike has the vision. He speaks.

"I mean, this feeling of unity inside, of being together, looking out over the city, now, the four of us," the joint passing through the cans of light. It is no drunken fantasy, I mean, there are those moments, but drugs are medicine, the Indians teach us, and we go to those places for instruction, outlaw priests that we are, mystics without teachers, we have no tradition of our own, it is moment, faith and sign, and in this longer moment of our present, tonight, we receive our sign.

When we get back to the house, Sharon is worried; we were hypnotized by the power of the moment, grabbed at. Three days later the road collapses in a mudslide from the winter rains.

We go down into the night, a restless sleep of hours, and day's beginning calms the heart, at Easter, on six o'clock moods, I start my new writing. I throw my coins and drink coffee in the hollows of the morning, awaited by the beach. Danny got me a cap of mescaline in Mazola before I left, for three bucks, a two-way in chocolate milk powder. I pour half in my coffee and wait, I pour the other half on my tongue. Medium.

I get the leg of lamb out and stroke it with olive oil and fresh mint leaves from the garden. I slice short slits and stuff the garlic in, five cloves, Salt and pepper and cumin, let it sit, and we head out for breakfast, cousin Mike and I. We stop in Montecito for some Sherman's and two Tuborg's and he drops me at the beach.

Well, I'm not, what you'd say, wired, but the energy is there, the other. I watch from the other side of myself. A rush of feeling, excitable boy, *this is John Galt.* That's the work, to speak, to get it down, to look around and tie the voice to the seeing, to synchronize thought and voice, to make it whole. In the hot sun by the frisbee players, I hold my arm out and snap ten frames. It doesn't happen that often, but I check up on myself from time to time. The flat horizon of *L'Etranger,* sparse figures, Easter Sunday morning.

I find the hot point of thought deep within. Tom is speaking. . . .

"For my own fulfillment, that's what it's for, this art business." Really, those poems saved my life, if I hadn't been writing I'd have been just another cheap hustler on the run. The head swarming ecstasies of youth and life, the passage through the great fear, flying my own course and finding a way out, out and back, the great adventure, sure, but any man's, really, that's the lesson. I hold my heart out, for words, I scribble shakily speeded words, I peer in the sun from under my sky blue visor, "Pure Juice," really, the words themselves, the hand snaking across, jumping jerkily spears out at lines and lines. The moment enters my being, calls down to work, the image of the beloved etched on the inside of my eyeballs. The world is the beloved.

THE VISION ON THE BEACH / Easter Sunday 1978.

This is the voice which speaks aloud for the first time my own. The simpler times of life are passages where it follows the dreaming light. The color of the beach is said again, and I can hear the frisbee touch into the sand, the picture of the boat offshore has a man walking in front of it; his arms are swinging loosely around him, and he passes slowly back and forth in front of the gray green surf-waves. I heard

these noises make a center from where I could hear them singing frisbee songs around the bend.

This that voice and watched for fifteen the evolution and collapse of familiar lives, strained across the crack and gasp of tension unreleased. This voice said "Listen" to no-one at all. I listened.

From the silence of passing buses, the Eagle sliding swift and quiet, unseen inner cosmonaut, intronaut of future expressions alive in persons.

The lady in her graces passing through my heart. Tears around the sun and white horses in the water. We are walking down a road in Turkey. White light calms the eye, intensifies seeing and feeling. She says, "Look, the horses in the water, grazing on the watercress." Low trees wide spaced, where water cautions the ground a river comes toward the sea. And there are white houses at the edge where we were given a honeycomb from the jeep-riders. We are hitch-hiking somewhere.

Dream weaver, song, yr radio says the present is here and singing. She slaps the frisbee on her ass, gives a wide throw, rolling blue disk the negro lady chases on Easter Sunday at East Beach in Santa Barbara, the vision at the center of the voice says simultaneous, to catch the sign of light across the page, as simpler words are going slow across the page. Phenomenal.

Speak, it says, again, yr homecoming perfect return to life from fragmented balloons of mad air striking from all directions all at once.

Silently, he comes home. He returns. I am the same voice spoken from within these trips around. Calm surf breaks the sand a repe-tition of life, begins again within return, and calls aloud for brothers and sisters met between hallways, strained pursuit, the mad dream broken out at the heart of the mountains, very much my own story. I am I, is what it means to say. Slight encounters on the bus, the two brown boys sitting beside their sister, neither talking. She's buried in a fumetti. When I sat next to her and slightly touched to say hello, she slides toward the window, holding the tan and white pages. She's only fifteen, with braces and zits, a shy chicano girl-mama ferrying brothers into some new and innocent experience, growing up on the Greyhound.

How can this world be so exhausted, the fire runs me constant forty years flash by, another life begins. The seed lives within. A three hundred pound poet back east with no kids, who writes non-stop Voice, is he the laureate? Of us?

Cousin Michael drops me off. "I'll see you in an hour and a half."

Beach vision. No the voice does not come from out there. More like the center of my head, no cosmic allusions, only the voice that talks, blatter-ramble, chatterflap. Super-hip fancy of hours unrecorded senses going non-stop fantasy speech.

Look at her walk, fast but slow, bending at least from the waist, her tight middleaged ass needs the corncob I have hanging in my bedroom, upside down. The kernels popped off up to the graceful yellow penis-end. All the ladies like it, "Ooh! What's that for?"

"Come on, I'll show you how it works."

"Oh, no," she giggles. "It'd hurt me."

"I won't," I say, "I'm a gentle-man."

Or does that mean what it says to mean. The voice that talks is not necessarily the one that remembers. Milking the right vein, the left hand wins. "I should practice the right hand," she said.

"We all come from somewhere."

"How, or why, this difference. Is it just inertia, or solitude?"

"Oh, all that, all that goes by and stays. You are, you know, and what's the rest?"

Oh, but so long not knowing.

And you. Who are you and why are you here.

No, it's just "The Return", that's all. It happens in ordinary lives, not those artifacts they handed us, so easy to split or fall away.

This is the voice that speaks. Tightly colored loops recall the action of the past. I am remembered. And then this other one, the one that remembers and talks.

Lists of bibliographies have dried up inside my speech. Fill in the speaking lines.

What is this blitz, man, who caught us back there and made for all this silence? Who opens the door if not me, right here and now, and listen, out there, the calm returns, I am neither mumbling lunatic beach stone nor fruitfly cosmic soaring unknown seeds.

The calm return to life, the beach is sand and silence, open, you are the Sea, lady, brimming on my shore, realized, touched, remembered faces. Dark in the middle of the field in 1960, lying in the grass. She ran from the little red house after two days of What'd I Say, then, and waited blocks away in the field. I crept up to her. I circled around her. I could not touch or take. Shy eyes tremble.

Mescaline edge crackles at the edges. The handwriting spreads around. But the calm light, center remains. The core of belief, the passage through the mountains and back to ordinary life. The vision at the end of the trail.

Up to piss, stride the solemn gray skied cool-beach. Immense man blue suit beard rattles his keys as I pass into the large cream white room, piss cascadingly into the quiet empty room, he's seated by the window outside. Give him Dustin Hoffman eyes. Rattle squeak, I go out the doors, the keys rattle furiously, feverishly, I give him no-eyes, pass slowly under green wood arches, past the fat pink suited Mexican *buns, across teeny-bopper bodies flat and munching apples, smooth across the sand my spot, two beer bottles and a pack of Sherman's. Folded Penney's Plain Pockets. The very day.*

So a day is all the same, here, even, rebirth among self, the mountain muse another housepainter squatting in morning light before an open garage door, brushing out a dozen birch veneer shelves which go inside a hollow door birch veneer sideboard, built-in, specific.

Mike, anyway, is soon to be back from seeing the old Roland, who, he says, is getting his mid-thirties crazies and drinking too much. Those good ol' boys from the beach, they didn't make it. . . .

Ordinary lives recall the larger adventures.

"We're going to have sticks everywhere."

The lady in the long green thing is collecting wood for a fire. Calm surf, the air returning to light.

Look, we have come through. "He's trying to pull my pants down."

And love, the calm center of a man and a woman, seen in the center of the year, yr voices speaking.

Floating on his board, a motorboat pulling him, a guy floats out of Sight. And things seen have weight before the body knows. Hook the eyes into the dream, but be there, looking back, is that so very mysterious? Who led you off, you who don't look back; touched, the eyes slide off, the other lines are spoken softly, she danced around the room, I danced around together said, we are, lady, reunited after long darkness.

Love returns, the beloved speaks, one on one, the flesh, the perfect center of her body and I dive in, I hold my own, I come forward, touching her cheek where she smiles "yes" at me, and we go together softly onto the bed, holding, rolling saying yes you are, and yes you are, an awakened presence, a song along the day and dreaming forward.

Now he's up on two yellow skis, gliding by, Mike peering around, here, here, the voice that speaks.

* * * * * * * * * *

We are across town, I fumble into the studio, babbling, I got the voice, I got the voice. Tom, at easel, Kent from next door, a young Brookie. I throw the shadow pictures out at Kent, the fifty best of three hundred negatives, from three months work in '72, in Sacramento, when I was building the grammar for the private language, aesthetic for light events. Dramatic. The photographs are like a meeting of the unconscious with the real, where the film stops. Between the visible and the invisible. And they are jokes, too, the shadow on the laundry, the shadow with the cat inside it, the shadow with a child inside, the shadow flying away. The event of the shadow.

"Well, how's the art spirit," Sharon calls to us entering the sunlight of the garage-studio. What a day. It's time to put the roast in which I do, and collapse for forty minutes, shedding the mescaline. Silence, and no more doubt.

Really, it is a feast, on the old-new wobbly picnic table under the grape arbor in the back yard. Cloth. Plates. Mashed potatoes and asparagus, artichokes and lemon butter, mint sauce and gravy and lamb and biscuits and cheese, the wine flows, espresso and Sherman's. Art talk art is real, which lives, and in us spoke.

We are standing in the kitchen, Mike says we should head for LA, I have to try to get hold of Willie tomorrow, Sea says it's important. A seed, a nut, then, of information, the ominous shadow of Scientology somewhere quite specific in our conversations of the past week, friends gone under to mystical robotics, whew, look out. Sea's notion that I should head for Boulder. For Trungpa.

"And Waldman?" We pass in the dark. But we are standing in the kitchen.

"We did it. Pushed the rock away and he's gone. All right!"

Slap hands all around.

And in the living room, sitting on the floor, in front of Tom's four foot by ten foot rendering of the photo from last year's family reunion. Bill at center, beaming, Polly the same, all four red-headed children smiling in their own smiles. "Miracles" is on loud enough. "Just an ordinary miracle," she says "you get a second chance. Really, that's what we need, just an ordinary miracle will do. . . ." I get up and do my dance.

At the door, she says, "But what about buzzwords," hugging all the way around. "Oh," I say, "parallel languages, on two tracks," going down the stoned steps and into the car with Mike, buzzed cooked, smoothed, flown. Juiced and buttered, loose. Vernacular Holy Day.

As we leave, I yell out, "More!"

And driving to LA, I am amazed. Mike tries to talk, but I'm lost to thought. Really, it is event, and I am high on it, samsara, synchronized.

I know who I am and where I am going, the return of the spirit in the half glow of Easter Sunday dying off, the glow of the cars whistling through Carpenteria and Camarillo off the road on a short cut, driving in a car. And I know where I've been.

Really, all the lines are down, the war is over. Since Watergate. Crazed, slightly over the peak of it, in Mazola at Chris's house, watching the tube, the cosmic showdown, the great shootout, when the media finally shot down the government. There is no more government, the hot point at the center of my forehead, there is only media, and us, whew, look out. New languages. And California, homecoming

63

and return. The Silver Surfer gliding silent through the air, California is the world, man, call it what you will, the war is over when you've won.

Closing in on Santa Monica, Mike gets angry. Going back to work, I suppose. But he's right. "Macho fucking drivers, you son of a bitch!" Really. "You pass and they speed up." Honk and cut in. The finger. No radio, mad drivers whistling back and forth in line, push and shove, the LA 500.

South of Oxnard, the dog on the road, his head mostly taken off, by something, a car, "Ah, LA approaches."

At the light, where 101 goes from the beach and a frontage road splits up the hill into Santa Monica. Cars stopped, lights, people out, trouble, we slow down. A car, stalled in the middle of the intersection, people out, pushing in headlighted highlights, arms waving, more enthusiasm than trouble. LA. Really.

Book Two
VISION OF EAGLE

Summer of '78   Summer of '73

CHAPTER 5   **SOUTHEAST OF DISORDER**

Mr. Jimmy

We must go out and mingle freely with all sorts of people, friends or foes.

That is the only way to achieve something. . . .

Wilhelm

This is the deep remembering, clean clear fall into madness calling a name across the air, my own. The remembering takes place like this:

Deep within the core of what happened, I mean what happened to you in the summer of '73, for instance, fix that point clearly in your own mind, relaxed, falling back across the years, the past few years, even, the beginnings of books clear in your mind, a few islands and stepping stones across this, this something of the past few years, *melange*, I calls it, the chemical soup of the final mutation, the survival of invisibility which makes the dramatic event. . . . possible at all.

You'd settle back, then, and call recall the name of the game, and— cutting back and forth is something clear enough for "far dancing," the long clear dive of people in costumes, I suppose, another picture like this.

The white pole rising. Close, she stoops backwards, bent over the table. You speak her name and enter the tight ring of muscle, ah, and in the darker hours, a tunnel of light throughout the whole body, back and forth the muscle plays, you are, you are, the marks along the floor are wet, arrived, perhaps, like the sense of some other, uh, feeling, and it stays like this for awhile.

But the remembering is slower, even, than making love when it is all thought, or all thought about or what you might call thought, or all thought about or what you might call thought, or what you might call making love, remembering is like that.

The light on the surface of the white paint, stipple of roller marks, the insides of the drawers still a flat yellow, "all visible surfaces," of the windows, for instance, which didn't really need painting, or the day arrived in work, the name of acting, the body goes along almost automatic the cool drift of recall makes another surface to the seeing actually take place.

It is really the things of thought which pass for action; rough disclosures mean that the passing of events have made their mark upon the personality itself, or said relief is more a quality of perception than the stuff of recall; open designations of the real are marks which clear the forms of seeing from their own distance, loosening up the hand is said enough to tell them how we are tonight you're dreaming of what I said last night; a memory of '73 is clear across the day's behaviors moving slowhand saying this or that, and still, again, the texture of the act remembered flash of feeling, really, and image simultaneous moment.

You made the deeper acts revolve like the center of events, a situation more real than the even flow of speech which closes acts to more than mere disturbance, slight positions more than clear, nothing is lost to what is heard, the selective ear for which the moment itself is a surrender or a salute, the even flow of passion through the centers of light again. . . .

The deep base of light paling outer, coils the depth of light play-ing here and there among the memories, the hot pencil thin light; intense choice says "here" and the white needle dives in, erasing an image. One could go through his entire inventory piece by piece and clear it all out. . . .

The little rat girl, I have seen her here on the streets for two or three years, she is lost, fattish, strange scooped eyes yet look back, her thin strange yellow hair died back black yesterday, with something, and clear etched, no whiskey eyes were seeing this, but the same black wool coat slithered back across drooped back across her shoulders almost falling off the Charlie Tramp waif reborn, it is that, that she is so much the reborn waif-child avatar of or from the movie that I doubt her, uh, authenticity, floating child of Mazola streets, except that, one fears, someone will kill her. God save us. . . .

The remembering of grace is yet plentiful, the source, perhaps, of light, I mean, around your body, in between sentences of light I call recall the job, or the hand job of all time; I have the story here, right here in the summer of '73, not so very far back at all, the drone of acid eyes crazy meadow the hot dirt wind blew the virgin away, the pole of flowers, the tree of life it was, dried away, even the chair burned up with me almost in it, or Tom, we jumped back and forth. Crazy eyes.

In the recall of the dream, a song of light against the hours repeating here and there the same lines remind us that we are, then, returned to life beyond events, uh, it happened like this, the deep remembering stance, or trance, or the diving in to light, or life, or both.

The same with running tapes: you just go into the situation and splatter the shots go down the line she says yes, dream, remember, even the cold white light of early '73, in the trailer with Jody, falling on the bed one sunny day, the best ever, we said the sun was yellow enough, my prose, perhaps this melting line across the air.

Across the years I chased the demon poet, I rode him hard down the lines of the past years and their currents of present air, vapor, less than serious, really, the magnitude of the planet.

You call my name for something closer than anything remembered by those who are too close to tell anything. The clinic in Palo Alto, the doctor in his office, your frail position endangered by the close call of death.

So remembering anything is remembering everything all at once, from the present vantage point, that is, and let it fly outer, out, further, forward speaks the air of your own retreat across the days dividing hours hot along the matter on the wall. . . .

Day at charge. Other markers flow, and seen like this, that words are things, he sleeps at flying currents soaring upward, then, fulfilled at life's dream lived in, then, and then remembered, told, let-in-on, you are, it's like unembarrassed teacher makes mistakes, can't spell for shit, laughs all the time, but wait, there, it is more the drift of easy thoughts, from where you are now, the summer moments flown, it is about the same time of the year now, the same May days which make you say, yeh, the year's cycle comes the great wheel, and every February, ah, repetition, the trance and drum of cool remembering: the same the same the same. And I suppose that's why the age is suddenly classical but not boring.

But coming of age is the topic, really, of the vision, and it is from life-as-art and life-as-myth and life-as-personal that the drama goes to life. I know the old ego words for being crazy, but if something large goes off in you, you might want to put your own life, you might want to put your own name on what and why but that's rare. . .

But if you're direct enough not to say it all at once, how, really, could you? This is coaxing, after all, the reader and the writer both relaxing after the morning colombo and coins, another wave of the hot true stuff emotes your stomach, head, the day's job a half an hour away: easy enough for this prelude to thought, or thought's behavior, it was the long hot summer of '73 I lost my lunch, or what you say, the larger lines defined by this: context of choices: "I'll try anything, I'm desperate to know. . ." or the old art-lives attitude of what-the-fuck-go-for-it, really, now, it's a little bit hip to be crazy, and I thought, front runner high stepper to leap out flying fantasy superman the way is clear, I had spent five years assembling this little package of information compressed or reduced, miniaturized microfiche of private communications, I had this assemblage of cues, the whole shot on one page, I imagined and I knew the concept of the jump, really, from Buber, the style, man, the voice.

You call the days your own, even, sometimes the cool expectations of life invade description, I had these cool pressures wrapped around the socio-psychic not of definition of what a life is, not a man at all but such a student, channeled into, whoosh, the gestures grew more mad, "This is my brother, he's crazy," from winter '62.

Wide Gaviota rumblings. But Montana. Listen, the scale of the cloud pattern, a place for sky stories, rush of size, flesh of rolling hills, the glaciated sculpture the size of which immense we are the men walking around in this light, here, the wind an easy breeze from the left it feels the distance it really is, ah, the woods, seeing it, roll and flesh of carpet green and life.

Seen along the way, or the other signs are left clear enough to see, if only you looked. Any saying is quite the same, and the experimental attitude of OK as long as you are not committed to completion. She stays away, usually, different people looking for different things, the arousing of life, or for life; the same density is more or less overpowering, or you call thought and memory different planes of the same modesty, vocabulary and surprise: smooth and longer calls at air remove the sailing lines.

You are, and calm remembered the hot point of flashing lights, things seen along the way, those are the snapshots, then, and there is the deep recall, they are not quite the same hopscotch across associated feelings which reassociate or mutate to new images, flux and gloss the movement shows you how the rest locates wet between the legs, she stands and tries to talk about it, and has her hand between her legs, and sees you come between her eyes, a spot, a tongue, you are, again. . . .

Avid recall of the senses. You might remember the summer of '73, as smaller houses, no light in your basement heart of flowers strewn around the nest, the day, even, calling out your own names are flying colors in retreat the massive columns in their statuary, the evocation of the wind is clear enough, too, by the sea and not remembering how you are this madness left away, the dropping of self: the mask has slipped aside in mountainous elegance, they peel afloat the tides of reason ply the coastal waters inside less popular discourse, as inner leaves have paling lines no platform but thought in its essence in fantasy feelings called erotic substance, even the shape of the pole itself arising from the center of your body has newer marks are called the flashing and immediate description of unknown substances or manners of occupied persons where they fall, clearly, into the passions or the frosty valves.

This is an example of what I was talking about. The grace of the drift into the exact space of five years ago.

Not awake, yet, you think; the now of being involved, even, at loving, where are there words for it, even, among our short staccato barks and grunts, "Come on, baby, come on. . ." and she gives, suddenly, shuttering and flaking out, legs waving deeper shots the calm release of light from the exact center of her body, you are watching the dark gift flower in front of you, underneath you, from around you, eyes across the light carry volts of energy transferred once to the other it bounces in and holds, feeds the fire in the center of your own body, ecstatic heart glow transformed from the body's act provoked by, what, hands and fingers, your own fantastic replays of, of whatever sequence of struts and pumps the heart's spasmic lines evolve throughout a long arc of remembered pleasures, there, and there, ah, and there again, the circle cycle reflex brings the head around to the feet, he coils back into the perfect circle comes an imitation of where he is, in fact, inside a woman who circles encircled completion her legs around her man, the circle of her mouth is open and shut, you are.

You spoke repeating hours, once, walking across the light, I saw some other workmen leaning on the edges of hoes, or feet, or work itself, the words were less cautious then, unseen things the words themselves immediate or crossed-over, it was the world, actual and resonant, a shorter line than laid aside, a ferment.

You called the rest were called aside before, when I met the actual term of darkness a long wave deep inside events themselves, or poled the stream a floating pad revolved at strata formed beyond the shape of seeing left beyond the hours themselves, a pattern said, remind the fall of the year, the terms revolving in forgiveness the lesser actors speak aloud, you'd have to live somewhere, or stay here and be the same life rotating speed-stick, he says relief is calm enough to be the rate of skill, the room itself, her flesh opened to touch, it is the world, really, glistening spot, the body in the dream, was immense, perhaps, dark, entry, at the edges of an empire, the Queen's own body, below, vibrating.

Which makes it plain enough, I guess: the last thoughts are the ones which come first, no organization other than the one which is, there, immediate sensation of the old life, shell of, chrysalis , substance, your own manner transposed in old conversation, it's so cool, what we're doing, man, in the middle of the silence, a lake drawing upward along the side streaming hours have your name along the room you left alone too long, lady, you forgot to respond, now, a little late, after he has already left you decide it might be worth it, but alas, he's gone, the cool million just another substitute for love, or left alone, finally, you decide to cry, but, really, it's the giving you forgot, the afterlife of the fire might be a reminder.

It's all the same; living the style of tourists when you have no money. I think they forget that, that no-one might be listening; for myself, I can't believe you're not interested, I just can't believe it.

Cosmic shuck and jive, you said, whew, clear enough. With no risk it's all jive, and well enough, I'll let you alone, and be happy at that, it's the tendency to use each other which puts me on the run. "I figure I get a free fuck. He saw his old lady when we got back from Mexico. . . ." is all right, for keeping away from each other, avoiding the close chit-chat.

THE MATTER, or, what's the matter, you said, I'll mumble to myself, I'd rather be alone than have another frigid basket-case, with nothing coming back is not all the same to me, "just bend over, I'll drive you home. . ." ruffled like a chicken; the matter, the flesh and blood of it escapes attention, vague nuances of discomfort or boredom: go jerk off. But the matter of it, of, what, Ezra Pound comes up, "He had prostate problems," "Really, was that it?" "Well, that's what I think, that's why its a classical age, being a poet here doesn't work as physical types. They never get off."

But that was, uh, Wednesday night. In 1973 I thought my asshole was the ring of fire, what goes in comes out, or what goes in goes on, it's the rest that takes account the perverse silence of the macho, where's his asshole at, you gotta find out and everybody's sensitive as hell about his asshole's pleasure, or even its life.

"Well, I know   what you need. . . ."

"What," she said, eyes afire. Or interest.

"I can't tell you, really, the words aren't right," play shy.

"Well, what is it?"

OK. "Well, uh, you need to get fucked in the ass," she fluttered a little, "it'd change your mind about things, I guarantee it."

Like giving, or giving in to it. Well, she didn't understand, really, what I meant. "Well, I'm glad to know what you think, it's really just the opposite from what I think." Really.

The core of the outworks: plain outcropping of plain white surface is solid space perceived upward the light below the dark humor; lesser positions qualify the air around her body: various ladies in various lives, or the solid quest for conversation, with them, at least, you spoke another language then, and called the simpler spheres remembering, that you never really said anything at all, in the cool drift past naming anything at all, you spoke of this or that and left me all alone again the rooms are bare walls all around he grabs hold of something quite specific on along these airs are told, who, then, says anything yet so simply shadowed airs repeat the hours rotating disks repeat the light you are at large on the core of the outcropping left alert, here, spoken off the radio, the deep remembering says, you are. . . .

The stick isn't really bent, it is only like the pencil in the glass of water. I got up to check it out, no, it is one piece of stick leaning against the woven wall, a pane of glass and light.

But the odd outcropping against the wall a more conceptual space, they leaned across the moor of somewhere dark, an entire continent was laid bare, you had the harder courses lent, leant, the same wave remembered at the point of it, a rock outcropping into the water, gathering inedible mollusks, they were orange in boiling salt water, tasteless rubbery gathering we knew not why the streams bubbling at descent the purple hours recall the dust of something, centuries perhaps a call recall, the cool recall of doubt spoken waves are hours across your hands, even, less profunct than sheer rock, the outcropping of this distinction, auto automatic pilot for this one, baby, I shouted loud around the valley acid yelling hoots the forest rang the raven calling back, soaring dark bird croaking or speaking out in the woods the louder cackles more like words than sound, bird utterance.

You waited in the wings he rode away, black hours left alone too long the simpler messages read of higher wages in new towns, I just go along the walls are words enough for me to risk. Or needs, even, stretched across your hand: tell me something, who you are, deeper than said, a cool hand across your brow says, "Yes," and goes on into it, I don't care, but the depressions. . . . Well, they seem to be part of the study, the work, surfing downward glide of feeling, no, it is more than just needs, you might have listened in on the phone, somewhere near the middle, I spoke your name against the wall, hit the floor splash at least something left alone, I spoke fast and meant it, I think, shuck and jive, at least that, for instance, is calm enough to be used, just think about that, tough smartass lighter than thou, hoots on the front yard means that voices are poked or spoke, at least, you were here once before, at longer intervals perhaps a Bacchus sky-god from Montana, really, beachcomber's delight, or no more handjobs, at least a vow on that subject, leave them out of it for awhile, the silent darkness growing lawns are set aside the foremost topping light rays larger spoke than other names are heartless you don't know the slightest thing about me, Frannie, now do you? "Well, no, don't."

The voices of the few legitimate characters I've met are still fresh, Macrorie, Ferrini, flesh faced in memory's armory of light, Herbie, of course, and that's it. Names in books writ at large, I'd have their even tones throughout the music. But the ladies, type and song revived another full moon says eat it, or mark the gulls loosely looser said than nothing new today is signed with this or that. The Munchies. Unholy gasps of stone masons mark the mad air a footstep on the doorway unrelenting pressure of the left hand along the floor dragging knuckle-mounded patterns rip-rap letter from David and his PCP vision of the other side a collapsed lunge relaxing the hours say, then, this:

You left these phone numbers on the wall beside you, the left hand unlatched her hoarsely grabbed between her legs, too sudden to be love, but stayed alert, a man at least would share his thoughts no other would bother to do the same, and holding on, I'd speak in lower tones are pitched-in shut-down, plenty of time to go over all this and fill in the empty slots, add some details or brushstrokes, OK, go for it!

It spoke, against the air, perhaps. Or folded back aside her own particular waves of ice were knocked away. I saw this much, and let the angles fall which-way, newer, unreleased, a "potential sky" of gray clouds with light coming through gold shots the lines permit to follow in, the rest. As languages go, and practiced out as has the passions roused, would name it suck and jump her backwards or over, the random moon a newer act is spilt, split, spelt, the lesser madness driven back in thought, in situ, or hours fading back and forth, I let you up and down, sitting there, remembered, perhaps, the unspoken monolog another advertisement for pump or drag. Anyway, it fits, I remember that, and if it fits, the angle could be perhaps, hit the target at the back, let her gasp, you like the drive and bang, and gasp. But she never comes. She pretends, she says, "but not with yew," well, the unspoken conversation lags behind, but you don't really have the point, at least, of what I like. Selfish moons repeat the light.

Well, you said something, at least, that's more than before.

Pale pole rising, left alone, choice, song, the dream, all that. . .

Given my time, I've done everything. At least the cooler passions raise their own fruit. You see resemblance, the open door of recognition, the beginning of thought, at last, the sentinels relax, feelings are suggested, but cool to what lives between your legs, you say, that's not it, that's not all of life, at least, beginning or ending in sharp squirts. But let the sighs relax, or come at all, I'd be the matter on the table, on the table, there, around white dishes recalling other hours used or nearly broken down. The cold point of resemblance calls your eye a sharper tool than you remember, it surprises you with suggestion, even though simply talking is not enough, you got to get laid once in awhile, or make your friends get out of the way. No distance. And babysitting, watches the energy, just, evaporate, well no use being angry, you say, and why not, I don't care for these endless negotiations over a handjob, but there's nothing else happening, or is there? I tell you nothing like this has ever taken place, I've got you up for sale, do you remember that rap? The one that doesn't stop going on endless babble the short stuff grinding around the mushroom walls, painting windows all day or losing your hand. Cold point of light: the flower seems to have grown in the bottle last night its end floated a quarter of an inch short, today it has pushed the flower half an inch out, capillary action? Phlegmatic or cumbersome, it's my story, and really, it's the voice in the room that you know, so you'd better get to know it, me too, I suppose, the rush to get the news, what's the hurry, though I would like to get laid.

Still, she pisses me off, she's really dumb: I wave my flags at the mercy of her blindness, I ease my fleet across the wharf to foreign winds, they gasp and run before the wharves, the fleet ships and squalls, my heart, then, in this flux of reasons, love along the wall remembered a long time ago, love's long lines the vision on the way, more than making the time pleasant, there is more to love than that, there is the this of it, without thought, which seems to be the prize: the gift and the prize, and no more handjobs; oh, well, we missed it last night. I went over just as they were leaving, I didn't want to see them, so I went around the block and down the alley, circling back. Light's off, I knock a light "are you listening. . ." and leave the flower on the doorknob, long walk home, bummed out, I call her. . . .

I mean, remember for why? it is pleasant, sort of, in the present. Why add it up at all, why use remembering, what's there, and would it add, even? You assume you get stronger, by repetition, right? But remember what for who for why for wha. . . ?

Why did I say no to her, well, that had to be said. Unhappy though I was last night, Still I went to sleep, the ache was slow slight I did not hear her on the other side anyway I have these doubts about her in the first place, untenable child she is, heart locked up, my attraction to what, the unattainable, and the ones which say here, I flit back, scared to take what I want when it's offered, ah, that one, crazy lady three AM on the phone, going downtown to the address which wasn't, a few problems, yes, I'm working on them, Dogtown.

At least I don't lie as much when I'm writing. "Man, the lying animal," Jim quoted from nowhere Friday night, I had to shoo them out, bummed, alone, piss on it, I'll paint houses, which I didn't, went there Saturday and looked at those windows, thought about her and just, left, couldn't paint a window it hurt so bad, wanting. Whew, hormone problem, my ass.

The rest, really, you forget to respond, it is the chick's prerogative, I suppose, to forget to respond, but they are they, and ignorance is the cue; I mean, how is the cunt itself the cause of action, Tantra of behavior. Really, the pleasure drive, or ignore it, confusion of power and ego and cunt, and that leaves the ladies backed down into either selfish auto-manipulation, great dildo of life, you let these attitudes go their way, dumbly or scattered, the words fit close to this, your interchangeable names are this self-centered stroke, the same airs retrieve the light, and alone, if you have to insult, piss-off, ignore a lady to say hello, then, is it worth it, the body asks that. Anyway, you forget to ask, you forget to look, you forget to think of what to do, and that's the ego of the cunt, another easy name for handjobs, the conversation over paintbrushes, with another dumb one, "Well, I want a lady who's interested in me. . . ." "Is that how it is?" she asked, like, wha, you can't mean that "Yeah," I said, "that's how it is." Enough to be yourself. Try that, the egotistical cunt retreats, to safety, or just not-feeling at all.

An easy shot. Give it the left hand, over off the wall and screaming hand to hand, I don't think you know the difference between us, it's easy enough to be dumb and go for power games; I mean, I think you miss the point. Spoke out, finally, let the matter flow a little, drinking too much, extraordinary caution for equally extraordinary circumstances for extraordinary enterprises begun, I'd say, that to be specific carries the Queen along, her body is perfect; so there's the plan to consider, and the perfect lover, two quests rolled into a single identical fantasy, achievement, whatever. Well, the plan is the play within a play, or talking to her at the same time making love to the model and doing her portrait, which is the plan of the new world, buying as much of Montana as possible and retiring into the center of it, of course the cosmic fantasy carries the ego ever upward rising flame, a hard-on for life, or life is a hard-on. There, spoke.

I want a lady I can tell her what to do about making love, "Do this, baby," or, "Do that again, baby, come again, baby. . ." and that's the man's game, coaxing her into giving, and give again. Well, have you got that in you, be submissive in moments of play. Of course the man's game is both to give back and to hold back, not come, he keeps it up, and that's how they're different, chasing the only lady in town, beaver fever. . . . Well, you are this and that at the same time, the portrait on the floor is all the same I promised nothing, you said, or said more by saying that, I heard you well enough, I took the lead this time back and forth calm feelings say pervasive strokes have new feelings off the wall, get off, baby, on this, too, even before I come over, play that game however your left hand works out at 3:30 AM this morning dreaming a huge lady in the car, driving along the road; once in the woods outside Pullman, really, pissing a beer, she looked at it half-hard hadn't seen or touched her much, it'd been three days since three months, and she raised her hands, to her face, said "Oh, oh, oh," spontaneously jerked jerking off on the image, got off real good.

You gave, this. A voice on the phone said, relax, it's OK, gentle words came out of me, even, I said something nice, I am making a gift for you and apologized, said you, you were nice yesterday, I, I don't remember, I passed at 8 I am embarrassed about my drinking; the gift, frame, take it apart, ah, wash the glass, the AMAZONIAN COSMOS book jacket, auth unk, illustrated with shaman x-ray figures, orange yellow black, spray the edge black enamel glue the horoscope and sign it "Tom". And the flesh pink soft cunt tulip from next door.

Get the laundry ready, some paints; sit, write, get stoned. No mail and go out the door. The car is fucked, a V-7. Up and put the laundry in; down the street slowly thumping car: big 383 minus one seventh, I guess, and pull in, to the driveway, go in with two gallons of paint.

Back to the car, the picture and the flower. "Son of a Sailor," which I am, on, and into her bedroom, front door is open and I shut the bedroom door, over to the bureau with the plant, wall paper in a gilded frame; it's going to be a hand lotion job, I'm out and into her drawers, pawing around, left hand moving steadily. The pink jumpsuit, I throw it on the bed, around to the full length mirror, going really good, a little bed-magic from the Dog, I throw the covers back, put her pillow in front of me, the pink jumpsuit stretched out on the bed, and I stroke stroke from the depths the light breaks forward falling on I see her body back braced open fleshed fantasy diving in I fall come comes coming fuck the bed, a good, long, deepshot. And up, rather, rather, quickly; fold up the pink jumpsuit, dark wet spot at the center, and put it into the paint-bag, go into the kitchen to paint a cabinet, straighten up her bed, get the record and split: stop at the laundromat to get the laundry and drive home, crack a beer, wash out the jumpsuit, put it into the dryer and sit, spaced, good fantasy-come, a shot. Jumpsuit is dry, I fold it into a brown bag and drive back over to her house to brush out the cabinet. Jumpsuit goes back. Ah, the magic, I love it. Seeded, animal style.

In the afternoon, 3:30, she calls. "I like it, "the gift, really. It's a charm. Did you read the back?" No. And does. Good horoscopes today, 5.22.78. "Fuck," she says. "Let's," I say, all right, for 10:30. Get foxy. Baby, I'm coming over, calm light goes forward, I sleep a long nap again, falling sleep a dreamer dreaming, the magic, the magic. . . .

Calm behind these waves of light, separated from the rest, rests, as whole or part
remain the same related species of air you called my name and touched my face
along the dark was waves or waving fronds frowned front: the air beyond the palace
seeming let, told, the rest rescues, has the room another turn or calling: says, you are
and smoother, how the lines fall around the day at small or open, she has one,
opening out a long chase after myself, was folded floating slowly outer coils reserve
the doubt you left behind is said among the natives, foreigner, soil, the moon slips
away your finger on the slot, the magic spells have worked their own personal space
a configuration beyond the town, at the edge of the woods recalls who you are again
the fountains split or told have larger airs beyond the cliff, turning out as has, so let.
She waits, remembers, calls a name and fathom, the oars creaking at the side, you
said all that is remembered, "the way becomes manifest."

It is this mood of celebration relaxing between her eyes, a spot or marker moves
from here. What you want is not the same, at all, it comes from where you are
alone. Or were. But then, what you want is this or that, perhaps only a good shot
every morning at six o'clock, well that's too easy, you know that; I like
a lady can touch herself, but that's where I was, and in behind it's nice and tight, the
tunnel through to the top of the mouth, the mouth is nice, deep throat. But what you
want is feeling not acts, it goes with what you have to give, between your legs and
upper, stomach, heart, heat, the chakras of delight, names of airs reviewed, I'd call
you once or twice a day, I'd make love long hours, have you come again, or are you
drifting off, away, come down and roll around on top of me, sitting on my face,
bending over me, drinking us both to each is how it is today, I'd spell your names
the same as the original blonde who stays at large and steaming; I'd sweat on top of
you, and have your hand be enough some times, really, it's all things all times the
grand exploration of the body's secrets, now I am not so much afraid to give, it is
what you want to invest, feeling, the bizarre moments, from fiction to romance, and
from romance to electric lights behind. Really, it is the after-love that counts; after
they come, however they do, the souls mix.

Light causes all the rest, goes on uninterrupted, Jon Worthington's seriality, but
seen, is synaptic exhaustion slows you down into mute remembering, "no-time."

The erotic play of buttfucking reserved for women only is part of the sex style we
talk about, and related to genius and assholes, and Ezra Pound, too, I suppose, kinds
of space. . . . Erotic play of man and woman has to do with him and his hard-on, she
said; positions are the Play of the act in all its contexts, do you play? With me, too,
the gestural wrestling at play in fucking, simple, rides her down.

A sudden movement mars the eye a little shade lower, or slower; and speaking up, a
little off or Southern, a voice, or prose. Phenomenal! Success, the man comes
through, or all positive, there is that sort of voice, even, the manner working out is
said solid make her perfect your eye's mind speaks again, you are, inside the light,

ah, moon and marker seasoned out would say, too bad, this snow will break the air like trees buried in the snow, arms broken like trees covered with snow in early spring, the lilacs bent over.

A shallow end repeats her words: later, perhaps, is complicated by being true, also, just like you said. I listened all those years the same broken sentences only speaking out, broke the code and read the signs, whew. . . .

Or the car fixed, as well as it'll get before the rest goes down along the highway's son begins in June, another fly-by has the day's hours ringing in your ears have the longer rooms removed away and sending out, ah, heart, you are this moon along the day deciding now, the rope, her heart waving down along the way, a birth a day you had me heart to heart I poked her belly back and forth the ivy streaming on my face the slippery pipe internal flue a pressure up inside no contradiction calls the air a perfect residue of hours called from one side or the other, I mean, how the thing decides, anyway, to even say hello, you are, there, aren't you smoothing out along the highway dreaming now and then, at least, to recall the hours dancing calm between your feet, and settle back against these roses beaming left to right they shoal this, this matter of delight you meant no charm alive and flaming near to perfect reasons say, enough, hold, the hours clear or perfect, gone, along.

The rooster's hours calm design to newer loops the same, resist, outer, smooth, he leaps clear of the frost, less of the snow coming down now than before your guard is up, at least, in advance of the tides crossing over or forward, he seems extraordinary to me, too; I think, the oddest things most easily known are more than what you think, a postal route, for instance, even Packages Only, was not enough, no respect, was largely an adolescent reminder to keep on talking now that its really too late to speak any other roomers' name calling who the fuck are you, anyway rip-rap delight the words their own, too, smoothed out and holden, holding company out the door the records falling out the cave door already open into another realm of light her body open to you, now, and now, and now. . . .

Calm indifference, as the rule. Perhaps it is just, following, or letting the way become manifest, even eruptions of wrath and wrenching changes of movement, residence; perhaps, really, she will be there in the new life, a, whatever, nineteen and tight, they say, "Yeah, baby, like that. . . ." I think this out loud, and she laughs, or believes me, the Fox on the other side of the mountain who believes in me, waits for me to arrive in her life, there is that growing toward love which is all change and fantasy, you don't see any of this at all, "and how are you today," begins the litany, the un-roll of ancient song intent, that is, no self image but seeing sing-song, either the way of the hero or the way of the sage it says, though elsewhere it seems to hold to the mean and center of the way, ballast. Tough works, the Fox around the corner, I miss them daily through compulsive screening, I'm beginning to notice it, take steps to pay attention to the good feelings, no more dogs or basket cases. No more handjobs. or exclusion at large, the whole space before you says hello, the car's running better than ever, time to close the hatch and e-vade, loop out a high shot flaming arc's retrieval, the flight and pinion. . . .

The hard part always staying on the same line, almost asked him today, why is no-one interested in my writing, but then I knew better than to fall off that one, and satisfied myself with making an appointment I had no intention of keeping, I mean, telling me that his old lady is in Billings hustling her old man for the bucks to move him to San Francisco, she's pregnant; that's more than I care to know about him. Really.

Speaking of which: the room turns out, I see seeing, seems to be alive with energy from, from somewhere else you spoke aloud and called my name was shore and palm arised alive, I think. Or re-run lives, they seem the same as what you spoke again, gifts and favors say your calm intent is newer than these rose shots along her body opened up, I'd say the Eagle flows from the child to the shore and back again, a slight miss of water makes it look like further south: it says, then, of work, the hand should go automatic for awhile, a house to paint, then, and bucks for the journey down to where time retires, and me, too, this story might begin, "It was the summer of '73, of MDA and the Virgin, of the madness and the long walk, well, long enough. . . ." Dave remembered it last night. He left early, from the bar, bummed out. Me, too. Jane. Return, the one you picked out to head the poem, headers up, I'd say, and bending over, I'll drive you home, dirty songs to a lovely lady, I saw you sitting beside my desk stroking away while I threw the coins. For myself alone, or only, I'd say this.

The erotic play, mate. There is this between them, ecstatic energy, a volume, it passes back and forth, at charge, and not mere fucking, but it is both coaxing of orgasms from her, this giving, a feeding of them both, but his own seed stays, comes less often, that is the difference. Drama and play. "Come home at three and stroke it out on the bed, and I'll come home at 3:30, and, all right." Well, those are the fantasies, she doesn't exist yet. Most ladies see it as submission of will to lie about and stroke it for their old man, she said "Sleazy," she didn't understand, Pisces, but once in the sun down by the Jocko she lay there and jerked off, pretty, open in the sun, hard at it, head to the right and Bang! off she went.

Or a lady who can just give. Come in and stand around you and get horny, breathe out loud and talk about it, they always want to hide it, wet cunt and talking about the fucking weather.

Still, Imaginary Lover, really, you'd be a lady, Jane, and put your straight butt in the air, I'd slip on in, hang in there, "Oh, oh, oh. . ."

Straight back strokes the long thing sliding in and out of you, ah, banana, you'd have another stronger name, I have my dreams, lady, and call the air around the way a perfect shot between your eyes, a spot, a mouth, a long, deep, throat of, seed of, the sharp shot forward, "Ungh. . . ."

77

And again, she gives, legs, arms, the eyes open drives the energy back and forth, the eyes burn exchange, a tantra of living in the present. . . .

Really, no-one to work with. Jody knows, ask her. But, fuck, I say, let it in. Ask around, a very private thing. Jennifer and her colonic irrigations, she offered me her ass, but she was an asshole.

Whew. Mary Ann's ". . . and no grease. . . ." If she only knew, I was that quick. All right. ". . . .special," she said. The inverted heart with the arrow going in to center, it was a valentine, ah, return, the center of movement; I didn't speak too soon, or too bold, ha, ha! But ask for it, talk about it, over fun and games, love goes deeper in, it is no voyeur's game, lady, but the way it is, what a man likes, his lady between his ears.

And know about it, too, while doing it, doing what you want her to do, and her doing what you want because you want her to, and liking it, she likes it, doing what you want, and you can talk about it without being caught anywhere in fears of power or being used, it's triggering the good feelings, really, "Hey, jerk off, baby, I can dig it. . . ."

But they're uptight, or I am, just the old upside down. So I hang out, ready to jump, tired of the old bullshit, leaning hard on morning's six o'clock push me off the bed about a hand and a half, or more, stiff, hard, a fin, driven up again the single bed is big enough for both of us, really, roll you over on your face and grease it up get in back a good shot while you're trying to wake up enough to realize it's in you already off you roll over and stroke it out because I like it that way, and way out behind, you talk about it, and me, too, a morning's fantasy. If I'm to be wedded to my muse I might as well get fucked once in awhile.

The last quick Carol was too quick to be believed at all, but I got her six AM boogie she wouldn't come, "Are you frigid," I said.

A big hole in the middle, up at the top, I can look into it, see across your face, running close across the day, face to face I see her eyes burning light between your eyes, a spot or center trembling looser signs are spoken out, you are, a page a day is calm enough to lie aside the air is smoother now than meaning loosely shore and throng they call together piled one by one on top of the wall, storing up great powers, even Kerouac's fantasies are borne out by the sharpness of his perceptions, the arrow hits the bullseye more than once or twice, no, it is his psychological hangup which is so crippling to his flight, "wavering flight over the depths. . . ."

A model, a lady to work with on this, uh, matter, as in the matter of it rather than "What's the matter?" No, it is not so much a question as a substance, like, what comes, out of, and into, like Wally said, "Tom, wha, I don't know," driving the truck out to Ah-lee with a joint and a sixpack, in Tom's truck, "is what you give into, into what?" Well, Lady, that's part of it, forming on your lips, "Well, baby, what do you want?" Really. More. "submit and avoid. . . .correct behavior." Hard-headed woman a mile away, grumbling at the dark air, my hands in my pockets, scooped for my extra ten on a good debt, oh well, no more handjobs says what a bummer, can't even jerk off, the burning of my heart seven years of solitude in Montana, empty rolling hills empty sky, the mind goes blank, the heart holds sudden drops ahead, skips back, what am I doing here still this empty, hollow bunch of shit, no woman in my house I'm tired of it, tired of holding my own against nothing singing the blues on Friday night the book negative on my question well what the fuck just wait it out, well, what and where and when again going off the deep end with, as usual, two places into two lives where is the unexpected, or love, or passion or even a wet cunt this time of the year this loser bullshit no cowboy heaven lying around the house, the sound of the dryer the scratch of the pen a little windsong outside and not so very peaceful, just alone and quiet, not the same as loneliness Omar consoles today, well tell me about it, Sidney, I need to know, at least a good sleep and I almost didn't drink too much, did business OK while pissed off, depressed, just another day.

Ceaseless contact among alien people, us, together, bob and weave, you hear another term together has it all. On "just such a day," on, "just another day," one could fall in love anytime. The book says not, is usually a setup, or worse, oh I struggle over that book, and wanting a woman, we argue terribly over that, me and the book. I feel enslaved and rebel; nevertheless, I go back. I never get fucked, it is a sadness, really, I don't understand it. Perhaps another town, another life, new glasses, my body's beer an active thing, a lady, maybe, just around the bend, whew, wait, wave, collapse my heart, it was a very long day after a very long night after, what, or what!

Or a consciousness of long leg shots, how long? But goes on, development of the flower, and all that, well, a real lady would be nice, found a nice Penthouse today in the garage, in the garage, well, I don't know, I'm going to bed, piss on it. Or better, or worse, and finish the page off tomorrow, it's black scratch on yellow paper, call it writing, even, call it your name, call it a lady and send her back with me in mind, ah, fuck it.

I'm gone.   I'm gone.   Dust in high watery caverns.

At core, sharp shots leaving, in the air spoke or light, she calls around the bend from nowhere short again, you said something, uh, nice, perhaps, that you want it, that's a game I like, the high watery wind beating a name across the air, retreats inevitably, or flux-styles in "no action," she walks away, stays inside, the eyes turn from the dog to me, cow eyes, when I go back, she's gone, probably hurriedly, get away from that, beauty and the beast is not a pair but a meeting of pleasure and the ideal, most of them run from that as if it were a horror; speaks at other rooms, the same side wise scroll. Invite me up to your mountain cabin. Sit on my face.

Dreams fall apart, at least another quiet Friday night gives way to, to something, quiet, too, at least enough dope to feel rested, the left hand felt a deep pulse hit the floor at least release into what, he said, "How'd you like to be a big fish in fast brown water," Wally said beside the stream, white lines and colombo.

And that's what's here, folks, at the edge of the civilized ho-ho, we meet the dream at the emptiness of its location, cold point of the origin within a life where wanders poet or man, the man comes first, the lady later, competitive urge to orgasm less than unitive, giving into what, does this woman float in darkness, this hot wet cunt, is she really a pocket drama or a cult signal; well, having a good time counts for something, we say, and have at it again the rhythm falls apart, no trees call the air a perfect vision from around your heart, I saw the trees lined up one inside the other rising sixty feet or more, head and eye along the immense water from within aquarian moods, they have their sensuality, and what to do with it, his image of ripe fruit opened at the center, came through to me, through her, she was talking to me, what was the message? Was I supposed to say, "Yes," or "Now," or "Come," which I did, all those things unspoke but it is silent cow eyes need speaking to, bull in his lunge to heat, it does go back and forth, always, or in and out, as "Oh, oh, oh!" and leave heavy breathing for afterward, where the souls mix, mutant lore of specific love acts remembered .

At the edge of the world's beginning, a good fuck is like that, and when he says that the ass is mastery, ah, then, lady, I can see why you wilt and fade back, it is just too much submission, but really, it is the gift which returns translated, as a style is also a behavior and took off long ago, too long ago to be believed by "Modern Consciousness," aha, another way of being uptight or non-physical, they forget to work at it, this dumb romantic role play of giver and receiver, the old dogma of active and passive, is all subtle macho, hinging on the poles of poetry, position and success, it is the other side of competition fucking, the great low scene from Fellini's Casanova, the two-man fuck-out, oh his lady is hurt to be so used, squirting into them, it's not really like that, ladies, but then, who misses more, him or her? And when they're equally divided, how, then do we pair up not out of dependency or fantasy projection but out of the good sexual dynamic? What I see are the companionate thing, or passionless breakfast tables. Somewhere deeper, between romance and the erotic, poles of light revived.

CHAPTER 6
BOB ATHEARN'S WILLOW CREEK
BOTANICAL GARDEN

The superior man perceives the seeds and immediately takes action. He does not wait even a whole day.   Confucius

Really, have some class. The whole situation calls for the compassionate release. Of Her, then, tantra lady of serious pleasure, or cosmic joy, she's named entirely of light, panoply of air's essence in color, ah, the flux of transition; I can see you, there, walking down the dirt road for the first time in two years I was too uptight but really a nice movie, got the idea? You said, and I din't, as the kids go. But mating season carries with it a different commitment, that the mating should be perfect, I suppose, you give and that's your joy in being woman, ah, I drink from the fountain of light, there, between your legs, my lips parched from dried up dreams.

Anyway, I see you approach, both of us are aware of, something, and then it takes place. There are those moments, to take place in the heart or in the event itself, it is now, I say hello, "Hello." And that carries it, the tone of voice and the eye, for when you're serious, she knows it, I mean, didn't I ask? And wasn't I told? "How's she doing," Bummed out." Aren't we all, well it's mating season and if you're not, that conversation again, well I got lucky Bob says, "I know," I says, and we go on into the joint as after sandwich water hot to bath I go to this cabin where Alex is practicing Pachelbel's Canon on the cello for Tuesday night, I see you approaching and then I say hello, though I remember Friday night, "Hate to see a man in tears," I do agree.

Passes on into the white air around us, wet between the legs, an afterthought, or clothing, or a person underneath, Lady Jane arrives all of a sudden out of the air, point of readiness, coming out of something, you think of love's rebirth, the healing, going for light you pass through the dream from in behind I come as coming home, finding someone in there.

The cabin in the woods, about three AM, fire in the wood stove making light, the dark hours underhand, I find you saying yes, for once, and giving out, would trust to that sign, I mean, the signs are waving again, and I read them meeting one in one, you could understand that; I hope the same; I read the meeting in your eyes, Lady.

As he takes the lead, or follows on along the shore and waving one hand free, freely spoke, he sees the dream arrive in event, or the maiden and the flower: cool enough, respond, the air direct speech follows, has, through the music seeming seen along the way, she is these feelings, chest, stomach head genitals soles of feet the forehead, hands sweating, even the book in order (even?); or maiden in head, or brother and sister fuck, when they are the same, the man and the woman, how can they miss, the play, the hours flowing rapidly, the near miss has receded, ah, she gives, he does the same, they trade attitudes, the play plays back and forth, did she remember the part about the fantasies? Or what they are, even, constant crowding of air around his face, even, and short.

It is how they relate to the target, each twist of the body frames the growth of the poem, and when he enters her thus or so, it is the stanza of the poem, when they are good together, to each other, she sits on his face and he speaks to the flower, he tells her what he sees or how he feels, stroking the schmoos, we talked about over the black water barrel, no-wind sky coming flat gray air brush high white stuff pretending raindrops the white surf rolling forward booms the false air white wet with beating off the morning's energy the same as any other day except for visits and arrivals long suspected rumors floating through the small community, romantic set-ups the mating urge an animal thrust but taste and class recall her perfect book of love poems to someone, collected thin and perfect face the resonant posture tall within small features can't imagine you being nasty, but that's attraction, too, the exploration of space, the tangent rumor from the village drama of most-important life, your own, to lose the loser in your quick wake feathering out behind the boat, he hears the rumble calling from the mountains, love and danger.

Would keep them warm forever, the scale of the choice is personal enough to go on into a dangerous future in hazardous circumstances, the love ideal deflowered, dispassionate companionate "relations" more the rule than compassionate release, but she never learned to give, the trade-off back and forth, he said to her,"Have you ever known a man, really, what kinds of men have you known, your father, your husband; my own father wasn't a man, really to me, but we understand that now, and it is forgiven, because now I am a man, but do you know what a man wants, there, as lovers, they are really different you know, man and woman go off differently, use each other for the mutual energy differently." Ah, she didn't understand. A week ago.

What they call the air resounds again, the air around her body, hands across, as light, beyond, the omens perfect, what does Omar have to say today, he calls her name aloud, now, "Jane," his friends next door, maybe they'll go for a walk.

As, at lunch, the raisin bread, egg fry, buttermelt, honey espresso, doobie, Bob says, ". . .ladies I could name," "We all know," and the topic of Mazola ladies, ". . .who forget to give, nothing, nada, not only sexually, but nothing. . ." He's pissed, too, expressed, "this epidemic of solitude," I'm tired of it. "You need, you know, I found a nice nineteen year old, who could give, and it was what I needed to do, that was six years ago, in Seattle, and I moved over here, she wrote me once." The example, yes, "No one to give to, you're drying up saying, wait a minute, it's got to be the weather," he laughs, the other, Bob, goes on, "It's all this gray, it's shortening my life!" Not really, uptight ice, "really, she looked like that in '63, snow on the eyelashes, all that," over the photo album. He says," Well, all right, she got a bum deal, he went gay and left her frigid, never took her, and she's bitter," "We all got a bum deal" "And we got over it, too, Jody's had some hard times. . . ." Some of them from me, too. "It's a credit to us both that we're here today, together," "I know," "And you, too."

As the sun goes down, today, an example of proof, or waiting-waking, or of the gift given good, or of making an inquiry.

Discovery is nothing. The difficulty is to acquire what we discover. Valery, M. Teste.

Is rather circumstance than the nature itself, or alterations of, of event, response. Nothing doing, sit on it, but the change is there, also the resolve, but passing through is something else, and certainly the Loser's Club will have something to discuss. . . . The losers have a way of banding up, of holding back together. It shouldn't be argued, really, that the same conversations between used-friends should be so boring, formula, unfelt, safe and restful. Besides, they say everything that comes in, a couple will double-chatter, simultaneous cancellation, it is their manifestation, of being, to chatter on about the work.

Basically, she's sitting on it, something safe and distant, a "couple of friends" she sees from time to time. The loser's game. And the conversation when he had come back from, well, he came on for her and she said Nada, he walked off "to shoot some film." Back in the cabin the conversation of the losers. "Mazola is famous for its un-glue in relationships." Bullshit.

And twirling through space, he cooks outrageous steaks with little interest, the moat around his heart is filled with the teeth of alligators, not really speaking, he is like that, refused, angry. A man who wants a woman. But simply, they talk about Frannie, who he is tired of hearing about, still back there liking a lady he spent a year hustling, she comes flaky with nothing to give, she's home beating her kid, "The new regime, no backtalk." Her business has failed, sold out from under her, Linda made some money on her hard work. He feels excluded, suddenly, he is looking at his second ex-wife and her current lover, the botanist, and the cool-mask pretty loser lady poet.

"I do not belong here, these are not my people, I am different, not really a part of this drama of northern absences, failed relations, too much gray and not enough love, the slow drift home, south, into the sun, time to evade mad mountains, Indian death, white money, the end of the trail, too much time spent at the end of the trail, it should be a resting place and not a cavern. . . .

But we have altered the nature of the beast, the nature of Him, then, well, we have come somewhere after all, and pretty loser ladies can go their way, he'll go hunting in other directions, the west of here, the south of here.

But the message gets delivered, really, poetry is obsolete, bunk, no careers are possible, but the tactics learned transpose to prose by expansion, the poets can simply take over prose and make it new, which is what's happening, anyway, they've simply lost the audience.

Cunts revolving, one is enough, the hard headed woman speaks well of you, this crazy back and back and still alone two years, Frannie doesn't count, little girl in woman's flesh, child-cunt, manipulative loser. Ah, I'm still mad about this. Who's using who, or what credibility?

THE BIG FIELD

Predictably, she shows herself. A dream would interrupt the survey, you would see her, suddenly, riding up on her bicycle. "Escape is out of the question." "A way shows itself." "The town may be changed but not the well." Enough.

But horny, too, and when she finally tallies off, he recovers. "The charm worked." Only an hour before, Sue left, with my priorities, finding a lady, writing and the kids, gotta be like that. Quick shots, he holds his heart suddenly, speaking, "But are you any good?" "Well, let's find out. . . ."

Really, she was sitting at the round table. He says, "I feel like I spent a year chasing you and came up short," "Well, why don't you take it," she said, smiling, he went across and picked her up, "Oh, I like that, then, I will," and went at it, ". . .the kids," she says, what a cliche, and stopped, it's not important, and then a day would be tomorrow, a time to find out, and say, then, "You're a liability," "Totally," She agrees, as, two contraries. He thinks to tell her what he wants, remember? Only yesterday. . . .

Perhaps they provoke themselves together, not unlike men, but they are different, in kind, they alter the shapes of things in argument, in alternation of superiority without constraints with observation without guile, but truly spoke, they are often without whim or character, and only merely react, where intelligence comes into question, at least as discourse permits, at least the model can provide that restoration of energies, then, she calls out as mask and line, they are spoken in the kitchen only this afternoon, even to, "Please don't go," and interest, too, in what is private, or serious, and he knew Jane had talked to her this morning, her car was parked outside; it is not worth it, this game of hearts and flowers should be practice for something better, that's how he felt about having his buttons pushed, retreat, here, leave, always turning to leave, taking his marbles and nobody really gives a shit, really, it was the most childish thing he did, the specific yawp. He'd miss it tomorrow, too, and wonder, is it worth it, partner thing? You really dance out there: he gave away the couch, decided to make some calls tomorrow and see what's haps, beyond the moon, in California, somewhere, wet thing waits, my name inside her middle finger, in. . . .

84

"I'd fuck you, really, but don't talk to me that's how I feel now. *One of sixteen vestal virgins who were leaving for the coast.*

And. This time I'm in it for love; lines along the ceiling, a special lady, then, then, re-lines the song you have to sing, again, against the moon, you do not understand, yr dumb, I sd, ah damn it, but in yr favorite snapshot or come in the back door, but don't call, a page a day I take my own liberties with the voice,.

Simultaneous Multiple, the code of the day, the even combination of various serial modes in simultaneous parallel, that's the modality to be applied to all media, that's the patent in the poems, the core of the mad vision in the woods, no, more, it was the things done that make the story true, remembered vision of actual happenings like this: the blue-van dancer girl in Sacramento, the tantra vision I missed because I was too uptight, and end up this loser's game for late night theater in a dried up gray-skied northern town, man, town, let me off this hook, for Southern California and sweet nineteen to sit on my face and give a little light along my seasons snowing this morning end of May, the heat billowing, late spring mating season blues, old Frannie I like a lot it's just not worth the trouble, after all, and, strange-heart, I care.

He told him that. It will work, even the beginning fantasy of a rap is hostage to the moment. You'd speak, too, as well, and words in their proper orbit call the flame alive within the sphere of action, description, love, even, between her legs, wet slot, home of, seat of, ah, choice, that's the only one I like the ring or the slot, pale pole rising, her outer rings peeled away in the green mists of indistinct thought he drives ahead, thinking all the while of the non-stop sentence which flies away at the end, colors of paint placed next to each other vibrate overtones of light, chord keys, any two words together make that explosion of double meeting, as, cunt : fox, means both and neither, where's the cock, the pale pole, as in rod : shot, or rod shot cunt fox, what a formula, he met her passing passion outer layers, on the bed he left a dream, he saw her flesh a fantasy on the pink hot pants, he drew the colors well he left the same eye-looping shots, the painting business (business?) in Santa Barbara, a long story short enough, he got pissed and drew the line, Francesca, last night.

He's in that direction, then, coiled blow of air between his legs, he rolls along the way and waving he didn't give a shit who knew it, really, down the road, he seemed to survive all right the voice droned on he heard these, these, voices in his heart and deeper layers of being, listen and follow, the monotone humdrum beating of waves along the shore you spoke aloud he seemed to move recall and flavor, got her down on her knees, in the mouth and sighing, all right, I'm sorry, baby, I never fuck in the cunt, I'm a buttfucker all the way or not at all, now stroke it up, baby and sweat a little, cause that's what I like baby, oh, oh, oh! And off the wall Montana headers on the bus, or smooth her back and forth these ladies speak too soon the dialog of love's behavior, mouthing the platitudes of the gift and the prize, they speak too quickly to be believed, it is the cunt I listen to, how it says "proceed," or "fall back," the wet vertical lips he kissed goodnight her musk and central flavor decorated light along the way and free to be me and thee, a dreaming Beach Boys slowsong, Alex on the cello, ah, the harmony says, you are the magic mountain sighing back and forth, the model, where is the model for this piece. . . .

The lid off. Feelings dominate, she is not the one, he is criticized for arrogant obstinacy, and feels a drop, a distance; self defeat again, my lady, no, she is gone, already or again, the old-ones, all paired off, his own investment did not pay off, did not yield the relationship, he asked for too much control, really, crazy. He held the edges of it, wanting someone in his life, these three year habits of alone-ness had accumulated too much weight in his behavior, perhaps nineteen will be there, in Santa Barbara, tan bottom, sitting on my face, the moon a yellow light on our borrowed bodies, the poet and the lady, in tune, in hand, in bed, on the street, at supper, on the long line long along the way and wailing waving arms and legs the calm arrives in sleep you dream this light is mood or chain, her business says goodbye he got the business, it was the last shot by the door that got her, but he was talking about himself, not her, oh well, "I don't want another frigid basket case," now is that to me or to you, the communication slippt, slid away, along, "Lots of them," Wally said. "Why do you chase her?" Ah, the unattainable realm, it called him down, the lady of the smaller dreams, even.

But the shape of it, even, is a reminder of the story, in fulfillment says, the master in his solitary state, what does he want? A woman!

Where does the need to control take the place, of, what? Images of relations: him-her, her-him, there is an older man and a younger lady, teach me both, or let the prayers fall at control, three more years the book, the book; he calls his own light to bear away, give real songs, make the moon another sign for all to see, find a good thing going down the road, or meet these foreigners half-way and sell valves for a living, micro-circuits or connectors, symbolic bridging the air around his flames is answered-out by the famous airs have crept throughout, the woods' full beauty falls, his niche safely occupied, a lonely corner, here, his own, the demon in the closet, love's distance the sweet perfume between her legs, remember, hardly, the gray gray air half way through the year reminds you, description, of the beautiful lady, would you come across the light, the old monks wearing, the cow, unprovoked, feeding it, giving something himself, then, for easier moments learning how we are, then, at. There was nothing to see, his affairs wound up, this lady, a year's chase, on his heart's mind, Wally and him talk about hustling, "There's something wrong, here, I should be getting laid more," "Mor'n me," he says. We go around the town is slow and empty we get drunk and eat late at night home in bed by midnight. . . .

Sitting in the stands, a gym, about a hundred and fifty kids, bows ready, the spring playback of Pachelbel's Canon in D, Alex back there with his cello, goofing then serious, eyes at music. His teacher talks about it after, "He almost quit, but we talked him back; encourage him." Last lines ease the air apart departs, the house is turning, music in the air is flying back, he had left the lady in her house, she'll play some guy inside the walls, this one that hangs along my, my mind, as not-worth-the-trouble, he must like her, but the game is a tight one, with so much criticism, but the depression is beaten back, the days are short for him and long for the sun, we might make out all right.

Even the fashion show at the Top Hat, it's the frigid losers on parade, saw Michael at the door, a tender moment with his lady, and then she left. "A lover?" "An old one. . ." "I've been writing about Mazola ladies, man, I'm pissed, I'm bailing out." "Really, they're so beautiful, and so many, and we could love them so well," he says. "Look," we grab each other. "You and I can touch more easily than they and us. . ." "Really, they're dumb, that's it."

But then he drives around his dark eyes slant outward, the last days of Pompeii and he's glad to erase this northern triumph from his vision, Mazola, Montana, the ultimate handjob, Penthouse alcoholism and gray skies. "Boy, I could sure use some strange pussy," Wally said at work today, glaring out the window. "I turned down two last night," he says. Twenty days or more, for me, my soul is drying up. Dogs and the beautiful frigid losers. Straight ladies at the fashion show "Nice chattering with you," and Dennis drunk calling me smart.

Sharp and further, the joyous is manifest second sun of sunny days arrived, joy as government, "Quiet, wordless," and not believed, that's the image of the reading of the moment. But I know that already, ". . .not that they noticed," unrolling canvas, the image of the model in his bed and center, no drama unoccupied by doubt, living without doubt, that you are living in the body's perfect tenses, unalert, or recognized, Space Captain to Crew, What? No answer; the ego speaking to its body, teaching silence, fathoming coolness, your hip disdain. . . .

A slow thought surmise, sense. She rolls around him warm, awaitment of something less frivolous than the Queen of Signs who the fuck is she, anyway? You spoke in correct tenses, and a silly meeting at noon, to make price and offer no tribute. But giving them joy, that is the matter, today, the cool clip of noises marks the air a perfect spot to wait it out, a writing space just ahead, changed, the story pushing out, his own vision in the wilderness revisited, his "second chance," to be alive, a man among these others is good enough when it's all you've got, no lady saying "goodbye." Joy.

It's the pictures, really, in no confusion but the reading hours. No pretense any longer, just being there, mood-visible, if not strung-out, just another writer , says, the visual realm is all continent, land, massed, the music rolling flat and perfect speaker-shot and moving slow oboe under strings the day's work lined out thorough and plenty of it, must see it all recede, the last impressions of specific faces drawn across his mind three years these changes led him out of his "mind" and into the streets, looking at everything and marking markers down he spoke aloud once or twice in this town the days were days, enough! A growth of hours moved him sharp across an unpigmented substance, a growth of light and showers, texts of feelings, a practicing of moods, he goes at large again a contrary return to beauty, or the manifest, arrival and storm, a voice among these turning lights within the sphere of action, the vocable present: relief, maps, words thrown loose around the world, a smaller place than, really, we ever thought, my longer hours spent, I call you souther speaking of time and love again.. . . .

The empty lines. Ladies in flight, creatures under dark skies, others, the sailing hours depart, no essence, gloom and unrelief, cautious hearts, childish tastes, disgusted spasms, the long stay and staying, you'd be the floating palace under all, or spoke at sharp the lesions under all, poked, straw heads, the end of the end, pieces of hot shit, sharp signs, hot cunts, empty heads and fucking pits of everywhere, black gloom, whiskey head, chasing nothing and getting lost, the shower of easy shingles, flailing past patterns spread out, blown apart, silly gestures on the monster movie, private pleasures of self denial, beating his head through itself, leaving town, clearing out, passing through, splitting off! Difficulty at the beginning, thorough bullshit, hitting the mark, pushing the distance out, not talking to them, pissing in the wind, missing the third nice day in a row, these cheesy cowboy cunts spread along the mountain, pissed off, bummed out, talking to himself, lips moving, time to move on, painting his last house, packing his goods, running his program, writing his book about this, about this, this petty northern fucking bullshit!

He slides back into perfect work. Such disgust, driving around forty-five tooling out, Wally takes this lady's car back and they eat breakfast, still stoned from last night's acid, body vibrating with whiskey hang-over eighty degree day, the third in a row, it's here, and all alone. . . .

Anyhow, two more gallons on the walls, the white didn't cover the job, he grumbles over the job, but Wally says the money will be there, and they'll paint windows in Ah-lee next week. Anyway, he rolls the whole house out in about two hours, "Slow down!" Sprays paint everywhere, and they start drinking beer already high at, wha, one o'clock. The daily day. They're working at the picture window, "Wally, you've caulked a fly. . . ." I look up sharp eye, nice brown flesh lady, thinly rounded nicely there in the sun on the grass a hundred yards across the street on the lawn, blue bikini no top, on her stomach, "Hey, look, ah, oh, look at that!" We all stare, "I saw it." we are all agape, amazed, second day of spring, or what.

He goes to the front door, eyeglasses man cover, with white paint, and hoots a high "Wow!" She rolls over, waves, amazing, he's stoked, and finishes up over another beer, washes out rollers, stands around the house with no pants on, ha ha, dresses and goes across the street, she's been on her side and pearshaped, blood says, "How's the water," what, she says, well you're dressed for the water, let's go to the river; and, well I've got to study for my final, they talk. The story goes around, gets out, "It fired me," about teaching. "Novel, about my love life, or lack of it. . ." It should be volumes, she says, compliments flowing slowly, nice brown short-hair, I touch it, "It's nice," and she is nice, thanks, I haven't had a girlfriend for two years, surprised, she is, "Nell, I don't understand, either," they all go dancing Tuesday night, she leaves Wednesday for a summer in the Badlands, whew!

The day is better, and there he is again, going after something he wants, oh yes I want. Brown skin light hair over the calm triangle between her legs, ah, a moment. After crashing out at John's he comes home and calls her on the phone, "Debbie?" yes, and, sure, at ten o'clock, still light, for a walk, or something.

Here is the air. He drives the nearly dark streets over to the University, and goes into the building which looks like a mental hospital but is really a dormitory, yellow tulip in hand, the purple shirt and this, this lady is there, student-clean and lovely, straight energy, healthy smells, the flower works, "Oh, nice man," and chattering, "What did you do this afternoon. . . ." And they drive the slow noises up the hill, talking about love and others. The air, them, the light, and hit the top of the city, the huge old mansion on the golf course, he holds her arm, and then she tucks her hand into his, it's nice. "I'm a real straight person," and doesn't smoke or drink, ah, a lady, the cologne, clean Ukraine-face, beautiful and straight. Twenty one and smart. Peaceful, tall, we hustle each other in a straight way, talking about sex and love and work, oh, he likes her clean honesty, this entomological lady, I call her, "I've never known a writer." And kissing, warming her slowly, talking about the light and running two hours by like that. I drive her down the hill. "I'm looking for a special lady, to give me what I want, I want some things from a lady. . . ." They go on into good feelings, ah the need for love, they talk about it, draining the hours of what they can give, I'll work on this, he says, the fact is I gave a hoot and you waved back.

House unfurled, coasted backwards, he moves out, "Son of a Sailor," and hash, a sun-day Miller Time, all right, the papers to the warehouse and wrapped in plastic fantasy floating by a lilac in the screw-eye at the base of the house by the front door for someone, left a sign for me to see, he sees it, moving out!

Sweep the floors away, statements about freedom, "released from indenture," at dinner the night before, free associating with Gary from Horseshoe Bend, "I'm a dumb black moron." "I'm a prisoner," he says. Ah, the signal, her cologne, the neck, and talking about it, gives a little clean and peaceful juice, but could he keep it up with so little foxiness? Ah, the random motion skips him by, ladies, the sun moves slowly by, and leaving Eagles, throw them back into, too, too powerful, the Deb of Rah, a North Dakota irony, he thinks about it all night long sleeps peaceful complimented by all that they find to like in each other so quickly and talk about it, nice hustling, to seem so proud and be so firm, a stroke or two would make her perfect responding, you're supposed to let your even breathing flow, and moan a little. . .

Energy complimented by wisdom.

"I spoke at you nice lady said hello, doubts were disappearing, and the abundant presents itself, as "inter-related elements come together." I mean, the nice feelings of, of, a discovery, then, of an imaginary lady, oh, yes, there you are, I'd like to stop and smell the roses, I think I like to touch your body, I want to know how we are together before you go, and still be slow, but give, lady, and tell me something nice, once or twice, I'm shy, perhaps, and ask for what I want too seldom, I mean, what I want by gift and prize, but then, it's moving day I got you on the phone, bright light coming through the sky all around me, today is filled with such good feelings and Wally waits to party-out, I stashed my stash too easily to be believed, about a cubic yard of papers safe enough for a long time, I think, at least a year here or there, I'd like to know how we are together before you go away for the summer and me too, to write long letters not so much from "wanting to know," or "being cautious," maybe it's just the meshing you look for, and I looked, and it was, was, just, there! Really."

Such hours call the game a newer play, another dreaming stance, a long shot delivered from beneath the sun, a flying ideal with pasted movies sharply spoken, nothing doing. But she sleeps, or waits, the rooms are undelivered quantities, a salient passion leaning hours forward, says, who left the flower, who was that specific, and today, moving day, he parties forward, says goodbye, Dogtown, he waits at the edge of the woods, his time there was well spent if too long, he saw a thousand ladies pass by; got a couple, but nothing held him there at the edge of the world, this, conflict, spoke-out, the appreciation was missing, spaced out with moving words less and less of the good stuff, he let them go over him, intent on leaving, or transforming the here and now of it, he made plans and met a nice one, didn't call last night and said she would, a lack of seriousness, he supposed, at courting, they spoke of it. But today is Leo's goodbye, unless he is surprised "We had a good time; and then we didn't." The double and the magic, but departing hours say goodbye and, among the leaders of the fray, he speaks his lines today and paints a house by noon. Both. Nourishment and providing of it. To move, this is the moment of the move, joy, this is the final element of the passage. No, one has not crossed, but begun.

He sees her flowering out as has the name beyond the palace, they are, as here. Or spoke. Reverse goes out of Wally's truck. Karen comes by with dinner. Earlier, Mick, Wally's dad confides, "He told me he stopped counting after eighty-five. . . ." And only yesterday Wally says, about calving, "You'd have to, to, reach in and pull them out, oh, I pulled a lot out, you can feel their eyes open in there, you touch their eyes and they'll close them, and I'd, well, turn them around and pull them out. . . ."

I think it goes along the road, you stop out about six days and go in and the food is there, and do too, deep remember, I'll tell you, but the long slow droop remembers, goes, deep, says, uh, "Hello," and drift to haze remembered. "What the agent says, does, doesn't do, matters, not, it's the story, tells, does, you should," it comes, out, as spoke, it comes, in, as told, as said, I'll say it out, or now, I was there, at the center of the ring, said.

The light begins to turn, again, the fantasies of large ladies bending over, over him, or himself. And tells them, there, at home, you spoke too soon to be believed. Still, the ocean is only hours away at last, and smoother friends pretend away, he is the mountain in these fragments of hours, he spoke too soon again, but called a straight one backwards into this. Still running his own program is prefer-able to being a loser; they collapse too soon. He strides along. A lady, though, that's the quest of the moment, the story and the book. Cloud-lines shrapnel light. Her oranges making looser sparks. The words of it, her names, the winding hours of the wind, have said, you are this: becoming and moving, meditations of prose, the special hours, and, of course, work. Windows and base inside, two coats shiny white, ah, names around the room. Anyway, he called her once or twice, whoever she is, and the hesitation set him off, away, but nice and tight and willing to learn, and all that, he'd show her what to do, and then do, he'd call her, uh, something, arrived, immanent, potential, horny, even, and cool, too. The day says move, he does; he has.

Here, it is the moth which speaks, or seeks the solitude of the mountain. There have been two, or, no, only two images, one in a special of Hustler rejects, or Best of, wha? Tantra lady in erotic costume, clean clear nylon, with cunt, knee, elbow holes, her, uh, legs behind her neck, feet tucked back there, and reaching around with her hands her flower open, face perfect. And in Mookerjee's Tantra Art, a sculpture of Her, spread entirely out, ankles on the ground, even, open, red, flower pink body center slot, the, the target, The book is specific. About gifts, the message off the wall and flying to some local hot-shot, sprung out between her days, a spot and center. Aha, Which is true, art-lives, on top and other, he spoke too soon, perhaps, and painted trim all day, it is, forgotten, this afternoon's important art-thought while painting; the figure of Rumi floating, flying spinning dervish dance, a sweet young thing to sit on his face, ah, today, weather perfect, he did three twenty-five dollar windows; and while the hours flew, he imagined a calm disturbance, between her legs, and saw the native hours tremble soft delight, again, they came. . . .

It is the task, really, and the rescue. Power you can understand, and examples: work, storing of energy, the quest and the, the holy bell going off, ring it! A wild moment, chosen from time, your own vision would prevail, then, in limitation, in preparation, in the cool appropriation of the task. Of course he wondered whether his powers were adequate. It is more than a story to tell. The power, the task and the charge. And the charge is either "charged with," as, a responsibility, or "charged," as, with power. And there is work to do. Not enough to say, "I have been there." There is the telling, the dream in its magnificence, doubt, even, to prevail over selfish vows, he held her close and firm, uproot of release relief, a dream of lady, at six AM again, rod-straight, children visiting at eight, the page and every day serious work and wondering whether he was adequate to it, simple? Tunnel. Like his "Honolulu, Ohio. . ." Snapping at Alex too much, too early, too quick. The straight and narrow, danger, serious endeavor, ah, yes, the occasion, transition, a new life, spoken forward says the day he got up early and went to work.   "Go for the tight."

As, going. Deeper thoughts pursue. I think the story is still all right, is, here, even; despite what he says, the fox is on his mind, fox-over-mountain or fox-by-sea. And the trip down is clear enough, a drift between lives, his stash safe enough, strange faces coming in loud and clear, the paintbrushes still wet, he calls you in, he has her in the closet, she pulls her dress up, and, stroke, he says, they're hot in darkness, her hand inside, she comes, breathing names and yes, on her knees, she's down and breathing, he goes in her mouth again the seeds are light along her throat, there's the order set to music, longer hours crowded down along the sea, as the last of the volcanic city, Pompeii, ash and blood, the eye's mind cool receding back and forth, the muses, the lady in the closet; we go back to work. No more the running fire, she leaps aside and says, wet, here, your lips, eyelids, finger on the button and talking, be cool, and hold the hours open clinging hand to hand, the woods or children, they seem to mark the days the same as painting houses, horses, lady's clothes the same pants dropped around her knees, lying back, saying something new, a song or larger, the rose between your legs is flaming.

It is in the structure of the arising, of beginning, that the ancestors are seen, or respected, and when the music on the radio says "yes," then, you speak; no, not too loose to be controlled, nor, in any alliance with, uh, fiction, per se, a guise of fabrics, effects, I mean, "They need me more than I need them." But, passing through, the clarity of the signs, if you care, are, is, such that the flow of the mood of the move is, cautious, necessary, happening. If the interest is there, then the irony of the shift, the move itself is not so much important, as the writing. I mean, Newburyport and Plum Island, early winter of '73, he walked into through Vincent a whole show, two ladies in one house, another, kids, job, bang! all there, but he hadn't gotten to it on his own, it just had to be an adventure, a hand job on the beach, it'd been so long he almost couldn't, balling her on the phone to Ohio up in her little room; and so he stepped back, to here, for five more years two more than necessary. But unimportant, really, the history of a person or his trip, Jon said, is not important, so what! You had a vision, nobody cares, is right to the point, especially when all you want is to get laid. So the town may be moved but not the well, they come and they drink of it, lady, we are the same; his weapons shining bright, he goes out, speaking, great offerings.
He calls the light, here, the town and the well, clear enough teachings and leavings; but still, it is a life, and who I speak to is my own. Jeff and I drove out yesterday, kids in back and fishing poles, we canoe upriver into the sun at afternoon and it is all light and, and all green mountains, meadow grass and roads are far away, we see Montana moist and empty, here the trail of it, his own seeking in the mountains. He told Leo his Eagle story before dinner, called the question on Dennis, sold his ladders to Alan for twenty and went home to bed. Today they finish off the house and now it's three hundred for the road a hundred for now, including the lady in the dream was woken this morning gave wet shots at dawn from still the night before, one at a time, he said, perhaps it's time to change, even yesterday's "the lonely sage. . ." got to him a little, but still, it's the only game in town, "Those visions, no matter how cosmic, are still personal experiences," he said to Leo. He quailed, "but

others. . ." "Well, there's community, but the dream and the vision are your own growing up." It seemed he didn't buy it, wha, a shared vision?

Immediate. Goes like this, passes ladies up, out, or on; even the strong and the weak should mix, and still he could see these snapshots turned-out, the progress of a breakout, or, up and on, he spent some days, a northern solitary place, and in the midst of what doesn't change, he spoke names, he called out, he saw brown ladies in his eye, instanter of, the right time perhaps, she'd lean around him, call the hours perfect, open legs and arms, draw the juices further forward, and leave the vows for perfect moods. "Don't be so smart, just write it." He spoke the same, or water in the brain. He thought this new town of speaking out would be the same new faces crowding in for love, or strokes around the corner, bending over her in the darkness, "Come on, baby," a sigh, "Oh, oh, oh!" and fill the air with slippery moonlight, she squirts across the room, even, and hits the target,

Through words and deeds, the superior man moves heaven and earth. Must one not, then, be cautious. Confucius. The easier trails are closed. On we go, where there is some welcome for the person one is, where the play of types recedes from distinct competition, uh, the delivery, itself, "Uhnnh!!" she gives, and the air goes out from deep within; the program, he said, is also apparent, in stylistics, but the anchor eases off, and lets the information in, you'd be in, to, or into. . . . traveling down the easier gasps, the unknown is still to be encountered, but beginning, arising, and the caution one imposes on his own behavior, is really the faith that the program will succeed, one will have what one wants, a beautiful lady under way, hand in, flowing, ah, elixir of light, a cup at a time. Still you call out, "The Dream", and say specific things to specific persons, teaching; but the lady of the plan, waits, the model in the diorama, eyes open, hands across the light, again.

As, who's hustling who? Our three way nowhere last night, the queen of the Loser's Club, or at least a charter member, talks too much, really a bitch, but she likes me and me her, and Wally her, and so we're driving around talking about Something, her old man who worked for me, she too, or the guy she split with to come with us for Wally to hustle her for her to hustle me for me to be depressed ah James Dean Bullshit by ignoring her I may have made a point talking about leaving and Mazola ladies, who knows, I imagine she'll stick this loser life "up here". Dancing, arrows shatter hearts, the random generals peel away, "More dialogue, less self indulgent, uh, purr-rose!" But, but, it's what comes out, or, too loose to bear down on it, it moves, and on center, without doubt, union and fixity, the poles of the hour, monuments paling out for favor, for fervor, for rest, at last, the last house buttoned up.

In the fullness of the moment, river at cross and pattern, "no-interest," in "no-matter", but call her in from the cloud heights, bearing down, would move around the lady bending over on the beach, on all fours, she makes noises, then, comes, there a flash flood of energy, with the ocean leaning forward into newer days again, he spoke too soon, perhaps, to be believed inside, inside events, a dream or dreamer, at the end of the old life, to say something, uh, profound, like "hostage to the moment," or "eye of the instant. . . ." But how much does one want, is it clear or only another imagination of wisdom, or only voice being interested in his work, to ask questions of "them" or even go looking for a gentle, docile, beautiful creature who's interested only in him, is that the nadir of darkness the point at which a newer fantasy of a lady begins growing in the mind's body, a big one, and he goes for the tight, ah, the green banana, and then eating it, or what's left, and then eating what's left, suppose she comes away in love, or stays for more inventions, the image, the image of the erotic player with some devotion to the game in car seats or traffic, a California fantasy, and gray-sky Sunday had him packing for his trip.

"I know what you need," "Wha," "A good fuck in the ass," and she does, it'd settle her posture, fox it out. "I tried it, the other night, and I didn't like it," but then a half way good dance, at least, shy mood of almost touch, she had grace we went together. Everyone agrees I should fuck my brains out, and some think I do. Talking to her about being bummed out with Mazola, tears come to my eyes, I stop them. Driving around, at home, awake at four.

It is the picture of progress measured here, there is the root, the blind obscurity from which one begins, a promise is not given, not even suggested, and the stages of development for the idea are as profound as the life itself. Progress and process, the same. Really, dinner with both ex-wives, over the three boys, he did the steaks. Jody's Bob is such an improvement over me, at least for who she is. He could see the same house rendered smaller, cozier, more compact. Sue's red hair gleaming, they chattered after dinner at the table totally ignored him, he gazed at them both, loving them both. Different pieces of life. The boys outside chasing the frisbee song with some skill, it is the fruit on the branch, really, he felt freed to leave to be himself, or as he thought, driving home, the big engine blown muffler rum rumbling All I need is a lady to fill the holes in my scene. Work around the clock, beat the depressions back and "Heap up small things to make a mountain. . . ." His own, really, and your cards and letters along the way, something real good, is all I want so far so good, jobs to book, even a year from now, his painter. Al right, and the smooth clear flow of black scratch on yellow paper.

Just before you leave. Really. He goes into the P.0., a few days back, and, it's she even, working out behind the counter. So blonde and clean and pretty face the right little breasts is young and smiles hello a gentle a nice. It took about three days' infatuation and three tries before lunch he got her name and phone and left a flower poem note in her mailbox yesterday talked over a Friday night date, my heart is pounding my head, too, "you like to cook?" "I'm a great cook," "Me, too," "All the signs are right," they sign off, with three or four yesses, whispered, "Listen to him," she said, he was a romance of chatterflap, no more quick shots, a nice one, even, and looks as if she should give.

94

So he paints windows with Wally all day and leaves a note for evening tea with another flower, on his way to work. Alex has a sore throat and Yar is playing seven-thirty sunshine has my heart afloat after years of hard work, he felt her coming closer, lady, and called her names all night, stroke, give, banana. All the avatars of touching, ah. . ..

Goes in the book and sentence, calls the day perfect, clouds dispersing, really, all the signs are right on the way and saying yes, hello.

It is dark in the room, couch slants diagonal of corner, the room clean clear almost moving around me yellow bedspread yellow is the color of the teacher, uh, I read somewhere, her face as round as light, blue in half-dark room, "I can't see your face; I can't see your face," she-voice says, as if he had disappeared, ah, the visual and the feelie. When he's gone it's dark. "Beautiful and ordinary. . ." Again, after they had done eyes, falling through eyes into each other, "Come in," he said. She did, he let her. Heart feelings, between the legs, eyes. Ordinary. "I mean, at first it's special people for special reasons, as if you wanted to work through that special person to some ordinary state, that the special relation is the agent of the transformation. . . but it's not that way, it's alone." There is lady-shot of curve breast through unbuttoned blouse red thing on chain held the mustard flower between her breasts, "I like your shirt, I don't know why." It is this etude to her body, curve and touch of someone there inside her floating free through space wing presence the left hand before I go to bed, again, you speak perhaps of, of something there remembered. "Do, I mean, uh, men over thirty-five, they don't like to make love?" "It'll always be with me, when I'm seventy."

White bird, you are that name you asked about, leaving the house. "I'll walk you to your car." "I need a name," my own perhaps, you are too young you said not yet a woman, no your not the Eagle same as him you are the White Bird of flames entire opened up between your legs, a spot or two, actually, he goes for the tight, and calls her name, at least rightly, "Come on White Bird, give," she does, and stays wet all night beneath him, on top, between, behind and sitting on his face, would stay or say" awhile", and mean that, the term a man and woman stay together is just enough for what they are, she is the model for his scene, which comes later, and comes again, underhand, your own, Lady White Bird sails a season through the air, remembered, a picture here will speak for who you are, and not some other time, but now, across clean rooms the hours bending over behind his tipi, he'd say this to her, give and then receive, it is the man's game, not the writer's, and he'd speak like this to teach her how to love him, now that he knows what he wants. "Give me some time, I have some things to share." "I'll share with you." Spoken with some delicacy, close enough to touch, ah, again, "You're easy to love." Banana.

Really, he passes across the waves, just like that. The allegorical voice recedes, disappears, becomes a poem, even. Tom comes by with colombian and a long rap about Wally and Aleister Crowley, the pieces fall together, he speaks about the book.

"It's that old romantic concept of genius that's the enemy of the third part. And Pound. He never got off, and the artist heroes have got to be sexually normal and male, that's got to be said, Tom."

"I know. One old buddy fell off a cliff, my best friend ran off with my wife, really, and she was getting seven thou to write a dissertation at McMaster's in Religious Studies. . . .I was resident hippie but it was a conservative place and I didn't have enough money to go to Toronto." Pause on the front porch. Long black hair, Crow blood, waiting for his coal money, or a construction company. .

He looked at the gray North-Side Mazola street, wire fence around the school ground. Didion's "nothing" close to mind. The day she canceled gracefully, I'd better write a note or think tomorrow about what to do.

All night long the skies are falling, he dreams sleep flying anchors, or entering her from behind and no sheep for it, Michael's poem on fucking sheep, a recitative, must have lasted twenty minutes, laughing out loud it was so good. The same one stopped him in the Hat to moan on women, those who complain are the losers. Is that how you see yourself, the midnight meditation, I am only copying, he thinks; facsimile duplicate imprint of the cosmos, who is this Crowley? And his "What am I giving into? Into what?" The feminine cosmos found at the climax of the erotic meditation which has her on her stomach he slips her tube the bright tunnel upwards seed hitting the top of her head, soft palate opened fingers of bone part partly symbolic fucking the white arrow from the chakra center of his body, prostated words, entering her, shoots the tube, splits her center, line out to target, he could draw it, a diagram, ass under cunt-flower, shaping up the rest of the world to meet.

So he writes a note, Saturday morning before Father's Day, asking her to model for the scene he wants.

He paused before moving. "Another satisfied customer" stopped by last night with a half a bag of light brown weeds and seeds. The picture is clear enough. Art is war, it seems, it has become a, a vanguard of mutant thought, conceptual Darwinism, even Santana (ever!) is part warrior and part, uh, ammunition; he thought of the battle itself, between the machos and the fags, the lesbians massing to the left and the cunts and foxes in a strange but, ah, loose alliance. And Bilbo not lost. And Eagle, his other, or alter, or   counterpart, this high flyer, he saw him, well, not centered, exactly, that's the old schizo center of the picture fantast, watch out for the voices. Oh, the model and the lotus, or the norm. L. Ron and Crowley, what a match! Harvey at the head of the fleet. Hefner and some chicks partying off left. Flynt-flags (upside down cunts) flying at half-massed past fast ass. . . .I mean really, it's not that serious, then, but ladies in retreat, en retard, doing gardens or, or something else; and dinner tonight with restless Gemini, flashy or flamboyant, her wimpy old man, more like a lady, really, and I thought I might get laid for, for, that is, Father's Day.

The enterprise of it all, or, all of it, really, as enterprising as his voice itself. No, it is not so much a matter of being impressed with the gravity of your own thoughts, or the Modernity of your cinematic perceptions, aha, all that means is that he knows he is a product, a product of his time and a victim of his senses, his perceptions, uh, the ear and the eye and mind of it, no it's more like, are you getting laid enough, that's how, and not all macho hedonist, no, not really. . . . well, he thought, next week should tell the tale, the tail end of it, a blank hour before sunset, her red waves trailing backwards, the back door open, she says, "Ah," and on you go, you go on in. Rest respite despite the rest. You Asshole.

Jumpcut. I thought I'd mix them up, he thought out loud, I thought I'd mix the layers of the story, but, really, he had just started writing, it was like that, and that was only at Easter, we should be done by August, at least that's the plan. Meanwhile, gray Mazola streets indicate quietness, the day already gone over into sameness by nine o'clock, a little sun, the mundane river excursions.

Anyway, his plans were made. The new life and the new move. A pause before action, well, I'm into that. His car ready and willing. Old Santana on the turntable, *Samba Pa Ti*, the center of the erotic dream, played over and over coming down the mountains in December of '75 from the vigil outside Auburn, when she died, she went across the line over grief of the child he kept alive, he had some psylocibin she lay down in her dress we ate some food, she lay in his arms and gave it up, went small for a moment the hours and shapes were ominous in the air; dark wing-things half perceived but there in consciousness, sure enough, the huge black crow darker than midnight came through the trees just as she was going smaller and soft, he reached across the line and grabbed her, just as the clear vision of the old hag rushed forward at nearly the same time, angrily showing herself, running, swooping down for straight ahead right-up-there, he pulled her back sat up abruptly shorted, brought her back, put her in the van and went down the mountain where she did it again, the music on the tape, over and over. . . .

He went forward, then, in his thoughts, they were drawing the story out, the story and the line at the same time the lady coming forward from the other direction. A pause before movement. It is all motive and movement . Sit on my face, baby. So it is hippies and slots, chicks and squats, further and deeper. Sure, it is mother and child, but there is more, inevitably more. He sat at the table, a Miller's and Steely Dan on the radio just before ten in the morning, waiting another week to get off the ground, finally, after two or three years of, uh, getting organized, Prince Chi. It talks like that. Dream drawing down. Notes to ladies, spoken songs, celestial fox, her back to him, bounding up and down over him, "Oh, oh, oh," and then coming off of him, forward, onto four, he grabs the Vaseline and then pushes in behind, time to get off and into her, push, she's coming again, the third time, "Oh, oh, oh!" he drives up the tube, pushing explosion getting off, they both fall forward, her spread apart face down, he up the middle, relaxed between her cheeks, holding her breasts.

Dark eyes I at last close into
  your deep bilinguality
beside me, braille and beholding
the power of your love
without a nerve or vibration
  this second,
with slow dithyrambs coming
  over, overcoming me
so that I lie dumbly still
while you read by tongue
the poem already transfused
  through the blood of the flesh
you taste
wine of my darkness drink
in the snakedown deadless acid
of sweet voudoun
where I am crumbs of the sun's
reflections,
a landscape under your mouth
deaf to all other sounds
but the poem of my own submission
  to your tendresse spreading
winged style over me
turning ploughing up my kisses

Jack Spicer

Chapter 7   AS

He fought white lines throughout the last nights in town, driving Blackjack ditch
with Wally all around nowhere, really; and breakfast at IHOP, Casey, Jon, Striz and
Claire came, silent eating flat emotionless, lots was said, really, the only ones to say
goodbye, like that, he drove the hill, out of town, the first joint, forty-five miles an
hour, light, light, the boys in the back of the station wagon, driving around the top
of the hill, sliding down out of Montana, finally, the breath of the Clearwater
bending the earth's rebound and clamor. It's all horny, every ounce of day, the trip,
the fantast of the quest for the fox-in-hand, the light in pools all erotic blend and
twist, the vision of the day's body beside him soon enough to make her real enough
moments become the voyage in the book's heart flowing forward. Stops to meet the
air's breath flowing fingered outer marks, he shifted out of trance and stopped short
at the edge of the highway, at Whitehorse, and slept for an hour and a half. Two
weeks hard work, all over leaving a place. She has brown breasts falling through my
arms, she touches them and calls my name.

Even later that night, in Lewiston, after fixing wok-food at Paul's empty house, my
Pisces printer, the orange lines across the space between the trees, from the
Orchards, then, looking at the base of the cut, how far today the new emerging
fantasy, watched the evolving self flow out of the car, the boys belonging more to
themselves. It was a perfect tradeoff, life for life, and then moving on, abundant
charms. . . .

East of Lewiston, green flesh hills come out of the woods over mountain. Really,
it's whatever feels good, that's what a man goes for, he asks the lady to show
herself, and then respond; really, she should come to him. . . .

He ran the car down the cut, the Lochsa and the Clearwater rush and stop the car, at
one innocent curve across the river looking up the castle of some magnitude
remains, a cluster of rocks resembles the ruins of some Narnian fantasy, no, rush on,
we flew the hours out of town at last, and looking good, all around, flowing,
forward.

Passing lanes, the thrust of movement toward, uh, station it was called, not position,
really, or static, but, maybe, an appointment. The obligations of the past, of youth,
maybe, are, have been fulfilled; and the business of the wives. One at a time is still
more than one, and so the nature of the pairing changes, and a match for passion is
more "horse and rider" than earlier incarnations. The body's partner, the seed and
the light all meet in the maiden. Where it goes from there, well, a rainy morning on
the rainy road, the boys rumbling around departure and old friends to visit, last
night's policeman too clear and distinct to stay around, shall we return? Years of
letters boxes and changes all commit themselves to other lives, and the beginning of

life is part return and part adventure, where the calm light calls the stations on their way a study or a sure foundation. The mattress on the roof of the car will be totally soaked, washed, clean, put a lady out and leave your wet spots cool enough to lie in, the morning's magic thrush, lupine covered hills, all.

Quick, the hills roll flat yellow stripes, mustard; lupine pale purple swells some a mile long roll under high fastwind cloud sky some blue patched through, riding the High Palouse plateau into Anatone, green stem grass blown, flat at road edge from sleeping animal, wind blown, inland sea wheat harvest sign, the rhythm of Sunday morning at the cafe, last night's dance, a word or two with shy blonde braces beauty have her smiling forward, nice to the boys' father-man we come across high hills a road is less than real a twist or shred of line between the curve allows the room inside the car itself is large larger; an appointment of sorts they left that early, after coffee's page a day was tossed alert between sighs Wendy's bottom, going up the ladder ahead of him, above, he dug it. Paul's house, last night a typical shambles clothes everywhere kicked into piles (the high hills winding forward), dishes to wash, put the rice on, fix a meal quickly back again recall comes later and slower, calling lines are made the same, he drives.

High twisting land-scape, full of hill-rolls, blue yellow red orange flowers, portable, it seems, Arrowleaf Balsamroot, Paintbrush, a long high road through a series, steep passes, the Grande Ronde, into Enterprise, Joseph, Wallowa Church Camp, David's mother at the Manager's Cabin, gray and pleasant and quick old lady chatters at the door around me I spin out the door with Yar and down the road, where's David, on the way back coming across the bridge, I recognize the boy, and then gray hair yes David intense alter-person poet-brother of the Ahlee madsummer, witness and agent: his self gone mad Jesus freak poet ex professor just married in transit himself to the new life. Embrace. "We meet on the Bridge!" he says. And the boy, words, arms around, walk back to the house and family the gently fox-wife, devotee of David, too. The father, "Yes, he was incoherent." "They're very happy," mom says. And teaching, he is saying, "wasn't fun anymore," not that he ever did get laid that much, Wally shook his head, "I can't even think about it." But, camp cook is there, fixing lunch at two poets' corner, really, there, and even over Velveeta and salami grilled, jello carrot salad, David, "It, was in John of the Cross, man, that the intensity was focused, at the dark night of the soul, right? That emptying into the pit, those Jesus letters, nobody answered, but right there in the grit of it, yeh, the dark night of the soul, your ear for it, too, before, to say that the pain of the transition was of the creative changing into the receptive." we stopped to eat.

Or the awakening of the feminine in the creative, he thought. "I don't remember saying anything," he said.

"Where the dark night of the soul is the awakening of consciousness, you know, later, after it's the dark night of the spirit. . . ." He stops.

"That's the difference, there, the soul and the spirit." "Oh, its the psychological and the *nagual*, they piece together, the direct experience of God."

"Man," he comes out, "I am the incarnation of William Blake," and laughs, silly.

"And what you get, then," the kids passing through lunch, "is the bourgeois man, without any qualities to himself, a hero; we were tourists, man, and the Marxists knew it, that's how our genius was suckered into the battle."

"I saw that, my teachers, uh, disappointed that my genius didn't take a, a more acceptable career." Bombing out in El Centro, Ron tells him later of Matt Evans heroic "charge" to his humanities graduate students, he was Herbie's partner. . . .

No there are no careers left, he thinks, housepainter and, uh, his friend, they are pieced together after the fall.

They go out, and smoke the Columbian and head up the trail. Near the Scout cabin, they pause for ten minutes dazed by the dope, when David turns, "There is the purification and the saving. . . ." And he tells him the oral teaching, from the Jesus people, of the sequence and the timing of the events leading up to the Baptism.

"I want either to baptize you or make love to you," eyes wide staring stoned trance-head.

"Well, you better baptize me. . . . Look, man," large log no-window Scout shed, log. "The gelding shed." He is confused, his friend hustling him, and this time for serious. "Really, man, I'm worse than Anita Bryant, you wouldn't believe it. It's not in my program."

They are passing Wallowa waterfall the rocks around them, are wet. Little rolling path, woods place, zen steam hills up there steep, the pipe running through the woods up they pass, through some trees, a tent , there, and some more seen, the sparse camp of twenty boys spread out neat camps two or three chopping woods, Boy Scouts having a camp; and David freaking, a Groucho Marx bent-legged run up the hill, "Two here," he shouts.

"Those guys," Tom said, "in Detroit, they'd get in there to plaster a wall or something, of their craft, and, man, they'd hang a sheet up, and you'd ask them, what they were doing, and, man, they wouldn't tell you!"

So it falls into the Master on the Line, and they are talking about Christ, and David is singing fragments of old hymns and hustling him, they are sitting by some rocks and David has his head on his shoulder, high over the creek-rush below, how do you make it apparent, the flesh of this instant, the one wanting to be converted and the other wanting to get laid and both of them poets.

"It's the same energy every time erotic energy converted into creative energy."
They have run down the trail. "Crazy Indian, knock it off," he yells, halfway, David is intense, and eyes, and he is nervous, tightened-up going up the trail with his friend.

"I mean, when I finally uncovered my motive for being passive with women, it engaged all the dominant fantasies, and suddenly I want the dominant position, I have the same fantasies, but they're not fantasies but part of the shopping list, for a real lady, maybe you need to find out what your motives for power are. . ." he trails off.

So they pass up higher into the woods, and his friend decides, says again, that they should go up as they are and camp overnight, "No, I'm going to go back." "You'd either get converted or laid," he says. "Really, man, I'm not like that, I'd rather make love to your wife." "That's all right with me," he says, "tell her I said so." "But it doesn't work that way," he says, and heads back down the trail.

David appears to be jumping off something, reaching for a vision tonight, and I saw him off the wall, a long piss returning signs the close alcove bangs retort along the waving dunes, pretend to air the mystery and the sign, betrothed today by an end to maidenhood reminds me of the flat gray color of the cedar duplex semi-transparent stain, a quick, cheap shot, and the old man wants what he wants, prose, and a lady to play on, the top and the bottom see the specific playing out, lips, arms, no, a man is not in my program, certain things are ladies only, and suddenly I'm choosey, here, the open door is not quite so nearly always, open. But the man leads.

The Eagle went like this: in the backpack, a bunch of stuff, magical implements, his recorder, a book, Anabasis of Perse, some of Dick's watercolors. It was July of '72, six years ago. He was primed, really, just back from Sacramento's quick and dirty Master's degree, the writing of the microfiche of all thought, and the rescue poem, the whole shot finished.

Down by the campsite, behind the tipi he packed up and took a hit of sunshine red, three more in the pouch for, for however long one was "out". Up the road behind the houses, an old logging outfit narrow gauge four wheel drive lane, to Jerry's cabin. Mary Jane took some pictures and he scrambled up a steep rock slide into the trees. Going out, uh, to listen, it was a gesture toward the vision. Back around the edge of the hill to the power line road, up that, puffing rushes slow wind makes the mind flow, you reach out through your body, blow by blow, make the slope gain in altitude, he flew the rock slope one by one each step found a shore of rocks to sit on, puffing first rush the deep incredible sun-silence.

A sharp noise went upward before recognition, called the heart new sudden found stabbed aware the shock the noise a loud high rising sharp-noise, "Scree scree scree," his being rose, left him scared, vulnerable, he turned around, and flap flap the Eagle left the top of the tree behind him left the air rose and flew forward, at the sun to hide from his eye, but the announcement made, like, you are here, it is my domain.

Up the steep hills rising rock over, acid flung, across ridge and ravine green space the air the silence the pack the nature of the excursion not lost on him and what had

just happened the bird followed him up all day turning through the trees following the man below him, he let his shadow fall on his eyes, and circled round around, the figures in relation, the man sweat his time across the day up through the bird's territory, sat, later in the afternoon, finally, at the base of a huge dead Tamarack at the top of the ridge just before he
went into the trees, further, to camp.

He went further into the trees, the woods quietly invaded, investigated, poet-eye came in and looked around, the camera went off, the long night came to listening deep inside for noises through the wall of tissue between consciousness and the world, between the flesh and the invisible, listened, and nothing came, no voices murmured in his darkness, no lines throughout the cosmos, but the night's fire crackling, going out, even, and waking him at 4:30 half light turn of the night's ending, left him up and charged by 8:30 or nine he took the first hit of the red orange microdot blast off waited while "nothing happened," took the second, and got up to go off from camp, uh, to *see*, took the camera and the book and went about half a mile from the camp and read the poem-prose the hero-king founder of a new civilization; confronting the base of a dead tree which leaned forward now some ten years dead perhaps they stood together or fell that way the silence of the woods, the two live trees all of them immense forty foot Ponderosa leaning together to form a huge tripod. He waited three hours for the sun to hit the apex.

The camera went off. The base of the tree in the corner of the frame, the hot point of the sun at the center of three converging lines, the images geometric patterns with the hot center, all went off, the vision of the day, and rushing all the time, the perfect beauty of the conceptual and the natural events, a coincidence of looking and finding the sign and the time, at least, if the voices weren't there, as one would think, would it boom from the darkness of the "out-there" would it whisper from the center of the forehead, would it sing or chant or what, but the image and the book and the rest, he thought, was all he'd get, and packed up about noon and stumbled back, the third hit singing through the harmonica he stuffed between his teeth, breathing in and out two chords alternating pant and puff, down the hillsides high flying came through the woods early enough the light hot long hours flying down across the rocks and into the trees, rolling forward onto a clear out hillside falling down to a recent logging road, he heard the scree and saw the shadow slide in front of him.

Turning back and looking up, he saw the teacher: the bird between him and the sun, the skeleton displayed, feathers transparent and lighted, seeing the bird showing itself to him, really, man, this is how to fly; and saw the pivot ends from the tail and wing-arms shift and turn, his shadow still running in front of him, the bird floating above him, tracking him, hunting him, the man thought, if he just hit the air in a steep dive, feet first falling, then, by the time he hit my back, why, he'd be going forty or fifty miles an hour, splat, face forward, unconscious, why yes, an Eagle can take a man, if he wants to, he heard the story later, of a man on the Crow

Reservation who went up, who met the Eagle, and was attacked! But here it was all teaching and showing, and he knew he was vulnerable and that the bird knew it too.

All the way down the slopes, through the trees that day got back at two or three, the imprint of the bird deep inside him. "That was strong medicine," Leo said when he told him. And onto Jerry's front yard-like tree space, the perfect cabin in the woods and Mary Jane's camera again. "Mayonnaise!" he cried, falling on the dirt in front of his friends, doubled up in laughter, mayo, really, a huge cheese and lettuce sandwich full of white, uh, stuff, the cosmic sandwich. . . .

The next day, out in the meadow, up over the trees where only the strange neanderthal cackling Ravens flew, came the Eagle high soaring, with its two young, bringing its family down to see the man's domain; it was a proper exchange of introductions, he thought; and the next summer, when he went up with his three boys, to see if the Eagle could find them again, it was one of the young that flew in circles above them through the trees turning circles, passing his shadow through them struggling through the woods, "See, there he is, the Eagle" of domain, and name, a question asked, a sign given, one doesn't really ask about such things, as they are there.

What is it, makes the difference? The call one makes, to others in their, uh, destiny, melts, makes the way clearer; he thought about "last letters", or the distance between ladies growing longer than before, before what? Still, the day came beautiful, and more plans loomed along the way, to visit a distant land and hold to doubt less and less the future holds him back from the wanderer's quests are said to be the whole game is made out of pieces, of the air, he called for someone at six and went back to sleep, untouched, but here's the calm adventure, lying on her back, or saying something provocative and unaware, would say a thing or two to that, the morning a preview or resonance of the other ladies in his past, they had all passed out, left, and his indifference only a shadow of newer styles of relating to, to them, as he thought of it, and a story is made out of that distance between him and them, this she of the empty trails, where no meetings have occurred for some time, where the coiled rhythms lay unforgotten, lady of light, his friends helpful, a cowgirl takes it in behind, do they know, would they care if they did? He couldn't wait to find out.

He was always surprised. They painted the cabin all day. Just after lunch, half way around the living room, he was rolling it out and David was brushing trim in the nice old cabin. The time he met Christ: "It was after service, and another guy and I went out for coffee, and I had the feeling of my spirit, of a dark sun receding, of a photon of light emitted at ultra high speed, and I gave way; that night, at the meeting, well, for music they would lay down a chord and everyone would do his thing together, and I let go and gave inside, I cried and I cried, and I know I couldn't have if I hadn't had the experience at coffee that afternoon. . ."

The man his mornings alone has these pictures, then, milking a lady, into, into, into, on all fours sitting in front of her hands on breasts, the milk coming. . . . which has the day the same everywhere you turn, the same day says return, not to one day at a time, but to the same day returning daily has her there, and soon enough you'd say it matters more what kind of man he is, to keep her happy, or just to keep her; in between your shots, some affection, or names of children call the day around your hands are used, useful, rhymed along the signs she leaves along the trail and sentence. . . .

Or are you perfect? Hits the slower yielding treasures left aside. Left aside, no yearning after secret pleasures spoken hot between them, makes the large rooms grow small, you roll your cigarettes thin thin joints are less than the day's portions are lunging, lounging, staying drunk, they are, really, and they do and they will; but not hesitating at all, even, hardly, slower spots are seasoned here or there, she speaks against your chests, into the darker hours moving slowly longer striving out, the day's calm work repeated again, and climbing up the walls, he speaks aloud, once in awhile, "I love you."

That night, crawling around in the back of the car, arranging pillows, jars of food, he drops the rice jar, it breaks, filling the inside with drops of glass. Standing on the gate of the station wagon, broom in hand, he sees return from the run to the dump. "I broke the jar," throwing handsful of rice onto the ground; later Stephanie fixes him a new gallon jar, half full of rice, from the camp stores.

David wants to go back to school, get his PhD in the mystical criticism of literature, an engaging thought. It brings up the topic of outlaw art. "Can you really give up your art?" David asks after reading the manuscript of the Return. "I mean, there is that commitment you have to art, can you give it up?" "No, I mean, really, you're supposed to give without commitment, the here and now of it, I know. . . ." he says.

Still the cool wind blows rain clouds across the still water of the lake, the cool air turns the lightning out, and they gather his last night at the camp around laundry and the subject of the gospel movement they were both, David and Stephanie, engulfed in, in a quest for community.

"The ranch was just what I needed, I mean, I had just almost killed myself in Illinois, in a motel, and reached in the drawer for the Gideon Bible, really. Rocky Raccoon. But the community was there at the ranch." Upstairs, over the commune store (Religious Peanut Butter. . .), a guy at a desk, their Zen-Christ shootout, David ends up at the Lighthouse, old coast guard station and one hundred and fifty people in the summer, forty surfers in the winter. "Typical, a couple of Jesus surfers scooping the energy and good will of the others." Stephanie talks, after her five years at Outreach in Alaska, coming down to Eureka. "Talk about a bunch of losers, trying to make themselves important. . ."

"When I told him," David says, "that I wanted to meet some real saints, well, that was just about the last time he ever spoke to me..."

Still, there are the outlaws, artists who have survived the break of the wave, the schizophrenic shore of faults, art of the disturbance and the epidemic, the song of the darker hours still receding, falling flat, dying off, and the newer sentences of light, falling, in. So, they say, the outlaw macho is no single mood, it is a style of response, a content of the behavior one has, what's the matter with it? Do we look our for Barnett Newman or Robert Henri as examples? Probably there are none, macho priests, wandering from one community to another, mendicant scholars, renegades, the final pirates from the dead-end sixties, transformed men.

"You know, this year, at La Grande and Mazola both, tenured professors were fired, maybe that means they'll finally clear out the old guys and there'll be some jobs. In any case, they'll be the old remedial jobs, and not the mysticism of literature, we still have a de facto discrimination against the study of mysticism and consciousness here, and any talk of alteration or creative evolution helps the eugenicists in the med schools, not the priests. Really, a priest who fucks, salvation through fucking, the tantra, well they can't believe it, especially the ladies."

Something arises, the punks down themselves, the libbers go gay, now it's our turn. Use your energy, it says, boogie-down.

As, anyway, the landscape, the vista.

Afforded generously, from self-center described forward, as eye scans out from here, but as whole, first seen, then later, and the constant dakhini erotic fantasy, also, gradually receding into the, uh, scene. At moment, Three Sisters peaks forty or seventy miles away, mimic of lava slide forty to seventy feet away, the curve of the shapes; and then later, the pattern of horizontals repeated by cloud form above it all, above it all, really, and short shrub green bush-shape about twelve feet away, blacktop and tree shadow lines vertical flow, no real sensation of color.

In the fantasy, she is kneeling or rather standing on knees apart a stroke away from the light, he is meditating on the vista, she is focused on his out focused eyes, and blows into his mouth. Then, over bench from behind, the meditation on the vista.

A chipmunk goes flutter-by, the clouds spread, break into two humps, and the page goes down and stops, the bird remains below, nested, transition.

". . . relations with others are intrinsic. . ." As. "A stranger in a strange land. . . ." A little Kung Fu, perhaps, would seal the day, at least a little sense of humor is in order, to surf the times evenly brought up on the dry land of Santa Barbara beaches. True, I seem to know couples and teachers and people with families, this, this devotion to the cosmic, it, uh, intervenes, no, is the reality as well as being, "a view."

And this transition, from here to there, is, is watched aloud, would even give a reading as shift, center, recall, recoil all resound no flat disturbance, or, "a dull thud," no, voice is, has got to be a little more perfect than that, ah, the this of it (he always gets back to that) and the ever-wandering line, I mean, at least if there's something to what you're doing, then others fall in with it, I suppose the apparent, the appearance of at least even, there, having something in mind at all, is the Sahaja beginning of it, and then, no super-impositions from above, take care of me, but without impositions. Well, anyway, it looks as though there will be something to do in this new world I never left at all. The voice goes on.

The sand drifts, the star shines, the soul yearns. Through all, time streams forward or backward. What of the nonce? In the drift and the shine and the yearning, tomorrow is the mirror of yesterday. All days stand still.

Wm Carr Banks.

* * * * * * * * *

The vision went like this. A conceit had burns within him, seed-life, perhaps, but Idea and Genius nonetheless. True, his marriage had just fallen down, finally, burnt out at ten, and gloomy, fucking the life at Jody dark butterfly, Still, by 1973, the lines were light, drifting him closer to the idea of the work and the work itself, really, something was going to happen, now, and, prepare to get ready, the commands from the inner layers read, get ready to go, and a sort of countdown of the months began, terrified.

So by the airport, Bill's old red truck, he pulls up hot night two joints of Bugler and his own homegrown in his pocket, thirty-five year old hair-down-to-here and looking good, tan, walked into the lighted space of the airport to meet, now really, two of them, both fifteen year old virgins and one of them his niece his brother's girl, I mean really, burning at cock's center, yearning.

He was back on the Rez from Mazola into Ahlee and June wildflower meadow of love's burning in the heart of the poet, uh, to be in love, he was hot for it, thinned-out and perfect, he thought, cabin in the woods, the world's own poet, writing great, head this way into the Indian land around it, the house he built more and more his own, possession, Sue in town, him in the wood house big, church window box, the big room inside, and the loft, and the three boys, then, wha, three five seven. He'd taken them into custody out of the divorce, taken to the woods, ah, a woman would be good could he take her, could he take her, head into the cosmic trance-drama, I mean, thinking, uh, feeling really that he was in the myth, in the play in the drama in the poem itself, and that's what you should remember, as the mind heaves shorter strokes behind, you leave the body's wall and enter into dream and give up finally flying free actual into the dark space ahead without anything at all, his "nonce." But the airport door went open he shot through into the crowd, electric eyes said, wow, four, hello, she's jesus, jump, my voice faltering, as Uncle Tom, whew! The other, oh, my, reddish brown hair falls wide young boybody tits and mature eyes deep within, as, Allison or All-eye-sun, and then into Alleye, the other, Laura, jumpable at the minute I saw her, he says, the breasts of life, she's the one to bend over, on all fours, and milk her into a bucket, oh, and go in behind, and only fifteen year niece, they're both hot, for me, immediate. . . .

They chatter, "Tom, what a breeze, you're so young," 'Uncle Jack,' her father, wild bright chatterflash across, the years do not exist, they say, vibrating in the front seat, they ride up steep Evaro Hill in the darkening sky wide range bare hills behind town, a summer June blue night sky filled out with the wide span of bright points already seen, night sky of Montana remembrance, the night truck singing up the valley road they were all pretty well safe inside today was life the early 70's spoke that, here, it's summer and you're here, you won't ask why, and getting high, we'll find out about it today, I'd think, that soon enough is here and now, that's the word, the sword of light. He was hustling them both already teacher and stalker, oh, yes, all right.

Perhaps to revenge his brother by fucking his daughter; he had thought in February, really, the ceremony of the virgin, he wanted a virgin that spring, to have, to restore him out of the pain of the last three years of the marriage, both left numb and seamless by the default of the pairing, not strong at going through it, really, it had not happened at all, the intense gout of pain there that went back into his history, it slipped away and moved them back and back. . . .

The bumpy road into the meadow, evening at colorful best. Inside, Alleye, "This is the best cabin I've ever seen," he wants them and it is slow dancing. Ah, the shaman dream in the darkness. But tonight, they make a fire in the wood stove, cook zucchini in olive oil, close, talk, man and two ladies. "Do you know about. . . ." Impress them both. The older man.

In the bed, that night, they are both in the loft, for two weeks away from home in New York for a visit, brother trusted him, you might say, though later he called it, uh, like a sacrifice. Maybe, but, the game was follow and lead, and going off into It.

In the bed, that night, oh, god, wired and trying to sleep, he hears the smaller one masturbate swishing in down bag brief flutter, ah, asleep, intense light of darkness.

The house in the woods, illuminated by the full moon in its season he asks them soon, yes, both virgins, the smaller one, really, thirteen, her father dead, and Laura, the niece, that night, down by the river in the full moonlight, crying hysterical the blood poem growing between them all.

They live together those three weeks, the man, his three sons and the two virgins. When he takes Alleye to Jody's for a shower, to clean her, there, priestess-like, Jody refuses. Really, it is no memento to nostalgia, to go on, the heart cares, the heart leads across the line, into the, the yearning. They make fires together, as the room enlarges over ice fires, leaning across the table, Bangladesh, Asylum Choir and Powerglide stream across the days hyped out on cokes and Hershey bars, the high winding energy run goes off at the end.

After the first week they call home. The drama with the brother goes on, his photograph appears, one he shot in February, or is it, no, a gift from home, her mother sends it. The deep remembering. Or walking up the hill in mating heat, him and her, the Alleye. After the first week, he got a huge twenty dollar bag of MDA from Bonnie, and they all do it. Watching slides at night, the bat flying into the house one night, sitting with Alleye while he strokes her hair, she at his feet, back on his knees, rubbing her cunt under levis, the two weeks flash forward, like, almost getting laid.

One day, she makes the Tree of Life, an old branch stalk covered with new wild flowers. They talk about the older man and the younger girl, his daughter wife mother child person. And her from acid at eleven, the play.

Her body blue in the five-thirty light. The policeman came yesterday, she had to call, "The next plane," the plane leaving at noon today, in the blue light she gives herself, finally, "Tom, I don't know what to do" and in he goes a perfect fit, and then reaching around behind or her butt, it is all wet, he goes off, boom, sending seeds deep up within her.

The other shots. Eyes across, or brushing her hair, the calm persuasion, the day of the deeper hours. You see, of course, must have dressed and left still wet with me, on the plane for New York, I am crying in the wildflowers as Tom's truck goes to the airport, whisk, she gets out, boards, the plane leaves, the seed gone, he falls into two weeks of MDA three times a day and listens to My Sweet Lord for thirty six hours straight into the earphones as the virgin flies away, it is the tearing and the falling which carries him through the day.

The rush of time between remembering, falling in love, deepening-out through the girl, and exploding far behind doubt, the lunge-thrust, the male father seed driving forward, the light drawn forward into the world, the sign given outward and taken in, it is life given over, the seed of, the beginning of, the once of time he comes through, he gives, where there are no consequences to be ignored, where love flows strangely cornered into here, he says, and her, the clue and giving sign, where the sky stays calm again, Alleye, as gift, comes across, gives, then, all.

That happened. No point to telling other, or other-than. Authentic or telling, no story, but what is. And spoke. You see, he fell out immediately went insane, not the ordinary love story, those parts were there later on, seen in the headlights of his brother's station wagon two months later, after the madness, and unrecognized at first. No, he goes mad over this later.

But the girls come, the niece leaves when she should, Alleye stays and the seed goes out, he gives his life to her, that she is made woman, and that is his grief over, the grande passion, to send her away, is not like the seed and the egg, when she gives child, is more the heart and the deeper sighs give way through the third eye, drives character upward, into passion makes the man whole, it is the girl made woman makes him man enough to take the grief that follows, singing, even, in the sweathouse, and not alone there, but singing high into the night's hot dome, the grief of his love lost faltering echo in his brother Tom Indian's song-voice, ah eey-i ah, the cry goes, this is a song to the beloved, he throws it out, you hear cello music from somewhere, cars. Train horns.

The mirror of yesterday. Goes forward, the intense pail of light makes him man, that way, the old way makes a priest the effort at dawn, to go across thought, or love, even, to capture the virgin and fuck her and let her go free-woman gives him the grief of his own possession dying off lived out, made priest not celibate capon-monk, but seed-man, at the beginning of the marriage, to light, she seasons the grief of love's loss away and foundering.

He hits the peak, even, walking back from hitching into town.

It is the other way around, perhaps, the dirt road immense sky and no distinction between forms, the high and the low are more or less arranged to, to produce, uh, noises, speech perhaps, man, and love in love, he says,"to yearn is to love" and goes on, love is the heat and pinion of the core, sex arises through the tantra, not in kundalini but in release, in orgasm dynamics, the energy program; and when the energy is cosmic, or when the view which runs the program is, it meets love. Ideal. Sex and love combine to produce the passion in the work, the work-person.

Or is it all letter and sign design: the relation to women as well as to her, they become the game, it is no problem, there are good players, like the distinction between macho and ego, no difference in the desire to exert control, only a different pleasure in either case, ego being self conscious macho, Ed said last night by the store.

The high dirt road, wounding with presence the anchor and the spirit bending free and clear, a high run outer left apart, they arm the air with newer passionate positions; at Fox, Oregon, where are you now Linda Gregg?

Ta Chuang. They were not all that interesting, those ladies of the last few rounds, in his attitude he found married ladies more mellow, though usually not too well meshed with their, uh, mates. The drama of possession and submission that the single ladies seemed unwilling to experience was, in some, a fault and in others an ignorance, but they were none of them, now, aggressive for love, not the way a man is, horny for love, for love. These ladies, whew, no pleasure but in doing, always retain your identity; no, really, he wants you to give up in him, go into him, it is no death, really they think so; no, they go in together, at merger, and some seldom seen, sighing always in retreat, they were not really all that, like Gertrude said, more interesting than occupying, oh yes, they are occupying all right, but in the play between fantasy and the dream, well, he said to Dennis and to Wally, too, "Well, they come and they go, really, man, they come and they go; a month now. . . ." Mostly they go. But I "Um-hmm" a lady at the meat market, and turn around at the front door to a very interesting look. A little fat.

But, well, that's close enough to home to be, even, convincing; and the slow rap of these disturbances is more like, like waiting for her to come to you, really; it should happen that way, like, what do you want, well, come on, I'll tell you what to do, and, go for it, heart signing down, the lawnmower buzzes in the back yard, he comes through the dark to take her heart, she gives it to him and he takes it takes her keeps her because she is what he wants, and then it is over, that, anyway, the taking and the keeping, do you remember, and, really, it is not final, the renewable, personal, moment, after all, continues, he thought more than he should.

Well, so what if it is boring, she said, if it is what is happening then it is true, and if it is boring to you, then that's also what the world is to you, and if you are bored with the world, your art is trying to tell you something, and if you choose to ignore it then something is wrong with you, you should change directions until you are always feeling the same and always feeling good, that's what modern art is all about, and fucking, really, fucking the dog, little big hand.

But even with that distance there, that on-falling darkness, still, there was the possibility that he might get them out in time, the wound was slight, only a light cut in his upper left thigh, on the outside, in the meat of his leg: he got them, spoke to the others, and left. It was the only thing to do, not so much a, a retreat, but a withdrawal from a disastrous situation was what was called for; power sudden uprush light beneath the waves, so what if they are not very interesting," a woman is to fuck," Jerry said one day, I liked that, for fucking, always get a woman, why, they should like that, engage in it, more willingly than they do, but then most men are such wimps, stoned out, or kundalini work-heads, or just, over forty and, really, dead to it, and the ladies all bursting with the need for release, well it's no wonder they all jerk off, all of us, it seems, they tell themselves too easily, but they, they should do it together, "pleasure shared is pleasure doubled," ah, you might relax and stroke around the pond, one layer after another, just try being a little foxy; but then I suppose most men fall off in fear, whew, the lack of confidence, uh, perform!

Eugene, blue-jean, gray-sky made him pause in behind Ed's house the little shed, the boys clustered on the floor in sleeping bags, Bert a day away, his folks another, and then the short specific run down 101, one oh one, re-run return, at least at last something he wanted to do for a change would be nice, or right enough, to call collapse the inner Nile, and forge ahead all foreign dues specific, yes, he would actually track after Linda, he must do that, she was the total fox he'd ever met a writer of the stream, too, where are you now, foxy lady? All compass marks indicate the south-west is still the place to go, and that could be anywhere from Tucson to San Diego including Santa Barbara or the same El Centro, I should find Vanderford again.

I suppose it is living by formula that gets them down, looking for shortcuts. Really, the essayist has no idea what he's talking about, he is still trying to find out what it is that he's talking to, not the easiest sentence to write, even, out, the rest, down the tubes and falling out, or in, the sky emergent surf rolls back down the line clean air resembles what's between her legs, honey.

Really; stoney, driving lines. As it were, all recall the lists of ladies met and missed and known, even if, even though, more than a few came on, and of those that stayed, probably the earlier were most promising, though to refine your judgements from single cases would be, uh, flawed logic, less expertise, nothing to say but "her" or "mine."

Stoney cave grunt, or a release of doubt, or neighbors, even, sleeping with a lady in a car all night, boogie in the morning she's still wet and opens easily, your knees ridged from the rubber mat on the floor, but in and gone away you'd stay awhile, she should accommodate your whim and pleasure, says the book, it is like that, lady, says "No more handjobs," and lift her legs up and apart and slide it in to mess around, really, the birds whistling outside say, it's 8:30 and all right!

Wet line surprises, cool mist on the windshield, the old pickup goes by, three guys just from moving sprinklers, the green bush under the gray sky calls your own freedom Eagle or turned-out, or simply going along the road, you were less than cautious the other lives, all lived, finished, rather, finished off, finished up, goes on and on and on. . . .

Even so, the day promises to be more than that, promises everything, as if what you'd call a drug, or a ceremony, or a lady, is all the same underneath, and calling the middle lane "control", well, that's all right, but the empty road between beds is longer thought than one would think, the random tunnels are more spoke than sentence, even left two of them in a house, a setup if I ever saw one, but, ah the old days, had to split, couldn't leave my life unfurled so easily: a new spirit fills the air, what seemed unending ends now the day's own independent reckoning, an outer coil from which remove youth's lessons are not removed or left behind, there is still, still, the rest recalls the higher jumps, made alive, allowed, then, perhaps the resonance of it, the things seen, even the mist on the windshield drying down, we've left the doors open, long enough, it's time to go inside and be private, or physical, or personal. Locked outside, the doors pursue the hours roaming golden golden sighs the spot is magic markers moved from side to side, they were, uh, still quite specific, and the ladies moved, return, the man they almost remember from somewhere else, you are not entirely off-track, off the wall, off base. She thinks.

But really, a little interest would be in order: your smoother thoughts should find action, enaction, like, do it, they need only to hear the tone of voice that's right, and a "come on, baby," you meet them in the dark, a breast under silk swings by, don't move your arm, she brushed by and leaves a harder nipple under all, and faces pass by the swim of feeling at market measures hours (quick receding) speaks at moments unrealized, you might get laid anytime, even under cover of strange cities leaving the hours at recalled distances, markers, posts of, white wooden posts driven into the ground around the parking area, seen.

112

Really, I think you left too soon. The ladies do know these things, they have not been awakened for some time in them, and no-one has spoken, at all hardly anything has been said at all, and the main thing, the main thing, is to get laid. And why not? The main dynamic, the main flow, is through that energy line, the rush and flow and motive that is male, he gets it up, and that's the clearest sign we have he's alive and, well, kicking in, getting into play, ah, the play of her, next to you, makes it right, and right-on, enough, to say, here you are, lady, there's nothing left to say.

As, uh, something. Parked along the Oregon Coast Highway, in a dirtpatch at the foot of Humbug Mountain, really. Yar and I walk around to the tube under the highway, dark space-out leading to river, campground, walk along the, into the wind, the high highway over pass around, following a saucy twelve, to the ocean he has never seen it nine years old, Montanoid almost, a "Wow!" and slow to focus on the magnitude of it dances along the line the waves' edge leaves at sand and dollar makes the wind the cosmos in his future sighing ever the first strong image, with Tom the same at Bolinas in '67 coming around the edge of the cliff Bang! into the dark night wind, no, today the sun is out around us blowing the heart clear we close in on California, and make a journal, entry and calm, the claims their voices make again and over all the speaking sounds, "Gross!" "Shaddup!" The boys at play, here it is purple and green and blue rush of the water, the two boys dancing along the edge of the sea, I hit the free shower and wash my butt, the road goes South, as California Dreamin, almost, says,"Come on," it's this family sentiment has crowned the trip, returned, Eugene and outer.

Ah, not so much a matter of finish, the finish, as of carry-through, the long haul through the lighter hours, he calls them down to meetings in among the healthy well adjusted voices, voices calling simple half paragraphs, utterance of, the river flowing downhill a half a mile away, you'd spell the name you brought, against these vague feelings of emptiness in the midst of, well, of salvation, is what they'd have you believe, that there is a refuge in the present, or in the mind, or in fucking, which is probably true, or, I'd rather believe that than something equally vague about not fucking, well, we've had enough of that, butterfly-form in down bag, he's doing push-ups over her, oh well, the early hours are more recall than flower, he thought, you are the same, I am, that to this, and skip a bunch, the rest is, the rest. . .

Learning to speak, the rest are hours in the dusker shapes relenting private songs are called to life or say, alight, room-fathoms spared at showers for his other ladies stayed at home and the newer ones are in demand, as, uh, material, to be shaped within a newer mode, response.

Through divisions in the woods, one sees the hours made of, divisions in the plane of light, words go out as lecture's lessons in the thwart response, he sends the liners out a nether state of being calls within the rounder skies, at perfect showers repeating this for that, they never fuck, I'll bet a dollar on that, but let them think they should. And it withers, no, it is the mutual vibration, of getting stoked both ways at once, is forgotten songs have simpler lessons to perform, I suppose, as he rages off, slamming the door of the trailer, disappearing into some childhood wobble of frequencies, she smoothes the hair around it, lays it open between index and ring, lets the middle do the work, sitting in the car beside you at the picnic tables, the kids are off playing, "Come on, baby," "Uhnnhh!" "Really, you're beautiful;" goes on down the line a thousand cars parked at the viewpoint vista point, the real compared to what, and we go on then the line, Trucker's Roost and Carl's Drive-In, logs piled overflow corpse of the woods, the lady in her down bag, spread eagled, the left hand stroking fast, the early morning light. . . .

In simpler days were we ever more direct? The flatter of fantasy, or power in direction becomes less imaged, resident hours more occupied than resistance, or, have you ever thought-off, bending over, strawberries. . . .

Ah, well, the morning has its California transfer, and what we missed, uh, in there, should come along as, as wanted, as spoke, the easiest thing in the world, to talk about what's happening as long as there's been devoted practice, ". . .a virgin of 36, looking for a lady of the same. . . ."was, surely, a put-on, to give the column writer an opportunity to talk about old people (old!) playing with-it, keep those channels open, folks, give him air, give him air, as the lady pulled up in her VW bus just as I parked, and got out, "I'm an epileptic, I, I'm going to have a seizure right, now. . . ." And, going blue dark light the cars parked between us and the street, she goes down into her tension, insect posture, dance form, the physical tension arouses in me intense sexual desire, she is stretched tight the body's muscles tension moaning the orgasm of spasm, the hot noises, "Uhnnhh! Uhnnhh!" coming from her being, I am bending over to grapple into her body when she goes limp, it is over and she is collapsed on the grass, thirty half miliseconds, and is then returned, exhausted, beautiful, the way the stylized dance of the orgasm is mimic here the shadow of no-problem, energy circuits enhanced, perhaps; "Always avoid energy rip-offs," Edward put it, "it's a matter of energy and balance. . . . "

But the rush is over, there among the giant redwoods, as Alleye has grown some newer life, so, too, does he. It is not, all, jumping, as she asked, did they fall in love merely that he could jump into his dream-being?

Passage and distance, straight line tough, carry-through, hit the beach, at full trot, and scoop the old waves easy, easy now, your own subsiding hours, a more modest enterprise would succeed, one says, ah, but here, in this turning hour, a latent song your name the markers strewn with light along your body, signing.

CHAPTER 8   THE STATIONS OF ATTENTION

Hot summer of dark remembering. By the intensity of the days, he recalls nothing. There are the days of MDA: "Have you had your MDA today," he sings to himself and the others. The steady diet of coffee, beer and dope has emptied the body, the body is this tunnel in the air, muscular tube of light, entered, fed from both lines. When she's foxy, body erect, her chin goes high, the throat gets tight constricted tube, the lips part or open, the eyes look out or back, the throat insert, tube-tunnel, you go into her mouth and stroke her neck to feel the seed swallow relaxing back and back into recall the hours were hot the sun the hot line of the days were seen, at dream a quality of life left within poetic fantasy a myth deluded growth the growing is, however, real enough, real enough almost to justify, the excesses of feeling aroused by the, uh, madness or passage or chemical flowering of the soul's glands secreting fluids up the spine driven seminal fluids the medulla exploded head spattered psyche unconscious needle of hot choice retaining the compressed readings moved across hot lines was what the academic process had yielded the alchemical reduction of character into faith and process, survival.

So the days in the blue chair following the departure of the virgin were rote phase and static. The inertia of the dramatic intensity of feeling, the actual confusion of the moment and the screen all conspired to energy and compressed accumulation, uh, psychic battery zooming elevating gathering speed the burst in the fictive wall, rent in the curtain, the specific dodge of the accurate drift, he sped slowly terrified by the locale, even; he had this: retreat into the mountains and, really, settling down among the Indians. Now there were hippies and there were hippies, and generally the fiction was a ready-made American myth of the loser as hero, or the other way around, he laid back and let go, this high running high stepper, going into his asshole, his head up his ass, or whatever they mean, colloquial folk mysticism shamic texts patriarchal authority macho energy freak the girl the girl he got that went away the virgin and the poet the fruit on the tree, the ego and the snake the image and the orgasm, the psychic body's peak and center, the jump the grasshopper leap of the man's moment in life, the arousal of the deeper core, individuating thrust of the collective personal seed.

I mean, the MDA was pure trance, was, later you see it, the alternate alkaloid, with acid's schizophrenic donut of light its dark-holed center a volcanic ledge to circumvent the whip-wheeling centrifuge of energy vibrating the body's centers, in which the orgastic release is prostate bulb root shot across the room, three feet splashing on her breasts; no, the MDA was central, center, higher up, head and heart and chest vibrated forward outer outward; the slide show was the cosmic moment, all the vision of the seeing, spontaneous gestaltic throwing of attention into displaced or central forms, the whole artistic erotic creative unifying of the act in itself was, was word and trance communicating through the gate, the hole in the bone through which the shaman sees into the other world, this corny bibliography of acts, all met in the moment of the breaking of the will into its actual falling.

The music was the gate, seated in the study at the back corner of his house, a four by eight sheet of plywood with Jody's grandmother's old Arabian rug on it, books, pieces of rock and bone, glass, feathers, drugs, poems, drawings, the power table, the reduction of the cosmos to these, these figures.

Compulsion rules the nest. The body paces energized anxious pain driven wired out of love and loss, reaching forward muscular genius woods-house hair down to here, the woman in the man speaking, "How far back in my life could I go and not find you there, larger than life. . . ." The deep remembering lets go, drifts free, the years of wandering Sufi myths the twelve years of madness believing actually swallowing too the poet-super-hero-god myth of self delusion vision in the photographs twelve years of various apprenticeships, following the solitary trail into the flowering the center of the body vibrates. Genital embrace, the genius seeded self-seeded later on the trail, this, this belief in growth or process let the dogs out. . . .

There were five or six dogs living there that summer, the lame Duke, Tupa of twenty two puppies, Ed's guide dog Gabriel; there were neighbors, across the meadow, Olson's ex student, a novelist, Chuck and family, soothing him, watching the onset of the episodes. Really, he was sticking his finger down his own mad throat, being a cowboy to his Indian self, this mix of fantasy trips was going to seed, going to explode, let the chips fall where they may, he said.

Really, between his cock and his asshole, that was the tension. Perhaps that was the Orobouros, a mystic fucking himself, "Go fuck yourself," now ladies, there is no image possible there, but the dildo does make the man horny, it is his release of fantasies you are acting out, always, it is the seed and the egg, the man is always there, and that's his dominance, his presence. Always, whether she loves herself or her sister or her man, it is the thrust and entry of feeling, is the male presence entering the body of feeling, though "different strokes for different folks" doesn't really alter the sense of the strokes. . . .

So he sat against the wall, in the study, in front of the power table, on a short ledge, books on either side, coffee cup at desk edge, earphones on his head, for the three days after the virgin left, the same song over and over, My Sweet Lord of Bangladesh, and the trance mode at the end, through the MDA, the ladies' voices lead the harmonies, the rhythm, the soul finds a small hole in the forward moving rotation of the movement of the song, finds this tiny hole and jumps attention through the hole in the reality, as if the heart skipped a beat, a rush of attentive action, he jumps the ring.

So he was alone in the house he had built in the woods. His kids neglected and dirty but fed, he washed his laundry in the ditch and spread it on the grass to dry. Bill sat in the chair and watched him.

After the dope ran out, three times a day, he went about four days and went bananas, went off the trail, lost his lunch completely, he thought, he never knew really what it looked like from out there, he had seen crazies for years, and all you could say, really, was that you were going into it, going there, that's for sure. The thought that you might or might not get back, ("Back?") ,all of it is left outside consideration, and the Mantra of All served to vibrate the body forward into, it said, the integrity and the intensity of the meeting itself.

He lay in bed without sleeping, or without dreaming, either. The mixture was complete, there was no distance between waking and sleeping, between fantasy and reality, the breaking down was beginning. In the middle of the night, a suffocating lion sprang onto his chest, strangling struggling upward seating, crying out.

A small kitten came up onto his chest, was he asleep? It was licking his eyelids, giving them vision. He was surprised, almost afraid. He read the signs that the selective unconscious gave his attention to consider, he saw what was happening to him, and that was the tension, was there really any story at all? Was the fictive in action? It was like a wave, a fragment. "Oh, God, I'm going in, into it, the great it!" You can't really argue with what's there, after, no, argument is out of the question when it's entirely a matter of choice.

There is a huge pile of old cedar shingles piled up in front of the house, over behind some thornbush. He used them in a random pattern on the gable end of the house and in among the cedar one by twelve's with which he covered the particleboard of the house that summer. In June, before the girls came out, his parents came up from Oakland to visit. He had cleaned up his act considerable and they were impressed. But the cedar shakes were still there, and one day he and Tom U the painter of pictures had thrown an old chair onto the pile and torched it. As the flames came up he jumped into the chair and sat there. "I am in the image," he said aloud, and then it was the other Tom's turn, fire brothers, the flames came up around them, and they laughed and jumped free.

Yes, something was going to happen. Ed brought over Jung on Synchronicity and said, "You might be able to understand this," but he didn't, not then, anyway, and when he did, it was only inside the personal system he was imagining. The main event during the three days entranced in the music, was the hot electric needle of his psychic editing. He had gone deep into consciousness and unconsciousness every time the record hit the jumping point, and he would dive in, "I'm diving in," and pull out an image; some he kept and some he changed and some he destroyed: the acid in the brain cells, but if I'm working on myself, he said, ah, then, I finally have control. "Beware of self castration," Chuck had warned, "I don't want to lose that," no, not really; and if he had control, then he could order the cosmos of this, event, really, that he was in, after the information he had, it was like that. The pain of the girl, the beauty of the mountains, blue sky everywhere white clouds trees the ponderosa, doug fir the scrub bush weeds of the earth all growing from rock and mountain, fern bush, blues and greens, the body of the lady opened out, his tongue deep between the folds between her legs, drinking from the fountain of light, he sat by the fire all night, under mescaline.

It was the night he threw his old jacket on the fire. Toward dawn, he got up, picked up the old brown duck coat and started to shrug into it; he had one arm in one sleeve and was twisting his body in a gesture, throwing the coat around and reaching around with the other arm to put it on when he saw the rote gesture of the old man, no, he thought, I would not go that way. . . even later, there was Waddell at the bar at Luke's one night, with Diane, Striz and Claire, and Waddell was quacking about cocaine, ". . .when I want some, I usually go out and get it," intense handsome Jim Morrison head, a true seeker, Striz had said ,"and when I can't, I get pissed, really, I want to be *transformed*!" And he had turned to look at him, as if, there, I've said it, and something, about, uh, instant gratification. He looks up. The girl on Sesame Street has instant flip-flop turned into a princess, two camera instant fade into double image, really, it was the double and the shadow, even Wally knew about the double, homuncular presence of growth cycles, but, but did the landscape ever, uh, appear to be different, where the fuck did all those dragons come from?
Really, down there, squatting in the dark on all twos, arms hung over knees in the Montana darkness in front of the house he'd built, gazing into the deep caverns of the glowing red coals, when inside, a voice growled and sung low chant-noise he did not know where the noise came from inside him it was not so much a matter of his will at all, his spirit was, was entirely quiet and observative of the, evening. But all night toward dawn, it growled and sang, and toward dawn, too, he finally stood up, went to put his jacket on, put one arm, the left first into its sleeve, twisted his hips and swung his shoulders to pendulum the cloth around him onto the right shoulder when he stopped, slowly took the jacket off, looked at it for awhile pine tree coven, and dropped it on the coals. Forty five minutes later it was gone.

There it was, power, authority and control, it was the vital fluids at play, between the testes and the prostate, his sense-body vibrated, and that's the game, macho or pussy, and in him the poles, too, began to postulate new thoughts, fantasies, erotisms, moods, diagrams, splitting and realigning into this: I mean, obviously, man and woman is power, really, otherwise, being alone is OK, or the clone. But breeding season terminates, and like the textbook primitive, we forget about the difference between sex and love, they didn't know that sex and children were even related, that much sticks from somewhere: anyway, with the kids around, they quit fucking, partly the old incest taboo, I suppose, she became mother, his mother, Mother, and since he hadn't accepted that, how could he accept her, and the old erotic element disappeared. But the macho self joyed in the child, aroused him, a hard-on for life, the poet said.

But when the Indians finally came it was different. The initial recall was when Toosi left, they were standing on the porch of the cabin, and Toosi and Jeebo had driven out, to invite him for a sweat. It was Pow-Wow and Fourth of July and the summer of Watergate and his madness beginning to bloom, the hint of initiation implicit in the invitation, he didn't take the sweathouse lightly, no, not at all, at least now when you went in with Vic who would be chief someday of the tribe, a bushy Aristotle, best singer in the tribe, some said, or with Tom the hunter, a fine tall powerful man, wild man, for sure, a stoner and a dreamer who had run against Mansfield for Senate. And Toosi and Jeebo, well somewhere between them the Shaman and the Bulldog of the Gate, Jeebo the fierce figure who ran the sweat-flap. The first time he had been into the sweathouse had been three years before, with Tom and Vic, and he hadn't sang that time at all. But now, here were the Indians, just as he was about to, to "go off." They must know that I am seeing, he thought. But Toosi, a fat eunuch-like knife-carrier, a castrator-initiate priest person, a wizard at the sweat, wild cackle-laugh, stories of his knife, really, he would cut your heart out: "Touch my kid and I'll kill you."

Going up the road that night, with the boys in the back seat squabbling babbling run of, term of, energy of, this. Stopping to piss, his cock hurt so bad, and bump-bumping the two or three miles down Vanderberg's never maintained road, around what became Couture Loop to the highway and up the hill a ways to make a left down and then stopping where Cold Spring crossed the road and an old house a new house too, a drive-on, the sweatlodge by the spring, beer, Thunderbird, joints, Tom, Toosi, Jeebo, Tom's lady, an exception to the rule, and two other white guys, the mood of the mid-summer synchronicity of time and event, of life's own ceremonies rudely interrupting the mundane flow of "nothing happening", of course, the total contrary flow of the nerd discourse of colloquial wisdom flowing around the fire with the rocks on it dark air the half dome of burlap sacks fourteen feet across seven people going in the Thunderbird passes around the circle everybody is really loose and the center of the spirit of initiation says, "Enter, go on in," and they do.

Squat on knees on ground, head to the floor naked men inside the sweat rocks in pit the water pot Tom tap tap taps on the jar with a stick sings a song Ay-ay, invocation in polite form to the ear that listens, he sings with, they all sing together, he finds his heart in the song, "I'm going to sing a song for the girl," he says, and lets go an anguished heroic howling yelping moaning rush of feeling tones beneath the darkness the body lunging out to say, this, intense pain of, oh, oh, oh, and all seven, pushing out through the flap, walking heated bodies over the dark moss and rock to rush of cold water lying down in it drinking cold contraction of a rush of clarity into consciousness Pow! the body's naked edges marooned crisp and certain he fingers his asshole in the dark water the men all gather around the fire to warm up the bottle

119

goes around he puts his feet on the hot coals. "How can he do that?" one of the young whites asks, "Because he has power," Tom Hunter says.

And Toosi tells the story. "We were havin a sweat you know up in the mountains in, well sometimes you have a sweat in January for three days, and all the old men get together up the Jocko and we were one time on the side of the creek we had just gotten out and were goin to go back over to the fire and we saw this small Indian guy on the other side in Buckskins and he was talkin to us, he was sayin things in a language we didn't understand and in the water he made some noise; but we never saw him again, that Indian we didn't know where he was from or who he was or anythin but he was from the spirit world and he was tellin us somethin. . . ."

"You know," Tom Hunter says, "There's a monster up in the lake at St. Ignatius, Tom, I was up there last month; you know there's seven people related to me died in there so far, and, really, I was up on the cliff and I was goin to go run and leap spread eagle wave my arms and legs yellin and go down about thirty feet into the water; and I went real fast across the dirt and, then, something said no inside you should stop and I dragged my feet and came to a stop and looked over the edge and there was a dark shape under the water, man, I could see it, and it wasn't a log, or anything, but I would have hit it, I know that. Still, I don't know what you'd do, how you'd conquer it. . . ."

"I guess you'd have to go down into the water and take its spirit into you like you do when you're healing, you take the energy into yourself and then you find a third person and give it to him, like, you tell a story, and, well, then he can pass it off easily, and it's gone, that's what you do." He said.

"I don't know, man, it was really close, I don't know what it was. . . ."

Then they went back into the sweat again, and again, and they all sang these, these chant-songs rising into the darkness and smoke and the tap-tap of the stick against the jar, and out into the cold water and the joints going around, the T-bird, too, and came, to the last sweat, Tom and Tom were in there alone, everyone had gone out, and Tom the Poet started a song and then Tom the Hunter came in and they went like brothers through the darkness, their voiced undirected and spontaneous going at a song neither knew the way it went but it did, and they made union over his cry for the girl, they met in that sphere of energy together they fell through the darkness and the healing and came out at last, to join the others, put your clothes on and go two hours had passed into the house where Toosi-priest had fixed a meal for the seven men, meat loaf and gravy and potatoes and so forth, junky masonite kitchen table, instant plastic house, the kids and ladies in the front room watching the tube we have made the order, of the day, and sit together completing this ceremony, this space, this attention gathering him and taking the narrowness of the old ways out of him, he is gaining power, gaining altitude, smoothing out. . . .

In particular, the details suffice; recover the whole, a generation, or, no practice at all no teachers at all, the psycho-types of, of the way, there is always a way, no matter there is no system to our uptight ignorant clutching after sighs and spasms, of course, it is, for power, the whole resigns its distance, the elevation, even, pursues the waves thought has, pursues the self's soul's journeys watched unseen numbness subsides, then, intense roll of mix at pain and pleasure have little to do with power only the gradual distinction of the individual under way.

But, what exactly of success or failure in this, uh, realm, it is more the non-competitive distance of the leap, there are winners and losers, we reluctantly admit, but the pursuit itself, even, readies the climax, over the long haul, like a prolonged lifetime body rush; though if you are committed to the idea, the idea of distance or a reluctant defeat, perhaps, no there aren't any dimensions to, to behold, perhaps a sensation of story, or the uncommunicated last ditch attempt to resurrect your own life, up from the obscure depths, the pit and realm, the open movies slightly less than depth, or the boys punching it out at the corner, sunlight evades the issue.

Water came across pools of light reflecting colors and visual planes of distance, he emerged into the seeing in the moment, the longer he looked at the landscape the quieter he got, and the seeing, it gave physical pleasure to his eyes, yes, the eyes feel, and when they like what they see, they are happy, and they feel good. Yes, the body to the point that they were no longer deciding what to do, it was this contraction, this constriction of the moment into its immediacy that left the hours flat, pasted against the light reversed the time the time and the seeing both warped to a center of feeling made the spirit fly into the composition, falling into "image" the day he was driving into Ahlee for, something, anything to do, it was that "nothing to do" sent him up the wall, the day they all piled into the blue van to go into town, there was an olds 88 with Connecticut plates coming down the road, with some people in the back seat he thought he recognized the virgin, and he knew the car didn't exist and he didn't look in the rear view mirror, he just drove as fast as he could down the old bumpy-road the same road he walked down in the full moon MDA moonlight with Alleye, he just kept on driving and didn't look back.

It was the world turning. . . he went back to the sources of his energy, and found inside, a time of his own mastery, and in that confidence wrote to her married with three children, really, but there was no doubt she would answer from even further back, the years do not exist, and what went out as passion was less sensation than cause. "Not so much a matter of who as when," he had written to Sea, but that had passed, too, angrily, left aside, or left out, or left. It seemed right, then, there, to call her back, the Other Lady, and meet this, this drama of his own life returning, to the order or structure of his own passion, and giving in return, to her, the real return, of first love. He was home, on his own turf, finally, after fifteen years wandering, to take possession of his own meanings in a time of cultural pirates, interlopers and wandering hustlers. He had always been California, as far back as he went, even to the old adobe of his childhood among the orange trees of his grandparents. And when the book talked of revolution it meant going back and taking what belonged to him in the first place. It became what it was, that's all, if you beat down the filtration system that consciousness provides, and let the so-called unconscious speak, then, resonance to direct speech is overwhelming, and even reflection says, these old hippie high stylers, fancy fathoms, shot shooters of the, uh, cultural runoff lets the audience as they say, go fuck itself, which, generally, it does. Generally, is, wha, the comic strip of love affairs, well, baby, I know what I like, and go on, rap it out, or hustle your own thoughts, that's the solitary of the hustle, I really only just thought about it, not to long ago; I mean to be any kind of cowboy at all you'd also have to be part Indian, too, like Tiresias being both man and woman, well that's too much for most, ah, Americans to, to think about, it's just so hard to think, but really it's just how much of your head you put into whatever it is that's happening, and if it's being crazy that you're into, you'll have to admit that the very quality of observation which is created by choice. . . I mean, if it's part of the program to go mad, then you'll admit that you'd want to see as much as possible of what's happening, really, not to remember, but to see.

To see is to be (*well*, you say); the speed of light quiets thought, even, just as the eye traduces the ear's six hundred and forty miles an hour slowness, he thought out that, too, and Fox-in-hand was close enough to smell around the corner, her signs were out, from the sly-smile good-tit at Safeway, asking about Playboy, well, not a Penthouse Pet, yet, that is, and Tom's studies for the two graces in the garage, a slick eight by ten with a she-shadow and a horny twenty, just, just about to start giving, pants turned down, hand at the edge of the cliff-cleft, he didn't say something, I think, he didn't sing to her, "Hey baby, feel good, just put your hand in," I could go on. . . .

Besides, Sharon had, this discourse on genius last night, the aberrant intensity which is polar to, really, boredom. . . as if someone interested in everything should be more interesting than someone simply interested in something.

Less than what they spoke, it was the ameliorative burst in the wall, edge, spine, hour, mist-in-trees, it is where he wants to be, against the Chief's disorder speaking lines he can't remember, out loud longer says the moving rooms.

Lifting back, before the mind's memories make you no-one in particular, but the child embedded in his play, or, or a man, even, there are some now and then, ten years is, isn't precious much the whole enlarges, I say I saw my death about halfway up the trail I cannot emphasize I had no idea where the trail went or why in particular I was on it, I had practiced sighting. . . .

The position of the body center of event, right on centers of attention, response to focal energies. He was at peak, in the meadow, sighting through space at motives, really, the thrust of energy through the eye, circumventing the rational, there isn't much dialogue because no-one said much. . . .dogs alert, Chuck and Ed and he all drop some Clear Light and split up, promising to all circle north and meet up at the beaver pond. Orange turtleneck, cutoffs, moosehide mocs, a hit of sunshine red in foil in the pocket, he went along the ditch saying goodbye, the air went tight specific holes in the air and went across again into the space of the ceremony made, made perfect silence calling, down the ditch road to sit on a tree stump, and rush-rushing, out!

Along the road acid heightened heavy weight went paling forward drawn at dreaming times made him move against (against,) the will spoke out, again sun's specific angle calculated, calibrations on the spontaneous eyeball leads the heart's beat tropistic compulsion makes the body choose, to go, that way, coming closer, there is noise, he hears a clatter of metal, drops down, into the low brush, selective attending, on edge, goes through the trees and finally comes up at the ditch behind some cover a gigantic metal insect feeding dinosaur-like chomping vegetative watersnake the fierce and sluggish machine-beast with man-brain synoptic flash, the beast if feeding on the green plants which grow choke the drain stop water finally, must be cleaned, the huge beast gulps and swallows farting bellowing clanking turns his head away sharply, goes down a few steps and, again, sights to the floor of the meadow, receives the body's command to, to go, and the line to a tree-form, out there in the meadow, he goes down to the flat, through the trees. . . .

Air bright and unsettling, light humming with energy, charged signs floating, foot first and sighting, he moved across the flat, white, grassfield and stone, to the tree in the heat, dogs moving in the distance, over by the creek, toward the mountains, he faced the mountains which were wooded steep slopes five miles across the valley. He walked across the meadow toward the tree.

When he arrived there, he turned around and looked where he had been, "Never look back," his internal monologue had been saying, and he turned around and looked back, and off to the right, something, a hundred years into the white bright sun. He stood, as in a daze, then moved toward the something coming up, onto the, circle had been dragged into the ground, a large circle about twenty-five feet, a trench etched by something about only three inches into the ground, a sky-target; and at center, raised by collapse into seeing what had been collapsed there, he saw the carcass rib cage, dried fly cavern dead cow-carcass lying sun-stained death-house the air trembling quickness if he didn't turn and run he would have to dive into the house which was like the sweathouse, and he turned and ran.

Back, toward the creek, aimed, as he was, toward the mountains, and he lost it in the brush around the slow running creek, the dogs met him and together they followed the water through the August heat and sharpened acid cleared out heated air the shimmering vision of the curling waves of visual distortion kept them together crawling heated haze the air hanging in his mind the bright gaze of stoned eyes at the ground calling forward lives they moved out of the trees and across the meadow on the other side toward the road that went down a ways to turn right and go down toward the highway. He tied the turtleneck around his waist and brown body floated eyes to the ground or fastened on the asshole of Gabriel the guide dog in front of him, he would look at nothing he decided he would not let them see his eyes, he said, and he and the dogs went the mile down the road, looking down at the flow of the clear water in the irrigation trench along the barb wire fence they went slowly along as a car came slowly up the road and passed him by he would not tell them he had already cut off his hair, the day before, in the cool emptiness of his house, naked, standing in the middle of a big orange piece of cloth, he had bent over from the waist a sharp knife in hand, they were always sharp, his knives, and he had held the long hair down over the grief over the virgin and his jumping off of his life he had cut one two three times; loosed hair fell forward onto the cloth he threw the knife down as Ed came to the door, "Jesus!" and wrapped up the hair and the cloth together one must be precise in such matters as hair and fingernails they are power and must be disposed of properly, it is told, lest they fall into the wrong hands, he wrapped it up. . . .

He was walking down the road toward the other dirt road, another car passed them by, went flowing off in the sunlight of the day his eyes were on the road or the dog they went slowly down the road and got to the intersection and went around the old yellow pickup parked at the edge of the field where the old timer was over piling up his bales, and they all went, man and dogs down the lane to the highway, he was standing on this main trail, looking over at Vic's house, thinking, I'll tell him I'm going, off on my quest into the mountains, to have my vision, I'll go tell him that and ask him for a piece of his power to take along with me, I'll follow the water up to the source, to the head. . . .

But he didn't do anything, he stood at the edge of the highway, not looking at anyone's eyes, watching the mountains, thinking, I must not look back. Never look back, it was some kind of Dylan song that pushed through his consciousness, trying to use whatever came his way in the random flux and play of spontaneous thought as it pushed into his conscious monologue.

(As conscious, thought-feeling, fox-alert, she bends forward from below the waist, thrust of pelvis forward, squeezing her butt together, tightening of muscles, from the slight tipped slope of breasts comes forward hip thrust, eye shot, eye at eye on brown hawk-face of pretty enough pleased smiled-out down the tight bark blue nippled underneath white flesh the push of the hips comes alert and drops down total eye on total cunt, the line of her shorts divides the flesh-fold the eye comes, up to say, "Hello. . .Montana. . .transition, are, you. . ." goes on brief exchange comes up to see the beach, across, over there the beers are, cold enough a bowl in the hot sun says, Bill and I sit all afternoon talking about that one, and the other ones, the promise of hard work to tan the body sweat out the beer and eat burgers the Sunday feast is shaping up.)

At the deeper wash of space, performs the wild walk across the valley floor five miles decides, then, to become invisible, but for the five dogs he decides to cease this planar surface dodge the intense rush the space between lives and utter realities speaks between them, man, shadow, dogs, facing the cleft in the mountains sighting sighing disbelief wanderer's core at heart, heat, shattered outer lines penetrating the straight line across the valley, as prose, as walking half naked browned outer cooked man five dogs lead and follow the sun's trail in the water all the way a hot day browns his shoulders streams the body forward rush of clamor settled houses frame the way along the shore your sailing ships renew the cowboy in the jungle, really, the blue light of the tube in the other room shifts attention off course of course they settled all dogmas moved all time the religious content context a long one liner spread her legs apart, pull her dress up, slowly, "Baby" says, "put your hand there, make it nice," she does a long one liner drifting back and forth would stare across noises bending for attention scattered forward, means, really, go for the tight, I like the, really, yes I do, the model may yet show up on time.

Wet feet along the streambed, trickles, really, rivulets of summer rainoff, run-fall, the forward flush of the earth's sweat-lady, climbing through the trail the water makes, he bends his line across the valley floor criss-cross over fence along bush trail, he comes to a treeline along the backside of a large field a machine coming down around the bend the edge of the way he hides behind the trees down on all fours makes his way through the bushes peering around for Gabe, to know which way to go, guided, at least, by somewhere between compulsion and a large dog, goes across deep folds and clefts of bush-grown, overgrown the body's lady driving forward hot acid sign seeing says, this: a fence he comes to is nonetheless on his straight line to go across the fifty yards on a side, about thirty black cows in the field, dogs go first he goes under the wire and starts out the cows draw back. . . .

Off to the left, the old guy, appears rather out of the ground, takes a few steps forward, and he is old his blue bib overalls are inscrutably dirty the gray hair of his beard altogether scrungy enough to be inside the small field all the time he looks at him and the dogs, brown man standing center situation from, from where, and the dogs milling the black cows also milling back against the barbwire they move and spill as water does, moving bump-bump around and back the big dog Gabe is barking dangerously holding them back, "You better look out," he says, the old man says, staring at him, "there's a bull loose in here. . . ." and he looks around him there is no bull. But now the cows surge forward coming toward them, the big dog barking, he calls, "Hey, Gabe!" he cries out "Hey Gabe!" over and over the dogs split the dog is barking out loud they move, the cows begin to break forward to charge them he turns and runs toward the fence the dogs ahead of him he hits the ground on his back rolling off his knee and face-up under the wire to his knees and up and out of danger on his feet and striding into the next, empty field, and, not looking back, goes into the brush at the edge of a ditch, runs into the gully, stooped.

It is this slow march across the valley floor that is, no distance made the steps fall quiet, goes through the distances of trees the quiet rush continues in the body aimed ahead at some gully-wide trench, the water always flowing down behind him, earth falling forward, the sun behind casts long enough shadow leads him forward, the arrow is the target, and moving silently swift he passes projects, he moves trees silent movement through woods the trees are not a maze, they have, this arrangement to him, the ground has become a poem to the eye, and the particular patterning of, this engagement taking place between the eye, his motive and that which is, the medium, where no trails lead but the clear path of water-ditch, shovel-line, hay piled at pattern on the level of the field his eye can read, he shuts the left and draws a bead against the tree-trunk, over there fifty yards moves toward targeted eyeball of light a string across the floor of the valley intense "Where am I," included now inside event, he is event itself, and moving into season, makes the grade, arriving hours, no destination but the valley he had seen from the other side of the valley itself, he is passing through the net, he is crossing, to the other side.

"I am on the other side," he thinks," of what?" The valley, no, the gap, the gulf, the yaw, the infinite distance of the march among the trees, and, walking on alone he finds the water leads him to the hill his friend is staying camp and children, brother Tom the Picture Painter long hair his immense beautiful lady, stories of fucking her in the mud, rolling in the total rainstorm, ah, friend, he drove the virgin to the airport, he saw the whole affair from the distance of the cabin next door, he walks up the hill toward Tom's camp to find:

No-one there, the coffee on the campfire, book open to bear-magic, perhaps it is a sign he reads, and, noises from the hill; the lady is up in the woods with the children, he hears them laugh and splash, before he speaks he remembers his vow to silence and solitude, "I'm coming down," she sings to someone, or to no-one, and he gets up and leaves, he walks down the hill away from camp, tents, campfire, carved sticks carefully handmade pit and center, careful camp with lady, kids and distance, vista of valley, water runs past the camp a few yards away, he strides ahead.

He went down a short slide, took a turn and found the old dirt trail for trucks down and around the soft edge of the hill. There were no turns to be made his eye read the nature of the distance. There was this ditch that ran water over the hill, around from, from way back over there they went down the line the water always coming out of the mountains, the water always running down into the hot meadows of the valley, he traced this root route of his own unconscious out from conclusion to source, backtrack and gallop, turn and run, he was walking up a dirt road, through some trees when he heard the sound of a truck back up in there coming toward him he went over to the base of a large tree and sat cross legged lotus position full meditation eyes crossed sank into attentive trance immediately spasmic intensity of madness and energy, blanked out mind, the car passed slowly by he saw nothing.

Then, slowly rising turned and went up along the ditch into the woods and made two or three turns, went past some pools and came abruptly around the turn a guy in cutoffs long hair beard low sloped body all short legs, the gentle face of Painter Tom

He fell on the ground in mock surprise. "Well, you finally made it over to our side," he said, they touched hands, and he said, "Well, yeah, I'm going up in the mountains, on this trail, as far as it goes, stay out for awhile, I don't know," and they stood there, he wasn't sure he should include his brother of his in this fantasy of the moment, did he belong, why was he there? "Well, I came up to draw, it's only a few minutes from camp," and they went on a few yards, he showed him the trail which cut to the right off from the main trail and up and into the trees, and they took it. . . .

And up they went into doug fir ponderosa thimbleberry serviceberry underfoot and close around fallen tree whisper of moccasin foot underground walkers, they went smooth into darkness, the huge fallen trees around along the trail over rocks up the huge cave hole Tom said he knew a bear was in there he himself was obviously studying the bear's power, looking for his habitat somewhere in the darkness of something left behind, they went off together up into the woods the one to guide the other seemingly blinded, stoned, mad, other, then went softly up into the trees.

The pool or runoff seemed to be about a hundred yards across light filled the space fully filled the air a cavern, made a, circumference through which the two, uh, strolled around about seventy five huge dead cottonwoods, water, trails, suffused light broke or fell into this, space, where low bush or shrub called the air green reflections, small white flower or red berry, twig, the vague trail that began back at the ditch road carried them up into the woods about half a mile, to this empty, cavernous, light-filled cathedral of calm insistence; the trees had, grown there opposed to, fed by, water from up there the bear, or, something let them in on, what was there, as if saying, "Begin," here the trail of the quest, the event of the moment; it was consciousness or structure called the moment in its observation a column of attention, really, it was the preceding days had led him there to, this brother of the field, of the art or madness, and Tom his story of UFO landing witness, in the tipi on their first meeting, Passing the joint and listening to his recall of a huge silvery disk settling into a Montana field, cargo-cult.

And they lingered or rather wandered through the impatience of the one's desire to be on and off up the trail, into, something, or, whatever was there was probably enough to fill the hours in his life, he thought, a central event in what one fantasized would be the core of his life, perhaps, or the success of his seeing, that from where one was, in space, could be filled with, these acts of seeing, enough to remind them of their, transigence, thought-forward and simple, they were hanging out in the woods and Tom was rolling a joint of some Montana home grown as they walked through this pasture of overgrown, contained, uh, space and light the silence of which said, this is a sign, you have begun, you are on the way, "I dove in" he had written a few days before, a short poem on a yellow note-card, thumbtacked to the wall of his house, the sign over the door said, *FISHING IN DISTANT WATERS*, rescued from piles of junk; it was this combination of poetic distances and abstractions filling the, event it was, with a dream-like double vision of the mundane and the abstract unified by the drugs and the deprivation and distance from the world.

He dove in; into it, across the valley, "on the other side," the voices said, and really, it was the very distance from all that had become familiar to him which heightened his attention to the vibrations of energy inside his mental-visual, uh, system, that is, read the code of his own surroundings as the temporal fell away into an immediacy of composition, that as the structural sensory meaning of where and who he was gradually shifted, fell away, he was left with only the persistence of his seeing and the arrangement of what was seen, no thought intervened but the rush and clamor of associative fantasy as the ordered program of what still remained in, uh, memory, clamored to exist within this personless immediacy surrounding, uh, the event itself. Which made the entire moment a heightened hallucination of the real without its usual definitions while the unconscious poured forth its imagery, and the ego babbled frenzied emergency instructions to consciousness, demanding that he organize this rush of perceptive absolutes, but no, it was no longer possible to do anything at all, he was surfing standing up.

He had already dived in. The entire situation became the illusion in the cosmic order: his brother Tom, meandering and hesitating over every leaf and bush, gazing stoned-out eye on the fixed levels of perceptive distance: "The longer you look at this, the more it changes" was, really, himself in his poetic passivity, they were, finally, interchangeable Toms, shifting in his own awareness from self to other, the double in event. Of course, he was there, or perhaps, he was there, but the visual maintained its specific, painterly, visual and abstract reality, it was arranged by the personal intensity with which it was seen. Light rays beacon-like filtered the dusty air of the patch of dead cottonwoods slanting reflected in the two foot deep pool of water standing at the foot of an isolated valley, and this trail, was prehistoric, was the line of the messenger into the sacred mountains, how many were there, and when one had dived in, truly, where did the trail lead and where did it end, but carried him through the museum of his own fantasies as they popped out, one by one. . . .

There. They were the stations of attention, these fixed absolutes which presented themselves to, the eye. Obviously, one saw every-thing, h, perhaps, but the eyes did take in all that was there, and as it focused down, into metaphor, perhaps, the image itself became the word for it, the selective organization that consciousness made, at the least, into some sort of serial motive, it was, a motive to attend, to include the thing seen in the seeing that was taking place, rather than lose himself in it, became defined by it, and there was energy there, even though it was provided by the illusion that what he was seeing was really there. Sure, what was there was there, but the seeing itself, what was that like, like, that and this, outer and inner moved together, a fusion, hydrogenate combination, fixity of purpose, departure from the distant elevation, he had moved so far into the poem of the moment that the particular itself had transmuted into energy and composition, and each of these "stations" became a line or motive in the whole event, a flow of seeing which carried him, flew him, surfed him, where?

So they dawdled around in the woods, either the other of the other, or the either of the either, it was that sort of combination of conversation, the poet and the painter, hanging-out in the woods, and Tom plucked at a weed and doubled it over to hold the roach, a natural clip, his spiral sketchpad stuck in his pocket, the other with his hair cut off, lying on the floor of the cabin it was, blue light entering the doorway, standing there, knife in hand, naked, on a square of orange cloth, as Ed came up to the door and said, "Jesus!" hands out to either side, "I thought something was going on," and the five dogs, ridiculous company of mute followers, the Duke, Tupa, Gabe the guide, a small fellow from down the road and a nondescript white. The master and his troupe, all of them a particular station in the flux of the event itself, all provoked by the one, the person himself, flying through the air, he was, or scuttling through the bush, the other coming up behind, "Hey, man, where you going, what's the hurry, look at this," but how could he say, you are an illusion along the way. . . .

So the matter of the illusion itself became important enough to push him up the trail; surely this is the first of my tests, he thought. Eagle at the start of the trail, held back by the alter-artist considering the outside edges of the illusory forest in which they lived, it was a pond of light held them on the line, and the trail wound up into the mountains forever.

He tracked out ahead of the spirit-brother-guide, his friend had become, he raced off from his, self. So, too, the present became the past, only five years passed, he wrote it down, but here there was nothing to write, and the acid pushed him up the trail, he bent over, put his eye on the trail, and ran up the hill, slow climbing meandering under huge trees, water tumbling down into the valley below from the clear cold mountain water on his right, he bent over and ran, and as his eye scanned the random assortment of rocks, twigs and leaves that filled the floor of the woods, they suddenly, briefly, amazingly fell into a pattern of brief and sudden meaning, a hieroglyph of natural writing which held him up. He stopped and stared at the floor of the woods, light, rock, branch.

So, then, suddenly, his brother and the trail itself were both transcended into the realm of the illusory present, it was presence itself had become an illusion of consciousness, there, he couldn't, uh, reason that, that conscious attending itself could be the source of its own defeat, that the problem of being aware, could even be a problem, he had accepted the limits of his own, uh, scene, for so long, had lived them so fully, even, that here he was, running up the trail along the edge of a distant Montana mountain woods, the trail into the mountains, surely it led to the cloud heights, surely he was "on the way," just as he had dived in, into wha, his own breakout image, mad Indian poetic leap from one consciousness expanding outer to fall itself the word-void populated, tree, line, sign of event, synchronicity of asking and hearing, his brother back on the trail wandering along lingering over the details of the vision while he rushed off, on, rushing toward the next unconsciousness or revelation or meeting of the mundane and the cosmic, there was a warp in what was coming back to him.

The image of the lady in the woods floated forward; the erotic thrust of physical energy pushed the physical body into a highly charged state. He sat down abruptly on the trail at full lotus and fell into a cross-eyed stasis, to calm the full flow of undivided bursts of his own free calm; even the air itself perceived this silence; solitary rush and clamor of attention calling for a point to fix itself, anxiety rushed from deeper centers, the body secreting ecstatic juices from within: his cock tingled, his asshole vibrated, his balls tightened with the climax of the spiritual rush from somewhere deeper within, the prostate seed-bag vibrating from the precise center of the body, kundalini thrust to the top of the head, the tunnel opening from dark to light, the woods falling silent the five dogs meandering up and down the trail, and his brother Tom coming up, finally to meet him, sat, relaxed on the trail beside the stream and rolled up some Prince Albert, sat, talked, waited out his impatient rush up the mountain the heightened sense that something was happening shifted from emergency breakout to a sense of vision, yes, perhaps this moment is the truth of my life.

The stations of attention and the illusions along the way, how could they be combined into release and ecstasy rather than the traditional breakdown? The alchemy of the virgin, he had given her his best shot, it had come out of some distance love and ceremony provided, it was the initiation and the jump, his grasshopper leap into his own being, and the awakening in him of his own particular secretions, the body changing thirty-five years old madness releasing energy, the illusions of the day he had been sitting crosslegged in the center of the meadow gazing out at the trees. The figure came out of the woods over there a hundred yards chainsaw in hand, rumm, clatta, started up, the fully dressed man over there head down cutting up the Aspen logs with his own particular style of push and pull on the noisy chain saw. "Who is that, over there, cutting up that wood, he has a familiar style of handling his energy, who it is. . . ." He had sat there some five minutes before realizing that it was himself over there, throwing logs around and sawing at them wildly nervously; and he got up and ran off toward the river on the other side of the meadow, not wanting to walk over to confront himself.

Perhaps the first of the stations was the introduction to the rest, to the others, the trees lined up in a perfect tantra of order, one behind the other, he could sight these lines through the woods, center of the body, eye, linear position of energies sprouting forward pulled the body up from crosslegged wonder, his eye on his brother there on the trail, he ran off with the dogs, he would leave this ghost sitting there in reverie, flee it, dash up the trail into the mountains further, where does this trail lead and where does it end, where is the end of the trail.
He came around a bend and sighted in on a four foot deep hole in the stream, a brief, cold inundation. "I must get to the other side," he said, "of what, of this." And he left the trail, went off the way and down to the stream edge, looking at the brush over there, tamarack and pine and berry, he took off his shorts, untied his shirt and stood cautiously at the edge of the cold, brief mountain stream with its two small pools, he leaned forward a moment and made a low flat shallow dive. He dove in.

CHAPTER 9   FISHING IN DISTANT WATERS

Soft eyes turn alarm intense, she speaks again the days are moved, across the light at forest, woods, or outer songs, the natural force, or the names things, uh, have, in distant waters, really, fishing for what, he says is true enough to be a rumor off the wall, he says again, "names", and waits at the top of the ridge for some feeling.

Day's pennants soar, reveal, term the lines, falling-out, driven further to the mountains, full or sending out, the same adventure speaks in all men in some degree, they say, we are all the same and different, I mean, really, if you were just good at what you do, it, it wouldn't even matter, man, nobody cares, and you can, he sd, put that in the bank. But ladies, raunchy purple outcome, they say things you wouldn't believe, I mean, who's to what, anyway, for whom or what, over and out, man, the same door opening and closing on your feet, your style, old friends faded out, the new ones yet to come, a lady in the folds, facing forward, pounding up and down on top of me, getting going, getting good, getting off and staying tight leaking the vital fluids, life's seed song strong, again, the light.

Persistent calm at the hot center of action, keep breath constant mellow flow of air as centers of fantasy merge emerge and go across the very core of the event, same mundane drone across the dynamic music of the particular situation underway, is what music teaches behavior, the composition of the forms are styles of responding, to life, where art's moods are specific lessons to the heart's life.

Still, the heart's pounding express carries through emergency states, attention is not lost to, mere description, perhaps, if you know the angle of entry, she gasps, "Oh!" as, who's chasing who, is not pursuit and capture, but rather a more specific dance the terms of which are not, uh, battle, but pleasure's newer stance, developed out of love's ideals realized.

Still, you see them, coming over with beer, "Hey, the grunion are running," reflexive hunter behavior, we go down to the beach, burlap sacks, beer, drink all night, it's a little like the wiggling toe on the amputee; but love gathers the edges in, is not always ecstasy and pleasure, love is the centering of behavior into its progressive definition of power and self and union, love is that becoming in the person makes him one to self and giving out her waves are truly spread.

But lets them go, these others of the world, you meet at hours unrecorded, dynamo in the bed, is, simpler energies are released, he greases her in the morning, even before she wakes up, enters from behind, she comes screaming pleasure to life the gray light wandering his strong shots miss the mark a stranger in the wings has strolled across the moon, a gradually enlarging sphere of action makes description a mark of friends along the way, a calm state always between passion and fantasy, is no macho dream is not so bad as, wha, the impotent general, limp logger, cowboy passive, or the man's beginning, power calls the balance a difference in body states they are all different, sometimes the perfect lady on the beach, is not enough, but, idea, as rest come out of private lessons for the heart the tip of the tongue, the fire between the legs, the heart's uproar and stammer, even the soul's immense wandering is more defined by love's passage through the body's body, the heart's mind expanding unitive fibers of dream and action, work, work, work, you say, driving down the coast at six AM declining drugs, driving.

The main thing, however, he sent ahead criss-cross anticipation of higher times, the salient angle of the jump or moment, beginning, wha, over the top and in, into more dramatic stance the opening cleft top-side richer dream angle taut shift aside AM news is, dramatic, all the same reading out your hours made like something, on-rush of, particular delight, horror and stupefaction, the model in the wilder-ness, or and.

But retread monuments, the, passage, or mysteries of men and their moon of, the same secrets are more or less wiped out, as men are mysteries, there is a cult of reversal, then, of having lived two lives in two worlds, of other dreamers lifting from their own lives a brilliance made the men the same victims of the esthetic rather than freeing the women to allow them, the freedom the men had already to begin with; after all, the inability of seeing particular relationships apart from the love drama they were drawn from, what's there to learn, anyway, what's this matter of men having mastery over women for everybody's benefit, it is rather a sign of another cosmic order, no, men and women are not equal nor are they unequal, they are different.

So he came up in this cold icy mountain stream, as cold as can be imagined a breath struck the air his skin crackled warning seismic fringes spread apart and opened up the pores of his being, even, the curious body goes flaccid, they do nothing here, these vacant Californians, he came up in the cold streambed revived shocked, the most beautiful place in the world, he thought, moss-rock, green light clear cold water of his own baptism, he had dived in this cold fast running stream the trail now ten miles from his house he left those few hours earlier, it was this: the manner of the frame of the accent, the proof of the machine, the view of its ancient possibilities were revived right here the test was made, if you went, almost a little like Faust, if you pursued your own salvation by example and study, if the education of your jumping forth were self imposed, a path or way developed out of cleverness, Gurdjieff puts it, "the way of the clever man," then, there would be nothing to detract from your achievement, initiation in to life, that is, if you had to manage the whole thing yourself, out of texts, ceremony and power, the same sign meant, arrive, or clamor, or sing the terrible news arrives, you are alive and well.

So he came up, cold, naked, clothes in hand scrambling out of the clear flow of light colored fast moving water falling through the half haze, dark-aired, woods of tree stream, rock bush deep within the gully, canyon, inside the mountain, really, dogs wandering by up and down the trail, the shadow of his illusion brother, dream finder, spirit song-companion left him down the trail, the station of the first illusion, he has sprinted up the trail and then dived in, to the cold, come up gasping chilled naked scrambling into, a brief circle of bush, brush, blinded by the closeness of the density and perfect silence of, the woods, he groped pushed, bent over and crawled into the closeness on the other side, I am on the other side, he said, I am in the dream he pushed along a log scraped his back on a branch through the tight bushes went along his eye led the way there was, an arrangement at the end of the log, tree-trunk, natural arrows a brief clearing space enough to sit and meditate, he settled down, he got into space and lifted his eyes, up.

It was: dismay perhaps alarm emergency of the eye-spirit, carried up, arrow at, pointed upwards into, the immensity of the roundness into the blue sky lofted, stretched-out the up-thrust pushing huge the trunk gnarled branches broken off rising pyramid-like from the four foot base he was standing awe-struck, breathless naked, moaning out loud, "Oh!" the dead tamarack rushed two hundred feet into the sky, yes, afraid to say he knew the minute he saw it, the dead Phallus, pinnacle of the male's energy symbol, but, dead, impotent, the bottom line of the unraveling mystery he was, uh, pursuing, pursued by or, on the run, anyway, here, approaching the epicenter of his symbolic episode and trembling in the admission of it, the dead tree, the dead tree, and sat down, rapt disappointment despair even thinking, if this is the main sign, I'd better see it, wailing a little inside silent whimpering cold as ice he sidled down the log, carrying his wet shorts with him sat down in the lingering patch of five o'clock summer sunshine through the woods, and looked up at how the dead old tree divided the sky, power pole, phallus of the world-tree, the sign of death and life.

Line of light from top to bottom, you are sitting on your ass again up the tree pole of spine intended sap-rush rise of energy the top of the center of the head a bright light rises up flashing upwards, same as this I see the same as this inner and outer find the mirror stand or sit stupefied silence of recognition or confrontation, really, final standoff of energy states met the sign and sighed, "Alas," this is it.

Or find out what, the calm center of the silent woods, the blue pact patched in blue skye tree top spire point of dead giant erect into center of, image of, what is seen is mimic or psycho-print the very composition and time of what is seen the primary cue to what is going on inside psycho dip-stick to cosmic order or constant ongoing developmental movie imaged out from event to center, a name, for this, I see, and, and what, the solar pole remembered, I should dance a little, he said, and reached into coin pocket the faded blue cord cutoffs Bill had given him foil packet in which, slowly unfolded, unwrapped the tiny red dot of sunshine red on top of this afternoon's windowpane should put me through the center of the knot.

The eye of the flower, a sign of the times, and slow moving, squatter in the light, body vibrating spontaneous spasmic postures, seated full lotus eyes crossed foot of the immense natural monument, a man in his woods of late afternoon sunlight body empty of all but the chemicals and what emerged from within the process of his,

own, unfolding life, the circle cycle high inside the mountains no feathers falling here he said, the slow work of the acid carrying consciousness into its frame and sphere, the tree was there in front of him the pole of the tree, earth root and sign, up your ass, and in, fantasy said, there,
root and line, the seed of life, seed of light here at the body's death and life, death to life, death in life, transposition of, energy of, the moment of, uh, crossing into the regenerative field of power, the silent drama at the base of the tree, this is the seed moment at large inside the tree, I am inside the tree, sawing out Osiris moving from death to life, seed of self alone inside the mountain breaking out, above, in the event of the moment of, time of, this particular edge.

So he poked the acid down his throat and stuck his finger up his ass, as he sat there on the end of a log in the cool Montana sun at August late summer seed falling mystery of the mountains, sat there ten or fifteen minutes staring at the dead tree in front of him stroking his prostate seed bag half a hard-on felt the juices flowing from his balls and his cock up the spine releasing energy the head clearing closed cycle circle of body's self attending the inner mysteries of the solitary path tantra woods-hole the outline of past information flashing down through print-off read-out micro-fiche imprinting, now, the unconscious releasing its internal information piece after piece, flowed out of the meditation on the log's presence inside a circle of tree and bush impenetrable to the eye protected solitude he felt his way from the anxiety of the moment, the terrible intense present moment without relief left him tingling peaceful seed inside the self's soul reborn at moment burst inside this flood of light inside the body, rising, floating.

The warm-cool air responding, calling forward, the eye's reminder, he spoke out loud, something unintelligible, a moan or spark of, after long silence where the parts of his soul mixed themselves together after return the mix of the soul's parts pass perfect lines along the light illumined the woods-glow his body rising slowly carrying his turtleneck and his shorts pushing through the bushes he spoke out, I have gotten off the way, I have left the path, the path up into the woods, postponed hesitating dismay, a side path, an illusion on the way, another, uh, station, the second station of attention, and he got up at the end of the log, head singing slow music went back to the base of the tree to the bushes, pushed through the bushes back to the cold clear silent rushing edge of the stream, he was on the other side, and looked back at the trail where it curved and rose into the mountains over mossy bridges filled with watercress, and saw him, dream-ghost brother sitting crosslegged at the curve in the trail, watching him, he had seen, he has looked x-ray through the trees, witness of, the moment, that had, just occurred.

Not only was the dead tree a shock to his, sense of what was actually happening, but that what had happened was such a surprise, that anyone should be around at all, even, to see, he thought so, even if they were both illusions, not so much invisible, no, but that seeing the frame in the wall, through into, uh, meaning, was too much to explain, was rather like telling someone what a poem was really about, no it was too much to, really, believe, and they went back up the trail again, the two men one naked carrying his clothes, and the five dogs went, strolling along, the naked man again ran ahead, up the trail at these, stations, pausing where one should or shouldn't, but, really, when one stopped something happened, beyond explanation, or entirely within the realm of explanation uncaused unthought unfolding of event or moment or vision was there the eventual pieces of information coming into focus, self-heal, self-seed, ceremony of genius and the marriage of the self in hand, the mystic's moment on the trail, went like this:

He was up ahead and running low when he saw his death. The energy was running free and clear alone along the way, he was back on the way, the trail, and the constant flowing fantasm-screen he usually saw through, it was a coalesced cloud of being a funnel moment of life expressed in his, moment of life, the flux-flow ran him through the day, and ended, he saw, somewhere ended changed, transformed, slowed down, went out, ended with absorption, expression in absorption was change into, the newer, regenerative thrust meant the gift and the death, the planting of the seed deep within himself had released the image of his own death deep within him left him without calm the great fear had lifted as death in life meant the expression of energy, at its fullest constant a transmuting and flowering of this event was, that, the moment of passage rather than the beginning of wisdom, it was how it was happening, this song along the biological highway, as the meeting of his opposites had produced a fusion inside himself, the creation of the homunculus.

And they went, up the line, self and shadow, self and brother, self and self, the meaning of the way became, more than a force of postures, rather a positioning among the elements of chance, he was a fragment in the arterial flow of traffic on this earth-body, a germ cell floating in the plasmic flesh of the cosmos, but he was on some ancient route of mountain messengers, he was, he knew, an ancient message on one of the body's forgotten routes. Not only was he there, he knew he was there, and he knew how to leave and return, he could bring them from the cities, out, to the mountains, by following the water up, from the fires glowing at the edge of the horizon, the earth spoiled and split, the red tide rising through the valleys, men and women and children lost in clusters groping escaping the holocaust of the final agony of development, he had found an ancient escape route, up from the last city on the continent, this, this last lost Shangri-la in the mountains, an old Indian route wandering from the Flathead stronghold, the last outpost of America, up through the peaks of the Mission Mountains sacred wilderness one side this whole backbone slope of refuge and wilderness, he was at the mouth of a feeder trail, as if, pioneering in Montana, for the survival of the germ cell of his last compressed and coded influx of images, the last poet of his order, he had chanced, wormed, struggled, risen, lifted himself, broken through into the strange space of the way, and linked up, met with the all but decayed signs of the previous order, he had met the trail of the ancestors, by which one trail met all trails, the arteries of the body were these trails and streams of water through the high sacred ridges of the last stronghold of the spirit up into the empty wilderness of Canada, he could gather the survivors and lead them on these trails, into some newer life lay up in these mountains where men spoke of seeing the grizzly bear play in the high open meadows of the wilderness scant miles ahead, there was death and salvation to this image of journey he was experiencing on the trail, the mystery of the prostate and the opening of the trail, they were complimentary miracles rising in his unconscious, he was crying and running up the trail, the mixture of pain and awareness told him that he was perceiving both fantasies and realities, that surely, the dead tree was there, and it was the choice he had made, about how much to give to it, to his seeing, and that he had given everything to the moment and to the seeing, and that everything had been there; no, it was not so much a matter of being able to see everything anytime, but of being able to give everything at the very moment one was entirely opened to receiving everything the body had to reveal to the conscious at the proper moment, ah, then, readiness and response, the end of preparation and study, that in a moment the information could be there, in its form and reality, and in event, that was important, everything came when it should, and he went up the line, dogs, his double trailing after him, calling to him to slow down and pick some flowers, still he rushed, where does the trail lead, where does it end or does it constantly interface with other highways, growing steadily into, back into, the mass, the intense and close community of friends and others.

A sign is just that, neither an extended moment of self esteem nor an exercise in, uh, chance; the lapse in cleverness, or, really, a confrontation between thought and moment, time and motive, the interfacing leaves from history and the unconscious; a context of surprise, a drama beyond the specific calculations to which art is subject, the man-object; no, really, it is, perhaps, the dramatic gesture of a man's life, he might say, there, and mark it out of the singularity of the passage, or he might miss it altogether, say the time was not right for his recognition, or, simply, leave himself at the mercy of his dreams, but really, the moments do occur, how could they not, could one pass his life without incident or drama; no, even though we fail completely we do come back in recall to signals of events by which the magnitude of life's processes were shown to us, calling God the distance beyond our mundane presence come to us in life, meetings in the mountain scattered out by our response to it, did we rise, accept the image, drama driven down by our own push after reality, or meaning. . . .

But the jump is such an invisible moment: the physical body living in its pressure and formality, we do see, that, the same clothes on the shelf, the ordinary flux of groceries beyond the intense unfolding drama of psychological development, deeper layers of energy present themselves, push us forward on our own trails beyond the assumptions by which we are, ah, ruled, and there's the moment: control, over self, response to the inner laws by which we, surprised, come around, to moods we never imagined, ah, surprise and the total warp of the all too familiar, "I want to be transformed!" Jim wailed at the bar, pissed over his inability to find any cocaine that night. But the secrets in the woods are delivered privately. Tom never saw what happened behind the screen. He heard the yell only later, triumphant echoing beast noise yell as he went back down the trail. Still, he had met something from within himself at the base of the dead tree, and it was, was what he had studied, he was there at the mystery, and now they went up the trail.

"Let's have a smoke," he said.

Traveling by bus from the south coast, up to Istanbul, ceremonial cigarettes are cast around; sitting on the aisle seat, he mumbles something half-way intelligible, the voice below understanding, the man on the aisle says, uh, yeah, the pack open, out, a long white filter cigarette, they ride along the dry hills in the Mercedes bus, smoking silently. Other cigarettes are drawn on various occasions, passed around silent communion of men at work, squatting in sunlight, moment of shared air, the slight high more a moment of friendship than an occasion for comment.

At the bend in the trail, they turned off to the left, the stream had passed down about fifty feet below for a moment the trail rising up and around a large boulder covered with moss and dirt in the dry hill, shaped like a woman's ass, gentle curve of the earth's female flesh they settled down and he rolled a smoke, two cigarettes, and they sat there breaking twigs on the ground casting them on the ground a small compulsive gesturing of passing time in no-time where they had nothing to say, but still they sat together there in the woods, resting in the flesh of an immense lady, and the other said, "You know, there's bear up there," and pointed up at the high cliff where there were obviously some caves in among the higher reaches of the mountainside, "Why don't you take half of this tobacco, I got to get back to camp," to his woman and his two kids. Now Tom and Bill had both been in the sweathouse with him, they were all more or less brothers in this together, but the darkness was coming closer and he was more and more alone in the perpetual silence of thought the imagined distance between the high energy fantasy of his own passing thoughts and the rote-animal functioning of his empty body, the drug running free clear energy through the specific system of his own release of jumping the loop of his own intestines.

"You ought to take this knife, you know, you don't know what you'll run into in you're goin to stay out all night." It was quiet and they were sitting there smoking in the afternoon glare. It terrified him, the knife and the particular, intensified anxiety of the moment. It was the sacrificial knife, it was the final initiation, the gelding knife, what this knife represented. "No," he said, "I'll be all right." But the other insisted, twice more he insisted, and after awhile he stood up, stretched his long waisted short legged frame up full, "I gotta go," and tossed the knife in its handmade leather sheath down by the bag of tobacco, papers and wooden matches. "Really, man, take your knife, will you?" But the other stood there a moment and looked down at him , naked in late summer sun, "No, you might need it," and turned and left.

He sat there alone, frozen with tension, confrontation, despair, anger and the reality of the knife on the ground in front of him. The moment at the tree and the appearance of his other had both been shocks to him, but this represented a threat and a challenge, it was the absolute moment, high alone in the deep woods, sitting on the fleshy butt of his earthwoman, a more fitting site for a sacrifice couldn't have been found, for it was that which was represented in the gloom of coming evening, it was the final macho of his mystical quest, it was, he felt, a moment of decision, and before it he quailed helpless fear and the need to, to do something to break the spell he was in, the state he was under, there was something to do and he was afraid and he sat there, he picked up the knife and held it by the sheath.

"My brother made that knife," he had said before leaving, and the pressure of brotherhood in the ceremonial knife hung there like a space between worlds, "Ah, fuck," he moaned and slid the knife in and out of the sheath once, twice, three times. It was there for him to make the final gesture, and he imagined himself, holding his balls in one hand and slicing away hot life, from him the hot seed making him woman, easing the final agony finally sending the pain away in whiter hotter flashes of light, beyond the world of his own intense fantasy, he was meant to castrate himself, and he shook sweat-fear at this moment of, of passage.

"Oh, oh, oh!" he cried and yanked the knife out of its leather skin and raised it flashing high into the air plunging it deep into the earth the earth the earth of his self and lady, he sat there stupefied released transfixed, and collapsed over onto the ground crying rolling in the dirt sobbed at the release of his self from the dramatic moment of sacrifice sent him wailing over this, this nothing he had passed over all of it, left the world alone amused above the world flying, called to his self and other, he rose after a moment, thinking nothing, he went to the edge of the rocks, and looked out over the edge into the canyon he had just spent the day walking through moist rock, fern, edge and clamor of noisy passage left him standing naked at the edge of the rocks the moss buttocks still there the knife in the ground; he looked down the ten miles and more closer to fifteen from the house on the other side, he looked at the wheat light of evening stinging the eye, and called, bellowed, yelled, a prolonged triumphant powerful cry, at sharp full throated volume, the cry of the warrior-man who survived, he shouted one long profound male noise out into the length of the light, and stepped back into the woods, retrieved the knife and stuck it back into the sheath, the stations of attention, he said, and moved back up the trail, saying, oh my God, where does it end, this journey, this, nothing, and looked down at the knife in his hand, running up the trail he slung his arm wide, threw both knife and scabbard out into the woods and darkness, the knife falling into the ferns, loose, disappearing.

Nor was it finished, this quest of longing, lounging out along the trail, the dogs ranging on ahead along the trail, his son's white puppy, the black bitch mother, Gabriel the guide and the lame Duke. Later, he found that this brother had indeed cut his old lady that night, back in their camp, had indeed cut her with a knife. It was beyond him, completely, this drama of the force beyond which lay the entirety of the unimaginable distance.

And still they went on, up the trail, into the higher reaches of the mountain. "Where does it end," he thought, one last time, and the response came "When you stop." Which he did. He came to a place where five rivulets came out of the hills into a meeting place, a conjunction, and the open place they left was a natural camp. He stopped and gathered sticks for a fire, emptied out by the release of his inner being, completed, by the events of the day, entirely removed from the fire that had chased him all those fifteen years, made something by the events of the day, he sat by the fire all night and felt himself completed, felt himself fucked in some way, felt as if he had been fucked, felt, really, as if he had fucked himself that day, lay back, impregnated by the poem of the moment, and what he was left with was these pieces of his own life, they lay all around him, to be dealt with, surely, in some newer life, for there was a continuity and a re-birth to be experienced out of this magnanimous passage from the darkness of his years of wandering, into the light that was the world's beginnings, from what was simply there, the inheritance of the species, and now made somehow personal in the madness of his own actions, it was the moment left them stinging backwards off the wall and singing out, the day was there, after all, his clothes dry, his seed self centered made within him of his own acts, and crossed to life from somewhere he had been left alone too long resembling some older form of magic moving down the side of the high Montana mountainside, back into the day's light, tomorrow, made into man by self and act, love's flowering and initiation made firm and following out and down and back into the world, beginning. . . .

Book Three
THE SILVER SURFER

CHAPTER 10   I AM IN THE RADIO

What takes place in the depths of one's being, in the unconscious, can neither be called forth nor prevented by the conscious mind. It is true that if we cannot be influenced ourselves, we cannot influence the outside world.

Really.

It is well to remain below.

Wilhelm, today.

Low key sunny Sunday afternoon, he put his feet up and wrote for the first time in two months. Well, the excessive self-consciousness of the age makes seriousness, uh, less than the form of play it, really is. Psycho-types, in the chemical soup.

Lila brought it up, friend, first reader. "You've read Malte Laurentis Brigge?" in the MGB, Baggins bagging. Her voice a little querulous tone of voice.

"Uh, yeah, why? The anti-anti," he says. "A real romantic bummer...."

"I mean, in English?" A pause, the right tone of voice: "I've only read in German. You dash one of my dearest dreams." Long legs, nice legs, Lila. "Of translating it."

"Oh, really," he says, the guy on the Shell strip commercial.

"O rilly."

"I mean, yeah, but it was old C.F. Macyntire, or whoever, a passionate Brigge, wow think of that...." He thinks of Palo Alto walls, four months later, after the jump, hanging out in Palo Alto small rooms with Alex in the first grade, lame welfare number, horny phone calls to Jody, whew, "Unnhh...giggle...." and the eye-of-the-flower stone that came back in the mail. But the Briggean paint peeling from the cool gray city walls, terrified him. The energy rushing up and down, still wired four months later.

But last night, sleeping on the cushions at Georgia's house-cooling party, guitar music went on til two, at least, the body listened, attente, in repose.

And now as you read this, you are the reader, the first reader, you are you, to direct address the here and now of the I and the you. I write, I am the writer, I am I, it says. And he is he, he that lived, he that is also story, and then, story itself. I and he and you, mixed effect, to mixed effect. I am in the radio, listening saying this, I do remember.

Romanticism at the end of its pendulum-swing, uh, perhaps, forward, into the now, where it catches, moves forward, into the classical epoch of return, the rules emerge, just as the new man, this, uh, silver surfer of the eye, as, he had said in the letter, and before, seeing is also remembering, him from the fifties and outer, standing up all the way down, like Bob Young down there in Laguna, seeing the light underwater, George said, he had surfed the big one, and washed up on some old shore, "Like Thomas Wolfe," Scott said around the round table at the storefront paintjob the other day, "You know, that you can't go home again...."

"Yeah, I was thinking about Wolfe the other day," clean even flow of sentences. You can't? he had thought, then where am I?

Going across the storefront, half-way up the ladder, how sweat-sun day last week, the blue visor, blue shorts, tan, dip the long roller-handle down into the paint bucket, wipe it on the screen, pull the aluminum extension-handle up, sliding it through his hands, turn it around, run up three steps and Wonderwall! Splat it up onto the wall, roll up and down and across, pressing with his shoulders against and into the work itself, acrylic sheet drying immediately onto the old yellow stucco surface, then back down the ladder for another rollerfull, all afternoon, dragging drop-cloth religiously across the sidewalk, looking fearfully into the windows of the place on the other side, "vampires", red and yellow and blue naugahyde benches for the aphids to lie back into, the metal refrigerator already humming in the back room, really, it turned his blood cold, and he hurried on across, not looking through the windows after that, just, not thinking, yes, where am I, this strange shore, washed up, but, whew, at least on solid ground, sandy beaches, the sun.

Something to do, really, a good hobby, poetry, but why not get a job!

"You hippies are all alike," David had said, when he told him he wouldn't work up there anymore for six dollars and hour. But standing up, there, on the sidewalk in front of the storefront, the door open, job looking good, Scott listening from inside.

"Yeah, I got enough to cruise til mid-November so I can write...." "You hippies are all alike...." "Well, a book is worth more than a paint-job, anytime...."

"Just checking up on you," David said, and jumped a little when he had touched his elbow.

The light a bright and constant thing here, palpable, made thick in the humid air molecules, not the mad thing light of Montana's thin air; a softer intensity making objects have softer edges when you look at them...

Well, he thought, I think I'm in the present, you might respond to that. Somewhere near the middle of the page, or somewhere near the end, or just somewhere, you look up for a long time, and try to remember this sentence, at least, where it began.

Singing "I love you" to Yar, the night before we took him to the airport, up Romero Canyon with Emmett, in the moonlight, just after a long beach-run with the three boys. I don't want to send you back, away, there must be some way, all those feelings; nine year old red-haired all loving elf-son, the big airplane took him up to Spokane in two and a half hours with twenty dollars gas money to get him back to Missoula, fancy dancer son, coming down the sunny Oregon coast with him, high water bucking outer pushes light the high line of seeing, driving along with the boys, speed day out of Eugene, that's what's happening.

Why did they want us to be Genius anyway, what the fuck did they care. *what* we turned into, our teachers, old Mudhen, too, we cared what we became, honest citizens, hard working functional beings, and this cultural war of transition and authority, this, us, adverse Kundalini of feeling. Georgia's reciting Amor and Psyche to the boys on the way to Ojai.

I mean, at the front edge of this silly fifties re-run, why not take thought that the sexual psycho-types it brought about, and why the teachers, themselves, working on their own reactive selves, tried to "go right" and spawned the cultural snobbery of the, uh, style of the period, but with our feelings at hand, now, and seeing what we do about those absent fathers of world-war two, why not, then, didn't the grandfathers, patriarchs of the preceding, older, decaying, Romantic order, incursive and familiar, invest themselves more fully in the groundwork of the present, emerging Classical dimension, this, episode from the dark side of the moon, *"there's someone in my head and it's not me..."*

"There's no doubt about it, there's absolutely nothing on the dark side of the moon..." and fade. Listen.

Just stay at home and listen, free entertainment, I think I'll watch my own movie for awhile, and he goes back to the source, remembers, the cooler hours of personal history are still there, "erasing personal history" someone had said, last summer, of his adventure, visits and re-runs, on the way by....

They were lying on the gravel fine sandy beach her red polka dot two piece suit was ok, the boys were all around the bend in the river. half way out to Lolo by the weigh station turn off, sunny Sunday, they'd boogie in the water or something like that, they were just lying there.

"Let's walk upstream," eye to eye, foxy lady Michelle, Pisces-lady, they waded giggling rather, around a bend in the river, the boys sniffing them out, eight and ten, and curious. "Come on," he said, and she wanted it too, hot and saucy, they went.

He stopped and yelled at them.   "Go on, dammit, get out of here."

The boys laughed. Finally they stood back, only to advance as man and woman waded along underbrush overhanging river bush, her bush was on his mind, they pulled around and he went through the growth along the river to a little, like a goat trail, the sound of Highway 93 just up there, rum rumble of truck and even moose, perhaps, for all he cared, he sniffed her and found her wanting, wanting, that is.

She was an adventurous lady, Pisces, she had laid down naked for him once, opened her legs, crooked them back, full open head back and forth from side to side, out there in the woods, she stroked and stroked, he stood above and watched, playing his own tune, she went off, "Unnhh!!"

But today, they scrambled up the bank, to reach a no-pass, came back to sit down her back against a little ledge, facing him, he looked over her shoulder at the river below, and really, at a small parking area, about a quarter of a mile across the tracks, not too far, and he said, "Take off your pants," she was sweating, and did so, and he said "Turn around, baby," she put her head down on the pillow of grass her bright butt up before him, flags flying unfurled, he came up on his knees and entered the secret room full, "Oh!" and "All right, baby, come on," she started stroking herself with the left hand her mouth pushed open by their pressure, he held her flanks and drove their hot line a mile or so, wondering about the parking area across the way and he blanked his eyes to all but the push and drove the hard pole centered on her rushing called the line, "Come on!"

And when she did, cold sweat stiffened posture, her feet lifted off the ground, toes arched, even, speaking sweet perfume, "Oh, God!" and flowing sweet energy up his own and charging him strong, he pulled his long middle finger out of her butt and pulled out drove it slippery pole straight up the line, gave, charging, full into the back of her, shouting, "Ah!" she shrieked a yell once or twice straightened out her body flung forward, they both came, came to rest and stopped, sweat sure and tight, closed in, finished, but the souls mixing, stepped out....

So nonetheless, it went like this; how could you have a fifties re-run, even out of nostalgia (frozen moments) for Christ's sake, a style is also a behavior, that's basic, and if you play up-tight, intense sex out of, uh , wha, withholding, the style of the late fifties, then, really the activity of the latent few, us, the surfers, well if you reactivate that fancy of approach, the cult-style business of mass personality trips, perpetrated by, uh, really cult-stylists, them are the false teachers, "of which it is written," but here's another, Eagle song, and pretty stoney, too, saying that the voice of the seventies is the vision, the straight line forward carries poetry, here, the song anyway, center to target and the old ways are learned once again, remembered, called up beforehand, before, hand, the eye is quicker than that, you said you knew my name I waited at the crossing, liners cracking down, the day's light marked a magic, moving, mountain penetrating the town below, below your arms, at the blood center of the stroke itself, comes the denser airs repeating once or twice the same call "Come on, baby" and leaves the riskier song for other days.

Cool gray light this morning, you don't even remember your name. "Interest in one's work" is what the book calls for, and you move restlessly for a moment, pinned to a thought, and then relax into the radio, black scratch on yellow paper at "eighteen after", the radio says, and then the music comes into your head smoother lines the light a course throughout the shortness, even, of your attention, look! And feeling rushes quickly, the eyes give feeling on their own; and quite lucky, to pay attention to thought, a pleasant coursing of movement, seen along the day, every day, as what you are doing.

Erotic fantasies crowding in from six to ten, again.   White spots on her tan torso, wet white spots you seem to see her from above. Charges. Or living in the present, in the radio, really, that's what the radio says, sometimes, All Right, it is Now. And today becomes today, a hot shower and errands, the least of which, to try and nail down these rooms at least for two months, whew! the shore should break some light a little, here, around the body, arcing back and forth.

Or even quietude. We passed all the outside markers, moving into the closer distance, through the layers toward what was called, referred to, as the Great Light, and of which nothing was ever spoken, nothing had been spoken, not even in the one surviving ancient treatise. It only spoke of the sequences of approach, of the tactics themselves.

How can something beyond description achieve to words? There is one's witnessing, the moment itself, then, but always culled from one's impressions, one's recall, one's mute experiencing. We were there, getting charged at the source, the object, no, the subject of our twelve year's quest, we were simply there, and then we were not, and we were changed by the Great Light, not that it, uh, spoke, or anything, it was rather the unfolding, the calling up of information and images already in us, in our specific DNA. There was the quest itself, which was more like reading the codes and following instructions, a kind of obedience to the signs. But really, the burst of energy each felt was precisely because the realization of achievement had itself triggered the rush of energy each was feeling within his own being.

All ornament is discarded.

Another day went whistling. At Edge's studio. dimension was un-comfortably a part of the painting we were looking at. He talked about the end of sculpture and showed me the program from his show at the museum, history at thirty-six, and thoughtful stuff. Dropped off at eleven, stoned again, to whistle through the porch and fifteen windows. Tom in the afternoon light, hanging doors at the duplex. Dead tired on the bus home, half asleep the seven minutes from the terminal, no wind today. Dick came by abruptly, for twenty one dollars for this summer's phone calls to Montana. "Can I write a check?" "Is there any money in the bank" "Sure." "OK." "I gotta go." And gone. The radio counts the hours over Robin's birthday tomorrow, and we plan a three o'clock shopping trip after school' I'll have to make those windows look better, of course, I shouldn't have written a note like that about my rooms, but I was too uptight about the house. Simple grace, whew, the evening's words after completion, and the good Omar says, relax, listen, and that's tomorrow folks, old bills piling in the mailbox piling up on this new shore already singing a mad song.

One remains, unentangled, the smooth road flows onward, or outer. Elf sails smooth, he signs the moon,"done," and shows the lighter angles left aside, voices from the radio, then, he speaks aloud, more than silences calls them back and forth, the work is constant, a rocket shot, a smooth return, calling.

Or are you spoken out, man, are you easier now than after? Or before? The names they give each other have the line sharp against events, but unassailed he moves, "a wild and intractable people," your own rattling noises pass for music's even flow of temper, or meant among these others' rooms alert her sighs, a younger day at Fox-in-hand, the query floating through the air in longer gasps, and no invention fills the heart but the real adventure.

So I'll go exploring, and follow the invisible traces out along the bus route, or angled down against your hair, I'd leave them room to stir around inside the hot wire, and the hesitant suggestion of mental images reveals the hot line of sense, morning's flesh is laid open at hand you make the air around your body tremble slighter marks throughout, or, seasons in the air and sentence.

At home, in the empty city, I come home to this, at three PM, George on my bed, reading *The Return* sections, looking for solace. All morning with Francie up in Monkeycity, matriarch, had her will out at the party last weekend; painting doors and doorframes, spotting tiny holes and chips with the white paint, peering still over the tops of my bifocals, the inertia of recall blows and falls, thrusts of recall blow and fall, thrust forward, rush, surfer sing the tide and fallow, the sign-rush is fervor, and clean through the heart he thinks all day the tactics of getting a foxy model, almost an intrigue, an erotic smuggling seance, calling, looking for what is wanted by way of the calm energy, "Uhnnhh!", "Yeah, baby," and song these angles forward.

And in the radio, memories hum, "He's fun," George comes up out of Andy Warhol's A to Z, a pilot program, really, encoded, jazz, or something, uh, accurate.

Keester weather-report recall, sharp intense voyage, Bill's car this summer through southern California Oak groves, clear dive along the coastal spine, you smoothed the foreign capitals where the rumor went, and rare error, he copied.

I got what is there to be remembered, but the pen falls out, or speaks, the dream image an erotic sentence claiming the edge of light a further action, the round airs wedged tight against her thighs, and driving in at dawn the total hookup, two batteries driving the long line outer, or forward clings the song, recall, flower.

The picture on the wall, of the desk itself at an earlier state, in Ah-lee, the picture of the desk and window, the window on the world, a dirty window, blue of doug-fir slightly out of focus at the eye's edge, it was, really, another photograph of both desks, a triple, really.

Hum of two stroke motorcycle, chain-saw-like, and the belch of chorizo and eggs over the beer, ready for another Sherman, the mailbox empty, the publisher "not yet back", from wha, they say. . . . And you know the rest already, tall wave, tubular swells and hot lips, Caiao, baby, the town's in an uproar of titillation, a slow perfume that moves without exaggeration, into the closer episodes of doubt and feeling, "a move from depression to obscurity," as George said.

The calm air returns, lower than the rest. What passes for morning is more silence than quiet. All night he tosses out this, not so much rest as not moving, but she scarcely yields, holds the hours at bay, there is no motion.

But today is longer than silence, it will erupt into event, no doubt. Perhaps I'll get evicted for arrogance; perhaps the model will show up, late, and yet, pull the piece together. No, the gray air and the warning in the book about gratification and desire, "mad pursuit," all add up to an uneasy morning, despite the assurances of the second dive.

Anyway, there is work today, and after that? One would like a love letter in the mail. And what's for dinner, anyway, not so much gloom as the persistent hesitation of the light. And the nature of the game, or, holding firm, a course is set and a good story is freely offered. Slow signs mark the distance full of details and closing in on the main pattern of resistance, you might be understood, is there a spiritual life to the country after all, or this, this zone of foreign invaders and youthful seekers; the indigenous values are, too beaten, back, obscured. Outside, a crow calls, yak, yak, yak.

Somewhere around the dance with the dildo, camera clicking, the fantasy fever blister broke open into a wordless state with no fantasy at all, it was a momentary brief flipping of consciousness, songs of longing and macho loss, uh, emanating from the radio, Rolling Stones into "Wet Dreams", whew.

Present in the present, brief openings in the wall, the daily ruptures encountered in the scanning shift and constancy of attention itself, the eye ever-looking inward scene, drawn like this, through the eye to the other, and into the ocean; eye to eye she came, we were on the riverbank, I got off into her mouth from a hard driving standing knees bent rush, "Oh!" into her, then sitting her down crosslegged in front of me, I handled her off, made her open her eyes when she came, took her eye-charge full into my own; and Michelle at the kitchen table, jerking off, "Come on, baby, you look so good. . . ." White jolt, "Ah!" her feet up heels down on the chrome tube kitchen chair masonite table, married students housing.

Late, after the music is almost over; the Fourth of July, '76, definitely a seed-day, I took some peyote and Jody came over, I suppose we drank some Miller's, she was sitting in the bedroom chair, in the corner, by the white curtain, the window open, summer breezes I can recall the game, a hard on for life, I stood in front of her a long time, stroking out, her eye was on the sparrow all the time her mouth open, or slack, or looking up at me, hot smile I love you, and back I shot plunged into her famous mouth and stroked her throaty song-voice and felt her swallow down my fourth of July fireworks that bicentennial year the other day, really, what a day. . . .

The long walk home from a Metaxa at 1129, to beat the bus, crackling of wild California electric-city bends my Chagall shadow distorted against the rock walls in front of the houses, white-blue neon mercury vapor glare the shadow falling flying along the sidewalk, the new moon over his shoulder silent cheap shoes walk across town, cars and headlights sneak by; the whole town under cover at nine o'clock on a Friday evening.

But, ah, the wizard; and Lewis, even, on consciousness in *Surprised by Joy*, states of, levels of, uh, persuasion, but nowhere the Rotic, except maybe in Reik (burned at the stake) does the "problem" of pleasure eg., as not, simply, other than pain, no the thoroughly Rotic view, of a tantra ecstasy view of energy maintenance and the good body view of, more boogie not less, is the, then, as the rule, calls the program a love-magic, power thrust, the mate-match, a la, precocious response is the lesson in-the-matter, uh, at hand, in hand or however you do it, calls these idle shots less than interesting let alone occupying, heaven forbid, you might yield an inch and lose ground, good heavens, not to lose ground in very important, that the thought itself could release such potential in-line, spoken, the clear rush across, eye to eye, "Take off your pants," and she did, and I liked that, I did, I liked that a lot; and his bum mood, as musico-logical as it is, as a good shot, there's no argument, one is, the light bending her hours around the long waves of white light, not "bathed in white heat, "the calm intensity says "shore, your heart resolves, even, the air," and breaks out.

"The possibility of exerting a lasting influence arises of itself, and no one can interfere. . . . " Wilhelm, tonight, and lets go, completely, the free fall of the music on the radio, the even prospect of painting trim for an hour or so, tomorrow, it all accumulates toward this, uh, something that is happening, coming into focus, like the main event in *The Man Without Qualities*, which is, somehow, lost in the trial of the lunatic, the whole is such an eternal, just-around-the-corner vision of vision of the new life; no, rather to have it be the here and now dynamic of this Rotism of the hot la-la, oh, baby, come on, the far dance says, you are, tonight, this motive in the flame and triangle, the hot spur of light within the sphere of action, but say something, will ya? And let it, just, go on, into the time and the time again this voice came out like this, presence-song, direct address.

I mean, it was after he came down from the mountain, feral-man, howling in his empty valleys for this girl who'd just, flown away. Then he gathered it all up in his old van and went back, drove to New York with Alex and no driver's license, even, made a grab for the girl.

Driving out, the mountain was in the way, in deeper sadness, he left them like a wanderer on quest, he took off with all the kids, got to the last steep hill between east and west, and the old overloaded blue van wouldn't do it, so they went back to Mazola and got someone to mess around with the car again; they met strange tight lines, Scott and Jody in her kitchen, "I already said goodbye, I can't take this," or was it the old melodrama of departure which had to go down, just, too many times, her intense gazing eyes burning, why not, but the game continues into, now. But he came down from the mountain and got stopped by another, and with only one kid, Alex sat there in the other seat those three months, really, took care of him by reminding him about food and laundry, gave enough order to the mask, they could pass through the net, sneak back there on a raid, and all across the Dakota plains even into Iowa wheat flats, fantasies rushed and clamored through his head, he'd be crying about appearing at the crisis-center of an imagined-real panic, television cameras buzzing; gnawing on the hit of speed Bonnie had slipped him before he left.

There is a moment in the Dharma Bums, a retrospect at the end of a long recall, like, it was then and there I could have had her, which is touching, even tearful over love lost, one says, yes, and eventually you bring up some of those moments, when you turned her down for those reasons you now understand, but the career of a whole life is not quite that simple, and while the false kundalini may have had its effect, nonetheless he called from the shopping center, scared, "I am in your town," and went up to the house, saw the yellow, uh, something zip the other way, the mother escaping the initial. Grabbed red-thick hair, ensuing events were: she shows him a place where he would be able to sort of, hide, or stay, they drive around that night in an old Mustang, go for a swim down in the moony lake near the small town, Carmel, and watched her face, nude body in knife air, they are driving up a short rise, a huge station wagon going the other way, "I've got to get out," Laura says, and he gets out first to let her out, off-hand glare of two sets of headlights smooth across the evening's air. He'd even cut the blue beads from her neck and given her some barley.

But in the glare of the headlights he makes out through the reflection of the car window, a face pinched with attention and wonder, alert; he must have heard he was, uh, around, but as he gets out of the car he knows his brother doesn't recognize him.

But they somehow get him and Alex to sleep at his brother's house that night; he is up and out early the next morning, driving the little car fast in thought, out for his I Ching and coffee and back to the girl's house, he sneaks down the hall at eight in the morning opens her door and strokes her hair and leaves.

It is mostly the atmosphere of energy and intense and poem and reality all confused longing for love and being, really, "out there" " heightens the drama, but he pulls back crucially, and asks her, no, to come with him, but she's too young and he's too poor, he never has a dime. All that day his brother drives him around and even points out a house he might buy and fix up, but this Eagle doesn't understand, and even yells at his brother that after-noon, "I can smell the fear coming out of you," Laura sitting over there, listening.

But then, caution and the heart, really, at head and hand, butted tight, there are some long conversations with Alleye and her two friends on top of the water tower, he really is, just, there with nothing to offer, too blind to see the offers made to him, and he forces his own flight pattern, pries himself, after a late night party, gets her in the van, the Spider Woman comes out, like, "Get out of here or I'll call the police," and he yells into the night, "Fuck you, lady," and leaves, calls over Alleye's calm voice, "Now don't do that, Tom, don't leave, you don't have to," and he drives away down the road to New York City, heartsore, the horrible intensity of the world's very, presence, coming down like a gigantic wine press, free fall into, wha, the hard cold it.

Walking about fifty yards from his brother's house, down to the uncle's car, she had put her hand into his elbow and they walked like mates down to the car, that was the moment, her barefoot new-dress, both of them fresh to each other, fresh from the time before the great fear, there was that, and crossed over, crossed out, the winnowing fen finally invented, the open skies darker sighs were coming later, the hard road's peril and clamor. Driving.

No, it doesn't, just, come down to that, or this, or any other, but there are moments and there are also crossings, there are all sorts of moments in a man's life (like, you say) , the movie moving on; and you could even get into "What if she still..." and other insidious games with feelings, with recall, sentiment and nostalgia all of which add up, to adding up, though love is hardly cumulative, or even information, it is more like a clean song in the air between them perfect eyes across that space they're in, hooked up.

It goes on. From Harry's house on Long Island, the weeks with Vincent in Gloucester, the old Hermetic priest; the aside at Newburyport and Plum Island, falling in on Jody in Chilicothe Ohio those three months, working in the nursery, wrapping trees like corpses, Christmas in California, Jody crying for her family. The blank winter in Palo Alto, writing, doing "the white room."

The whole adding up might be also another story, yielded from the deeper layers, stratum, of consciousness, remembering the whole drift of it, back and forth, back into it, swoosh, the clean lines pursue the man along the way, un-entangled, it says, but how long, he asks, how long?

At pass, at midnight lines, I send her home, before speaking too early to say anything more than mutter over ribs, records, wary that was what she said, yeah, wary; we don't exactly, uh, resonate was the other, I like that, I said, I'll take it. The hot juice not altogether there, what can I say, too early to stay up and nothing to do but rite, seek the level of utterance apropos to what you're doing.

"No, I don't know exactly what to do with it, now," he's said to Lila on the grass at a borrowed Miramar piece of frontage. "I'm just marking time on it," he said. "Aren't we all," she growled quickly, long legs dansk skin white cotton things around her legs, "Aren't they men?" the two slightly man-women, "Mennen, what would you call them," she cried. "I call them seedless grapes," he dropped in quickly; and later on, the thick hazy light, off the water, they talked about the light, there, as thick as Conrad, almost; more than one, lately, had brought up Huxley's novels," and how boring they are," all right, but even the tired dazzle of *Chrome Yellow* was an ease off Lawrence, and even as the old literacy surges back, or backward, we wait to see if, or whether. anyone has learned anything, in all these years.

Even the beginning recedes into you. Calling even shots, the energy proceeds along yr hands, even, touching without feeling, putting this together, listening to the radio today, the sentient qualities of the music, uh, structural simplicities, like "The Serial," give the impressions of continuity; she left a little while, I did the dishes swept the floor vacuumed my little room and sat down to this. You are the same voice listening to yourself read the words aloud inside your head in this moment you have stolen from nowhere, in this posture of attention the subtle buttons pushing in and out of the console, your heart palpitating for love, and the nearer distance, more of a maneuver than an ecstasy. Even the dreams were disquieting, no, you wouldn't buy him the levi jacket, even though it looked good, maybe tomorrow you will do it, and move the centers of choice, or decision, closer to the inner layers of response, "We both of us must hurt in the same way," she said over breakfast this morning before she and the boys went for the day, I answered softly, or as much as possible, replied.

"Not that it's between us, but that we have some of the same wounds."

"Yeah, ok," she looked up at him.

So after the dishes, a rather tenuous quality existed in the room, it was more than expectation and much less than courage, perhaps this was the day to burst through. He moved the mirror to the other side of the room, across from the bed, first shot in the morning, there! You!! Hello!!! And now sitting in the chair at the end of the room, if he looked down the length of it, there was the blank white wall and the rattle of bells he had made for daughter Mischa.

Outside noise, power mower, stops, and a whistle fitful, mower starts, radio is going, over a cup of tea. Boring, really, that's it, then, the problem, "Oh, God, I'm bored," and roll another joint; no, rather to space out on motive, or, mood, or thought, or then, go for a walk; no, bored, not, never; better to, just, look around, the safety of the geek in his cocoon of imagining, his hair flown less sacred ways, she gave me her toenail last night and I thanked her for it, it was power, even though she said she didn't know it, and I told her so, nonetheless it sits on the corner of the wooden box, over there, in front of the typewriter. And Georgia's lecture on Picasso's faces, moments in time, then, remembering the beloved, we agree, and remembering itself, then, coming at the this of it, that the photos have some distinction as time itself, uh, there: she turns and gives the eye back, back to him who sees what's going by, selective instant, "Ah!" and gets it; rather, the landscape, moslem arab of "no eyes" just, the pictures of the structures of things, and, light, transformation of the eye's beholder, it goes, like that, for a long time.

Up it goes, the invention of white light, seen, the blank screen of mortality, or, a heaviness from the more bankrupt of the emotions; like, freeing oneself from the confining attitudes of, uh, education, it's called, primal instructions which are meant only to last one into his adulthood, at which time they fall away like the husks of atrophied old cultural attitudes, and he stands more or less alone, alike no longer, this creature at the threshold of the crossing, the Silver Surfer gleams triumphant crossing in the light's radiance and glamour, a simple thrust of calm attention through the air returning light's love's airs return recall the moments of the passage and the hours of the return, the last letters written, whew, stamped and mailed.

And so the meditation on the present continues; structured as it were by doubt itself; but the present crowded in upon by fantasy and information, one almost doesn't turn and see the wind blowing across the patio, ruffling the bare tree in the pot the ferns in the barrel; I must water, black scratch on yellow paper, excruciating presence of no-recall, and, hurry, fill that space, quickly now the hours rotating off the blank Palo Alto walls he just sat there by the radio for a month or two or three, and, then, a year later, did it again, just sat there for three months. And the words, just clustering out, formulating strange intense space, notebooks in Wally's warehouse last seen, wrapped up in plastic dropcloths, his down jacket and mickey mouse boots, left just inside the doorway, he remembered standing on the other side of Wally's pickup, Miller's in hand, the old hot dodge they'd poked full bore the road around Pattee Canyon dirt road comes out in East Mazola, poked that pickup down the road, him and Tom, beer in hand, talking dirty to a couple of fifteens, "You want to get in the truck and me get in the car and we'll boogie," they looked at each other and, sort of, giggled, "Got another match," smoking hash up Crazy Canyon.

But even now, seven months later, he saw the garage door still sliding down and his insulated rubber boots, "I wonder if they ever got up the stairs," with the rest of his stash, the cubic yard of poems, papers, pictures, slides, his ten year stash, maybe safe, maybe not. It woke him up once or twice, "I should micro-film it or xerox it," and go back to dreamfilled sleep, the figures floating knife-edged through the air, recall and flavor, moving. . . .

Still, the sun shines outside, now, the gray haze given to blue with patches of white, the soft light of electric California wavers into my window and over my shoulder, crank, the washing machine goes on, and the ordinary presence subsides with its welcome relief, one wonders about all that, stuff, coming back into it, it's those really simple formulas turn out the truest, cliches of work and growing up, and even the plan of what would you do if, no, there is always that positive energy sufficing in the invisible realm for progress or battle, nonetheless he sets his goals and sets out to, to achieve, and does, then, get there in the miracle of his own presence, forgetting, even while writing, the hand moving across the page, the writing machine at work, the sunny afternoon, like this.

Sharp shadows fall, you let go, and the even smooth rush and pull of your own awareness is sufficient, you are aloft again, after the years of dream practice, you push off and spar free, your temples pulse and relax, and a spot on your head eases into "open;" rather it is the two horn spots, and your own antennae come into focus, laser shots infinitely deep the lines wave independently, feeling and sensing the dimense universe, its *epace*, and the fibers of sensation ring true and deep, they cleft forward or after, they cleave in and hold.

Still, the cigarette lighter holds, and gives remembrance of the long line backwards toward the first It is the root and the chain, and they come forward, the concept of her breasts, no, rather, it is her breasts themselves, her hand along and under than, stroking the nipple until it's up and hard, "You like that?" "You know I do," he says, smiling. But that's lightweight, really, and she holds tight, in formation her arms crossed her head to the left on her stomach, her legs apart, he vaselines his middle finger, opens her cheeks and enters, "Ah!" she jumps a little, and he pushes into her, slides into it, goes into her tight, "Ah, ah!" she makes noises, coming, through the tight, alive.

Still, he holds to what is firm, and the way opens, clear line throughout the open signs rotating, last week's beans on the stove, they might be very good, ham juice and port, they might be overdone, too. The laundry calls its signal, the day is all there is, nothing else is happening but the calm expanse of today the slow unwinding of page after page, going hunting out at the University Monday, you never know, but this calm repetition of hours implies success, or a message, at any rate, one would find out something of where he's at, I mean just because she wanted to stay didn't mean that I wanted her to, and that was awkward enough without the etude on role reversal, the Briggs amendment and the whole macho resurgence, not that far from how I feel, a reformed hippie, Cettie had said, "Like a Synanon enthusiast," he said, yeah, really, but there is the boogie in the sunlight to consider. Even The Doors is OK.

The day finishes out, there are plans, and the work goes on. Is there ever nothing to do? The human animal gropes compulsively for a stone on the ground, he polishes it against his thigh, or she. No, there is never nothing to do. With any luck I'll run into all of them sooner or later. The alcoholic in his hotel room, constantly giving him dollar tips for those ice-buckets. Eventually he got all his suits cleaned and checked out, gave him a five dollar tip, he had always worked, that was the way with money, "Money belongs to money," and even black scratch on yellow paper is an effort of concentration which is, uh, directed, and today's "presence," is enough to make you look twice or not at all, there is that intention to the view at hand, or handier than that, he says, the Chief just forgot to invent both sides of the dialogue, "Couldn't," you say, and there you have it, proof enough that seeing is also remembering, and clear enough. "I wrote this piece" the scratchy old throat-whisper garbles out, relic of conversation, the diminished present relaxation of nerves the black line smoothing out across the page, you are writing this, you are making these marks across the page moment after moment, the blue sky wrapped around you like something new, perhaps, the slow-low layers of metabolism are taking over, the regular systolic rhythm of breath undisturbed by the flow of the line across the page, it is this phenomenon of the present, yes, really, perhaps she is waiting outside and all I need do, really, is go outside, his heart beating. "I'm not used to coming forward," she said.

Finishes out like that. The model bending over, or something like that, is going around, they say true things sometimes, something is always going around. The most destructive thing they taught out there, Georgia brought it up. "I fought my way out of there," he said, recall of rage, the free flight into San Francisco in 1960, whew; they had it, have it still, that the posture or the stance of the artiste is not to interact with the audience, and that's why it's seedless grapes to me anyway, nothing out there has much erotic value, except certain monuments from Penthouse or Hustler, that everything is so infected with the false kundalini that the eye-pleasure has left the medium itself.

But the day still promises to be perfect; old Chaplin re-runs and fried chicken with Georgia and Emmett. Alex blooming out there, managing to get home Saturday wet to his waist from exploring the slough out by the airport.

But that the artist should not have some, uh, intercourse with them is to make them hot and hungry. "I'm not going through that ever again," Travolta said, mobbed in London after the Grease premier; watch out, there, they're nasty. . . .

But coming down the line, nothing could be easier than that, the thought rang true, like the vision in the mountains, this new light-like life was strange indeed, the geek's cosmic-trance-dance, a cool craze reeking of the other-in-the-one, if he had his categories well enough in order, seeing the illumination of the old heretical and sufistic visual diagramming of the hermetic states of relation, it was called, the one, the same and the other, in their forces of opposition, always turning, from one pronoun to the other, the points on the compass-line of projection the very ellipsoid of being, there in space, the one and the two and the three of it, look out, here come new cities, relocation of random herds of humanoids into various survival pockets, the uniformity of the fantasy goes outer, just goes, marks recoil, the center dream: upstaged lions calling back and forth, cranking, as it were, loosing the myth of the froth, actually, seeing or sensing the froth itself, leading the quiet hours backward further off itself, she leans backward beyond the air, falls, recoils, draws the dreamer straight into bankruptcy, and we laughed about it, and still, going off into Night Moves, the silence of the air following down these mazes in the air.

All beings stand in opposition: what they do takes on order, thereby.

Turns out, like the rest, a day on edge, like the guy down the street, I know when to stop, or do I, the acute awareness, like watching for the moment of the mutation, where the voice itself slips into true speech, the gradual transition from here to there so evanescent invisible gradations of slippage the voice suddenly resonates, so too with the excursion into a drama, or a book, or solace too for love lost, denuded, stranded on the far shore, heroines of madness, starvation in the psychic life of the ant colony, this, uh, collective unconscious exhausted, ah, the spark, the moment of the jump, the leap, the gap over which, without breaking step, simply going across over into, into, new ground, the voice across the light, and even into the change of the center of the Great Light about which nothing is written, she comes across, then, and gives, species of the river crossing, up the primal stairway into the light, she comes up from behind and opens the box, leaps out, leaves, asleep the rush and center of the dream he comes, at last, to free her, picks her up, finally, goes home with her at the end of the show, his hand on her butt, really, inside her pants, she turns and bites his ear.

And so Indian Hand dealt the next hand, they swelled the largest mountain larger than the next world. Indian Hand leaned across the table, "How do you like that one, white-man?" and the other continued to be pulled into the light and dark of Indian Hand's true story.

"It was after that they came together as tight as they are now, they weren't always that tight, you know," and rattles off the next three hours, marking time over the last few pages of the yellow tablet, thinking about the model herself, and he even talked to Georgia about it, she was very nice, "That's kind of being objective about it," asking for surprise in the play of the elements, no, really, as friends and lovers we cross the same ditches, and the young lady is more than fresh meat, as old Jane put it, rather coldly, just as I was saying goodbye to Montana, miserable at heart, up in the mountains by the fuzzy creek, marshy upland, Bob's boots and botany. No, there is more to it than what I hustled Jane in the reeds for, I was stoned and following it, something hot and lost, we waggled up the road, talking like strangers, I sat all night, I should have visited McGeorge up the road for that monopoly game and some Santa Barbara gossip, not that I need any now, but his time would have been warmer; he said, "You'll be back. . . ."

He left the house about eight thirty, win or lose, it's all the same day, he said, a small list in his mind, of calls to make, the on-going quest for a lady, a paint brush in his back pocket, ready to make a quick job better; anyway, he hit Milpas with no bus in sight. Down the block the 17 from Monkeycito came around the corner. He ran half a block and then slowed down; the bus turned the corner and left. He waited about ten minutes, the fat black lady and the fox with no tits looking elsewhere, the time went.

Off the bus, at the bank, he slips across the street and walks up to the window. A sixty year old man in a white suit is there in front of him with strange glasses that flip up; he has two expense vouchers. After a minute or two, he slides up, "Fifteen dollars back?" The old guy inside there behind the thick glass asks him over the tiny speaker, "Yeah," he says, and gone, back down the street toward the bus station, no, he cuts up the street and goes by a coffee house, closed, and walks on in the quiet early morning light, across town toward the small house he painted the windows on last week.

He comes around the corner, the fascia looks all right. Even in the bright morning sun, there are only a few shadows, one fat brush mark at the right end. And already paid for it. He turns and leaves, sticking the brush into his back pocket.

Back down the blankfaced street, where nothing is happening, back down the slow blocks foot by foot, "How long?" And goes all the way down to the terminal, still a little stoned from last night, waiting four hours for those last two pages, ah, then, event.

On the minibus to the University, the little japanese girl with braces and the black driver chatter away like lovers, they are obviously into it, and the energy they give off makes the road go by, dream song of rolling hum, her face somewhere on the horizontal distance.

He is sitting down by the U. Center, coffee, ten o'clock, Bob comes out, "Hey, Bob," "All right," "What are you doing," "Looking for a model," they appoint the lunch hour, and he sets off for Mudhen's office, but it is too early, only ten thirty, and so he waits outside, and watches a young fox dance away from a bee, there's Sharon, coffee in hand, she makes a turn and a slow smile and stops, throaty hello, and takes a pill jar and pops a cap, green and white, "It's for zits," she says, "I started getting them about when you showed up last summer," and laughs.

"I'm sorry, I don't think I caused them."

"No, but you know, I've been thinking about a new role for myself, the woman behind the man." But that's what I thought he wanted. "Well, it is, but I'm getting used to it." But I can still talk to you, "Oh, yes, I just have to be careful, I hurt him so the last time." Well, I won't come over unless I'm invited. "You know, he can hardly stand to be in the same room with you." They sit there over her coffee, "I've got to find a model," he says, "He'd never understand."

"I know," she says, looking at the coffee.

"And you don't have any friends, you're solitary."

"I know, I was thinking about that the other day. And he wants me to quit smoking. I could quit drinking and dope and maybe I could even give up sex," Wha, he thinks, "But not smoking," she goes on, "I went out and got some Shermans and smoked three of them, quick."

But it's time to go, and she does, and he looks around for the girl with the bee, but she's gone too; he goes down the hall to Mudhen's office.

In the door a turn, he's on the phone, melonlike Jewish face, the same glasses, brown on brown, at the phone, looking up, not remembering, "Tom;" he says, "Oh, yes! sit down, I'll be a minute here," which he is. The same books on the desk, Lawrence mostly, even the big Collected Poems. Graying in their cases. Flash of seminar eyes, what do I want here, he thinks.

"What are you doing here, how long have you..." I'm finishing a novel, six months, paint houses, he says, brandishing his brush, got any painting? "No, but, have you seen anyone else?" Old ladies, he names a few, but nice ones' I'm looking for a model. "What for," to use like a painter, for word pictures.

And they chatter, about his breakdown, his life. A young teacher comes in to ask about the past tense of the word "Fit", as, does it, and they eye each other over false conversation. A blond boy comes in, art-like, "Ken, this is, shall I tell him, Tom Eagle, E*A*G*L*E," he spells it outs slowly, "and why is that," the boy asks, the same critical derisive stance as his old teacher. I had some experiences with the indians in Montana, he says, and they get around for the second time to the subject of the model. "What do you want with a model besides the obvious..."

To cue up certain recalls, I'm developing an idea of remembering; and to have the erotic energy state ready to achieve them. Cue up certain locations and use the energy, a three way dive in. "Are you going to tell her all this?" Of course.

And he looks at them, what are you pumping me for, and Marvin, He is disturbed by the new name. That way, he says, if I have any success, I can be myself and still be invisible. "Oh you needn't worry about that," the old teacher says snappishly, "I mean, those People don't get bothered all that much," quickly, "But why did you come today?" Well, I'm going to do a portrait of this.

Even when the subject of the money comes up, the boy says, "I'd love to spend a lot of money quickly," and he says, no, I'd be up in Montana building houses, there is this. uh, you know, vision of the artiste and the marketplace as mutually separable. But business is business, really, it doesn't take much of a stake to start a construction business, but he is talking to no-one. Still the boy wants to go on a trip. Future novelist, he bristles.

Well, I've got to meet someone for lunch, and he's gone, over to Creative Studies' wooden building, down the back hall into Bob's office and there's Chaz, gray-bald Armenian face, Saroyan gentle laugh, small hands, painter of visual-conceptual experiences, both, and they head for a trough for lunch; "How's Dick and Bette," he asks in line; still trying, or now trying to fix up their marriage. "Seeing a counselor?" he asks, Yeh, "Oh, well, that'll finish it off, they tell you be happy." One liners, down the chrome plated tubes, a huge sandwich and too much salad, a familiar old-school face slides by, a poet; he goes to eat with the photographer and the painter, You know, he says, I always learned more from painters than other writers, they're more into the abstract, and the writers still haven't let go of the image, they're fifty years or so behind the times. "You know," Chaz says, "I told Dick he should go to New York, he has that kind of energy, you know, he's that, uh, wired, and the more I said that the more Bette got pissed, like, well, why can't we make it out here on the rocks, really, I'll have to stop by and see Dick on my way home," he says.

And poetry and dance, Chaz says, if you're into that, it's a tough row to hoe; oh yeah; and they go back from lunch, like three old lifers. "The mess hall". "I'll be glad when I can quit teaching."

He goes through Bill's studio, "A model situation," he calls it, laughing. Farmed out in a back studio, a second year class, the playboy art prof mystic, a little chubby. And he decides to split, her face hovering a yard away.

Across the bike lanes, a little, uh, deja vu on the whole thing passing the bus-stop to go over toward the bee-girl, and pauses, looks over at the bus-stop, really, I'll miss it, and goes toward it, just as two minibuses pull in, and as he walks up, finds the drivers all after a smoke. They stand around the kiosks awhile, and finally they move to leave. He goes to the big one up front, snubs his smoke out, gets a transfer and goes back to the rear, past two pretty but blank faces, and one by the back door, a big one, glasses, hair over the, he goes by, nice hair, all the way brown over the back of the bus-seat cascading down, along the, nice, he says, and sees her move, her face at the edge, the bus starts off, and he sits there, looking at the brown hair, thinking, really, I like the glasses, I'd take them off and kiss your eyes. As, after awhile, she actually turns around and says, "Uh, are you a grad student or something..." and he moves across the two seats quickly. "No, not really, I'm a writer I was out looking for, uh, a model, today," the eyes look back clean straight line of teeth straight line upper there is more beauty beneath this, uh, stereo of the feelings going by fast, the movement of the bus is a long way away.

As they are chattering, "Just moved from San Luis," she says, "Fran, and you're," Tom he says, "When you're famous," Eagle he says, there is a heart beat going on here, "What sort of model," he says, the artist and the model, you know, having that happen and writing about it, sure it's erotic. And smiles. They do. Are you interested?

Do you ever go out with strangers? "I have to get psyched into it," she says, turn of long neck, "Where do you live," on Soledad, he says, a place with me and my eleven year old son, what do you do when you're not doing anything? "Nothin." Me I sit and I smoke and I write and I listen to the radio. I mean, you look nice. "You're blowing me away, "Not really, he says, thinking not yet. "Oh, I've missed my stop, she gets up and pulls the buzzer, 5.2.1. he says to her ear as she is rising, "I'll remember that," he grabs her hair as she swings down the step, out of the bus big smile, crook-finger wave, he does the same, sits back, Ah! really I'll touch that gold again, he says, and the bus rolls into town, he sits there thinking already of the size of the kiss, the face of this France, Francesca, this lady of a mode, flooding his afterworld with light.

There the sign of the hours opened, and wet, he spoke with the sign and made a return the order of the day, a flesh sign that reason's energies accepted, it was a notice to movement, how the juices run, and crossed at eyes, even, he fell into Chase for two Dos Equis, is good enough; and listened to a long rap on paranoia from a guy who then split, two beers and a picture of a face floating in the air about two inches away, a name even, and, just, rode the bus around for forty minutes at least, just rode around and thought about the things that happen at the end of the day, when you, just, get on the bus to go home, and bang! there she is, turning around to say hello, and a keeper by the looks of it, and rides up the hill, a six pack of Lowenbrau and two pork steaks, waters the lawn, comes in to have a beer and write about it, his heart in those waves of brown hair, the fantasy of the model opens up again, and turns, even, into man and woman, and then back again, he has control, he loses control, and the idea, no, not the idea, really, the information recalls to voice, speaks, that is," when you're ready, you reach out and pluck the best of what you see, when what you see is really there."

Really, it is the quick hours receding, healing her underhand, the lady in your arms is giving, and going good, and that's how it is, she's nice and clean. . . .

You marked her sighs clear and moving through the left, the left hand wins these strokes along the cleft and clamor nails the day again, you are, at edge, at hour and smoothing out, the line is eye and set, or settled, taking a chance, that is. That a clean lady holds my hours close enough, after all that, you need the time along a cleft and thigh, not the "quick hours receding" actually, but the finger inside you feeling around your own, "Oh!" and "Ah!" has the less remarkable sensations made only by man and woman, well, not quite that simple, but the hours tell the day ahead, arrive let's see if she comes around, the pretty one, and call the others losers in the match for light it is the call and the called, they match mare mute vibrations the seed and the sigh, her quick hours rotating, "Give, baby," come on, the open door is quite specific makes the moment itself motive....

Chapter 11   ITSELF TO ITSELF

It is the tree on the mountains stands mute, rather, or stands, not so much alone as stands, rooted; so it is the emphasis of the image sustained in presence calls them forth, mute remembering draws the arm across the bow, the name across the air. The same preoccupation marks the time urgent or spoken, it is the same with the people, they tell you everything all at once, a rush of words comes suddenly spoken triangles of light, she leans forward across the table, her eyes open a little, eyebrows pushed up, as, sitting on your side of the room, "Fifteen years, I never made a nickel on writing." She calls him a holdout.

Yes, the times are turning on it, you've heard that one before, and the problems seen not so much new or revised, as, uh, constant. Lines fill out. And it is Valery, contemplating an act of genius "after which everything will be different." Or the letters to, to home or distance, back to the village in the mountains, his home, perhaps, if it is only the wanderer's luxury to have such fantasies, or the world made permanent enough to call motion the space of the age, commentary on the image, they look up. . . .or the angle of the passage, no more mute recall; it is perhaps the misunderstanding of the period, love lost among the shadows cannot recoil Permanently in this California fog of dark airs the drunks at the trough, a little girl in the arms of a father, perhaps her own, a Shirley Temple in her hand, "her name's Cheyenne," he says. Fags and cholos and uptight blondes, the macho distance no fathoms folded backwards across such un-named persistence makes the mute unspoken gesture more a con-versation about gourmet appetites than an enjoyment of what is at hand.

Or could such wisdom go entirely unnoticed? They have hardly even contemplated the sacrifice or the program. It depends, I suppose, on where you cut in, what exactly gets said among the calm disturbances of un-evoked thought, or the notion that thought itself could lead in one direction or the other, toward the muse, perhaps, even the music spilling from the radio calls attention into play; no, really, it is not simply that consciousness and being awake have something in common after all. . . .

Really, it is the interplay of the passions and the quality one has for observation makes the difference. "Reasonably intelligent" humanoids, cannons crashing offstage, mumbling functionaries stealing from each other, we should let them go the way of their obligations, where familiarity and the exhaustion of the period call familiarity and boredom more similar than uptight, or make our own distances more appropriate to the arousal of the new energy of, of some rebirth out of the junk of the present, a rerun unacceptable to the eye of the serpent, even, the voices clamoring for love's true ardor in the heart, if only I could weep, if only I could feel.

But we don't, just, break it off, I suppose, a revolution is also a return, and a return always seems to imply a death-to-life, not in ourselves, perhaps, if we are shy; perhaps one comes from nowhere and goes, then, into the world's light a man or other; it is the one made manifest, there is that example to, uh, mediate on the items of the chatter of the slaves in their traces, and even at two sixty-five an hour, they are still slaves. . . .

Yes, perhaps the arrival of individual achievement is no less heroic than the effort of the whole to participate in itself. "Itself through itself," is the tenor of the old argument, the one which penetrates the one and so becomes the two. And two in one is also three, and the sequence is born, begun. A sentence could possibly be an emblem for the whole, and even this signing on of opposites has come so suddenly, come from nowhere, as it were, arrived, aroused, matter made motion not so much a case for immutable law, the kind of absolute the romantic heart quavers over with rage; no, it is more Valery's case for mastery: out of the work itself comes a predictable payoff, that the enthusiasm of the beginning could mellow into a form of mastery, it is the same with women, one could argue, then, the man arrives at cases and emerges, then, released or revealed more to himself, and not simply engulfed by his own passion. To be in control is not to lose one's passion, then, but probably, to have more of it at the visible distance, in hand.

As turns, specific, made the same at light or pattern, would mark these shadows' names are sudden spoke, at large. . . .

Rather, it is this passionless view which persuades the others that they might not make it and calls this retreat from love the character of the period or the type of government we might make less profound than the sentiments at play between conversations, these easy riders between stations on the coast, a sudden deluge of unending motion calling out, perhaps, for life to be less stationary than letters from nowhere never mailed, why not the contrary alliance toward perfection, "but not for me." Completion, then, a more acceptable premise than perfection or death, but hardly different, are things different in their coloration or merely less unspoken than they, uh, might be.

Or does anything, really, illuminate seeing so much as thought, and how, such contradictory times, at first, to come into parallel; really, the speed of thought is probably as fast as the electrical impulses the brain offers up for transmission. Thus, abstraction becomes a kind of shorthand by which the idea and the eye come into the same trance progression from the idea to the vision itself, for in their mutual confusion does the new information arrive, sudden. . . .

And so might photography come of age and leave painting for the painters, an old notion, really, that the synchronous effects of light and color, eg., distance and time, spatial illusions on the plane of the mental drama; the sculptor's manipulation of cues in order to create mental equivalents not so much of ideas as of the stress of eloquence would the gesture itself bear down on the erotic mode, all these avenues of convergence offering the ear a line for departure, the norm itself. "But I don't understand," the popular voice whines; and well enough, they are sensations themselves, and the poor fellow standing in tension and confusion before the Rothko, or falling asleep at the concert, is not so much a fugitive from the period as cut off from his feelings, brutalized in the magnanimity of our permissive but passive icons. No, we say, it's OK, just do your thing, which is OK as far as it goes, it's just that it doesn't go anywhere. And described over a ten or twenty year span, then, nothing remains the same, even the permissive grows sour, we lose our mastery, we lose our vision and gaze around. Poetry collapses into museum enclaves of private secrecy.

No, it's not that poetry is, uh, out of fashion, it's that the very aesthetic upon which it is based has made it useless, deprived it of its sacred thrust toward the ALL. Ah, you say, listen to that, THE ALL; sounds like some other century, which it is, this one, I mean, the one you imagine existing has just about wound itself down and out of the game.

Raw nerve endings flapping eloquent rhetoric over limp re-run music without passion, the cool end of style and the tough sell, ah, the cool end of the new model, there's the re-run sensibility evaporating before your very eyes. Speech before silence, really, before the calm nostalgia gives way to newer imitations of the past's easier disturbances, a more mellow nomenclature of avoidance penetrating the secrets of the ages, that's it, go for it!

You'd hear these characters cawing forth, a little bored, perhaps, the quest for the perfect act, a simple gesture for power meets the day's revenues over to one side, he waits, he speaks, he meets these "images" in the mind and calls across to other, older friends, "Do you still remember? The heat? The calm precision? Devotion?" And moves toward rescue.

Well, that's it. A depression is depressing, that's why it's called "a depression." The, uh, economic dignity of names obscures from us the true content of the cultural drift, the lassitude, the hipness of the gay attitude, it is a turning away from the confrontation, conflict, the very macho of being itself; one must pursue his own being with some conviction that conflict is probably the root and core of the initiation.

We comfort ourselves, probably, with the thought of our own organization, denying the individual example of his energy by releasing ourselves to doubt. Really. I'm sure the conservative old mamas and papas could really dig this, ah, he's on our side, but they're as anti-life as the gays. No, it is really a case for passion and the private drama makes this poetry what it is. Well, then, you say, be comic, skip the shattering episodes, leave for another planet, call the woods the darkest place on the planet, but, no, it is the heart's woe to believe that passion has no end but pleasure; the skaters slide throughout these, uh, images. She leaves me, again, at five in the morning, the cool gray square of the window slowly turns back to black again, the tides. . . .

So a solitary expertise might release the distances themselves to more erotic, potent fantastic imageries without answering from any position at all. Your own units are practically exhausted. You called it down. Repose. No names have graced this, uh, penitent vocabulary. There is recall among the natives, and these less primitive forms of storytelling do manage to imitate the energies of the cosmic relationship, one and two and three, but we've been around and back and forth, it's the lack of cause from the neuter that bothers the main thrust of the culture, the seed and the egg do have to coexist, the child be born again to a more homuncular status, lost in the mail, perhaps, but no accusations call the rage evidence itself that such calm convention should be overthrown, dig on that! I never asked to be legitimized, you know, only acknowledged as the person I am, a self-soul driven along the shore, follower of the hermetic balance, paternal, smoked-out, retired within the line of the argument itself, even the hard sell implies a confrontation of energies constantly taking place within the sphere of action, look out, another voice. . . .

Ah, the housepainter leans back, reaches over across the porch for his dark San Miguel, looks up at the porch ceiling, yes, it'll need another coat of paint, I'll have to wait an hour for this, this stuff to tack up, and then lay on another stippled bunch of liquid plastic. Champagne white, out of tin bucket (when will they be plastic), into the tin tray and outer, after, other, over, drawn thin fine shiny the day's drops splattered on his glasses wiped across his brow, brush in teeth or stuck in pocket, credentials to the solitary mode, "Well, anyone can paint," and that's the point of relief, the unarguable meatball discourse of interchangeable positions, he leans across the porch and picks up the dark San Miguel again, moves the ladder over there, drops the roller down onto the tray, puch puch, up in the air a little dance, a letter in the mail to Wally about how lonely he is he hasn't heard from his kids in two months, how long, he asks, the night they did two hundred dollars worth of cocaine, ended up all night the forty year old lady's house on the hill, a nice looking old lady, big tits, tight T-shirt with "PRIMO" on it, bikini pants, good meat. . . .

What seems passion eases into morning's light askew, aside these angles the music flows below your arms are open, opened into the sea-sons of the year. I met them here and there across the years, poets in retreat, even the younger men choosing a life style for their art and energy which was, admittedly, passe, myself as well, and why? At the top of the line, poetic ecstasy, the headiest excursion into the cosmic-trance-dance, alchemic relations between cabala signs, light emanating from the line itself and more: in the attitude of styles, one found historically a grace of tension inherent in the forms themselves, of course, but the other-worldly escape from the mundane world of the great failure of the love ethic meant that one chose either to fall out from the pursuit itself or to make the experiment entirely within the realm of one's own personality: thus in an age without examples, the craft, a wooden boat set loose upon the waters of the spirit, the craft might be coaxed into return. How many readings did one go to. . . .

The excitement of the moment of the poem itself denied in the lax coolness of the reading. The poet attempted to give voice to the drama, the battleground of the measure of composition; he says, uh, I was sitting in my VW bus in the suburbs of Boston with a hangover when these lines "came to me", tweedy or stoned, it's all the same, one could hardly approximate the gut and bowel, throat-yell and psychic clamor, the triumph of the act in its very resonance, and so dissolve into self talk. But no, that was not the inheritance or the tradition, neither gave sense or passion to the actual triumph of the seed of light bursting in one's head, Flash! and moving quick at flesh-speed across the moment of the act, this monument to the success of one's passion, one dropped back into the cool depressed silence of the rimless glasses' glare of the audience. He wanted to say, This! here, a man's voice speaking out through the trance and emblem of the words themselves. No, the audience had been neglected, it had grown dumb.

And so the esoteric retreat of the line and measure into either obscure and personal, uh, situations, or the simplification of energy into, the image itself, devolved to an artistic heresy with passion downgraded; well, no wonder the erotic collapsed into the pornographic, or to be more specific, the expansive and inclusive retreated into the repetitious. But the failure of poetry to sustain itself has been, really, beaten to death, pissed on, and one would cease blaming the mode for its lack of integrity, it's uh, professionalization, specification, and wonder, perhaps, ask, perhaps, how the origins of the craft could become so removed from the cultural dialogue. And it is probably more closely allied to the religious atmosphere of the age: only certain acceptable stances are permitted, not because we are slaves, exactly, that's where we end up; really, the retreat from passion creates a dilution of force, as what was once central to the idiom of man's speech dissolved before the expansion of the secular universe, as the poem becomes the clerical accounting of attitudes. . . .

Rather, the states of being find their precise expression only in the poem. A broad enough position to enable retreat: as consciousness and the mind come into correlation with their related speeds, the speed of light is no mere matter of metaphysical calculation. Really, it is the voice in pursuit of the speaker, it is the release of the seed into the egg of the brain carries the matter forward, and where fraud succeeds with its imitation of success, so too do the mystical equivalents of the psychic glue dissolve to old wive's tales, really, the priests are allowed only those truths which the ladies would share around the ovens while baking bread in the communal kitchen. . . .

But this is quick and passionate. There is no calm embrace to the period, it is nearing the end of the night at last. Rather, it is the spirit itself demands this information out of its own instinct for survival. Poetry, we find, is necessary to the success of the species, and not in the moment of the episode itself, as Olson holds, nor in the activity of the trance as Gertrude holds. . . .

The Breakthrough itself leads directly into the Trance, and they both are responses to personal tension from within the sphere of action. The soul embraces abstraction; the growth of the spirit is in a direct line toward those simplifications which permit the growth of the heart's energies toward, then, completion, or death, or perfection, whichever word you want, they are interchangeable. And so the militant macho radical of poetry is yet to be expressed, and like any voice made visible after long suppressed days and nights of no-response, he comes boiling out after the career denied by the failures of the age, ah, then, there is this distinction between quality and instruction, he leaves the day's forgiveness unshattered, he calls the others forward to realize the specific nature of the absence: Look! It comes back on its own, it surges forward, leviathan beaches on some unlikely, heathen shore, takes root in what was already there, they are hungry, this almost forgotten pioneer race at the front edge of the world's last thrust, orobouric.

And so, look out! It comes all of a sudden, the revival of the poem is imminent, all one has to do is listen with the heart's eye, energy itself surges out with the sudden intensity of a fire-storm on the sun, the cosmic circle finds completion in a man, in an event, anyone can step forward into this new intensity of attention in which language and music, emotion and passion, consciousness and vision unite into this new atmosphere of genius. Ah, the final hype, from the hip. The machinery is there, the satellites blipping across the heavens, only the channels, the world's neuro-biology, it is empty and latent. Where are the pictures? Where is the ceremony of the energy-transmission, where is the sudden flesh-flash of light from within the person himself says, yes, you are, here, into sudden fissionable contact with the various parts of the psychic body, that's what the poem is, it is this, uh, moment of speech when the fusion occurs, it is the monument of the Great Light, he soars free and clear, from the chrysalis of bondage, free flight. . . .

(pause)

At the quick rush of the breakthrough, light pauses at the center of the diagram. The poem is the man's realm. The alchemist is also partly the cowboy in the heavens on his winged beast. All nations dissolve into some unity at the face of it. Really, it is the final, civilizing rush, the last rerun of doubt before an order presents itself on its own. There are no secret agents, only a legion of gardeners and housepainters. Even money is gone. We are all hungry for the food of the spirit, this paradise from the center of the diagram, sunlight evaporating the hydro-carbon mists from the planet Jupiter.

Yes, even the poisonous mists release themselves. We wear out our shoes as the circumference of the village withdraws to a larger angle of repair. All day he paints windows, laughing to himself. The twenty year drift into the cosmic density comes to an end with an unexpected rush of confidence, from nowhere, he rides up on his horse, at the last round of the archery competition, he shoots one arrow, hits the center, takes the prize and leaves, having never uttered a word, it is that arena, it is that gesture, long forbidden. . . .

In the museum of religious attitudes there is the modest accusation, direct and personal. He walks along another beach with his son, they call the day another perfect hour together. They have not eaten for three days. Their horse is dead. There are no messages at the house, old newspapers and Chinese treasures come in the mail. The music from the radio is repetitious, even though there is no one in the room.

His clothes are worn out. A box full of paint-brushes sits by the door. Nothing has changed, yet. And perhaps it is photography, finally, that creates the miracle. They speak to no one. There is a cool clamoring in the streets, a barely suppressed rage and hunger.

There is bread, of course, and the long line out from the top of the mountain. Years ago they made that journey upwards, through the white light of reversal into some retreat filled with ferns and dogs and small rivulets of clean clear water seeping down to the final encampment. Perhaps love's original agony was not sensual at all: the body's centers in the stomach, chest and head all turn roseate munificence patterning the day's forward moment. . . .

The stillness of the day is the passion of the age: make no waves, Ah, but the big one comes up out of the body's centering clamoring insistence after being itself, the seed and the egg. They all speak, mutteringly at first motive and recall, they rush hungrily after it, they want what they think is both a taboo and a secret. In fact, they have hardly begun to conceptualize its existence, "a wild and intractable people," only recently arrived into the sphere of action.

They expected the priests to be as calm and acceptable as they have become even to themselves. Hardly radical. I mean, why not remain just as I am, mortal, likely, predictable, ah, the bell shaped curve itself falling into disrespect. Worldly satisfaction, that is the goal of the mundane poem, dissolution of the cosmic ideal, wha, you've got to be more clearly, uh, whatever you're talking about, it's all new to me, I've hardly even begun to think at all, after all, and the litany is established, all too quickly removed, the clothing from around the body, scientists peering at the shroud, no, it's unexplainable, they agree, yes, it cannot exist at all. . . .

But passion declares the unexpected as, uh, fair game, one could coax the unaccountable from its realm, the cave made safe, the world made monumental, habitable, the conscious monologue entirely out of hand, off key, out of character. The universities are closed. The houses are collapsing under the bare weight of their inhabitants. It is the moment, perhaps, for new cities, one might take his wife and children and, just, split for the mountains before fires and famine break the old cities out of their final, static insistence. Of course, then, everything all at once. He calls them forward, Fox, Dove, Eagle, Bear, the followers of the clan. What do you expect? They don't answer, at first, there is no language, out of the intimate and personal compulsion to protect, yes, before the gasoline runs out, all the Winnebagos collect in circular patterns at various final water holes, and it is the poets who organize the settlers into their respective categories, according to physical size and personal distinction, something presents itself for survival, it has not been so very long, then, since these aptitudes prevailed as, uh, useful and necessary, really, it is the realm revived. . . .

Slow calls the iron across today, a newer climate has the distance largely surf, or friends, a pole and rhythm, the fat old man ringing the bell as the cars bounced through the liftgate, over the tracks, one, two, three, four, he'll never be the same, one thought, quaint memory, the angle of your disposition interior, outer, other, a new post and rail, her face a mile or so away in fantasy, you spoke quieter lines across the sentient beings solid or collapsed, a calm rhetoric set by eases clipped your shadow famous, shortened, spoken to the words themselves easing off the coastal waters shining shores at room and kink, her set, spoke. . . .

The photographs are saying yes or no, marking time along the coast in frisbee waters set sail along the warning showers shattered; at large, they say, these songs are also new, seeing the light behind your eyes is also new, a marker spinning centers have the air immense and calculated, here, alight or smoother, they said these things all night. . . .

Within the field of action, the laws permeate the substance of the act; or, the whole affair is set and turn, the apostolic future of the sentence itself, a rhythm of the air's denial, permeating the line around your body, sense and portion all along the waves at shore and calm your houses ringing foreign hours raveled leaning to the signs along the way and term: really, they shaped up for the hours, strung-out, fathomed, a purple motion broken showers meeting less than perfect hours calm repeating motives, "ultimate success," the pasture at heaven's edge, waiting, cheered-up, shoved along the room and sentence, she comes from somewhere far away like a reminder of the moon's moods, you are, or set between these edges, a rope or hazy outline, motive and stain, the claw along the ocean's floor was clinging out and spoken forward, ease along these private hours collapsed data, the root between her eyes, a spot or movie, magic mountain, master: rock along the day, gather stones, watch snow falling sudden after markers shorter comes a mouthful, strings, repeated. . . .

Less into, uh, intrigue than romance, the present situation, the illumination of the photograph itself, the markers left along the shore and season, have you half way across, feet still in both worlds, watering the tight bermuda grass lawn, pictures of Montana on the wall have tugged at the leavings of your own mind transposed arcs of association within the mode of particular eras subside in life toward the city in its open resonance, an angle or mark; or you'd say "ease off" and let the speakers have their day, the forms of speech settled down along your face facing forward athletic embrace has her sighing laughter a motive in the early morning light excessive seriousness even about, uh, pleasure a salient surprise would call the stream a trickle at no surf high enough to play the hours quite quiet, newspapers shuttled sudden harder moons are less than perfect between the hours moving one or two among them, costumes on the beach less and less: or move them back and forth no expertise left untapped is a mood you might restore within the heart's lines, slow, thoughts do not go beyond the present situation, slow or stopped, the foot half-hesitant up-rised or laid among the sentence. . . .

She called the hours motives in themselves, spaced-out, lost along the shore no calm nostalgia submits them silent shore and fathoms drifting the same, yes, as the one who called these streets your own another time was, there, without return, or re-run lives they went straight out and perfect runs along the foothills, the spirit itself another amazing grace and dinner, ha! left solid, part and passion thorough set them back and forth again against these repetitions, and the photograph, up from cool waters in the tray, play of light from foreign elements at four by five and cooling out in the trays, drying time under brush at elbow, he spoke them silent at last, the works working smoother signs are also songs below her heart or arms a friendly smile from next door would be a newer mode around your hair and cutting edge, the eastern letters slow to arrive, a fantasy, perhaps, is the season of the sentence unwound before the light breaks out to say "here", and pull her clothes off in the light, smooth, there, wet, cleft and reason, pale pole driving home at honor's game no frivolous attitudes left around the bend and bending over. . . .

Such as they are, speaking lines in the code of the dramatic moment. It turns out that common speech is really the simplest way of voicing the alarm. Of course, one could resort to enthusiasm or anxiety to color the affectations of his voice, asking for attention, powering forward. Is there any threat, after all? A threat is the distinction of the change, and where one man might argue that any change is a change for the worse, another might perceive in the balancing of forces inherent in the scope of the trial itself a pretentiousness, though the evidence is meant to speak for the situation out of obvious-ness. There are the natural cues, first, attending, arousal, possession; calmly waiting in the pit, the book says this morning, the reports are mixed, really, there is no sure movement either forward or backward. "Like Jackson Pollock," George said, "Or Bridget Riley," he popped. George shook his head. But the realities are equally indistinct. Danger there is, one can feel that all the time, akin to Kazantzakis' "tension," an ultimate feeling that life leads toward death. That and the dreams of fox-in-hand add up to the sense of unbearable and final tenseness. . . . Strolling across the plaza at the University at lunch time, her long hair down below her butt. . . .

Still, the accusations are made all too easily, and it is just a little bit hip to be gay. Now that's nothing new, but the atmosphere of rage and the emotional rejection of the seed and the egg, and the consequent development of the homunculus all lead one to the regressive stance of the boycott, the posture of elegance on her face at the edge of the curb across the street, waiting for the light to change, her white button down the front dress opened top and bottom, a thirty-two year old lady, and, really, very fine thin body, her breasts apparent between herself and the crisp edges of her dress. She had her hand in the hand of a man, air blown hair modishly breezy, his white shirt handsome face and European slacks easily fit the scene. As they stepped off the curb, I moved to the outside, of course, to pass her rather than him, give eyes. I give him eyes, we connect, his bounce off left; I get into hers, who's towing who, I ask, it is she leading him, and that's wrong. Simple. The man leads, the lady follows, but that's not cool, really, it's cool for the man to let the lady lead, a handjob at the drive in, she says, put your head back in place, bending her head down in the darkness. . . .

Still, the birds settle lavishly down the coast. You are no other. The monuments are altogether broken. She should hide herself less voluptuous, in the dark would come out of the mountain, or have you forgotten everything? The words are spread across the light, no it is not the words themselves speak, the pattern of the line is a smooth roll of feeling within the form itself, that should be clear enough. That on the one hand and the cool bummer advertised as a poetry reading on the other. "At forty," he goes, and   fantasizes a fox out of the ground, the lady who is not there and comes up to him to ask him to fuck her, and the empty, final vision of a chicken plucking the eyes out of another bird. The visionless passive hapless fantasy of failure derived out of the cool-hip voice of poetry's impotent stance in the world, the classic wimp located entirely inside the darkness of his helpless passionate retreat. . . that is the end of poetry, and the short lines mounting a fallen column, erect, reading down, top to bottom, yeah, you ended up at the bottom line, spoken out behind the doorways bursting through the light, a faith perhaps, that the procession of images could not cease forever words on their rhythmic angles, the fly settling on my hand, across the yellow pages. . . .

But your armies have not moved an inch. If I lost a child I would be heartbroken again. My own life this strange mixture of evaporating pain, infinite silence and unforgiving solitude. Perhaps the third time is a charm, tomorrow will tell the tale, of course, my box of tools stashed underneath a bush at lunch-time, the cadaver covered up at the end of the day, the assistant has stopped making jokes about the poor thing death has brought to the laboratory for the curious youngsters to laugh over, his skin stripped away, the gray sunken plastic thing he has become, smelling of formaldehyde, the cats pegged out in the other room. I don't bother to scrape that window, let someone else do it. "I talked to him at lunch, he said his job was getting him down but that he was giving his all to it."

No one laughed. And out in the hall, up on wheels, a black box that closed down from either side, held a lady I was told. The forgotten brilliance of living things and the curriculum of playtime, statistical disasters and the aesthetics of genius. Still, if a child were killed, ah, then, accident you would say, a richness gone out of my life, a friend detached from growth. The man his mind conjures worry, the parent patterns his self-soul'd silence again. . . .

Still, you are left alone inside the motiveless shadows against your own recalling fortitude, and the fine line of the prose calls this situation far from perfect: the easier grasps have left the doorways ajar, she doesn't listen to anything but rock and roll next door, the humping bumping grind of the drum a perfect fantasy against her open legs, dildo poised at the ready and selfless thrust inside, the to Montana with the thousand in your pocket, buy an acre, cut and peel some trees and, then, wait with her in the tent, fucking the days away and walking with her through the woods at night with music in your left hand, "Come on, baby. Take off your pants," and sail the darker rooms of history within the, uh, sphere of action, persistent. . . .

Still, they are no dreams. In Palo Alto, I took the bone she had found, with a hole in the end it was the shaman-bone, and I wrapped the handle with some cloth, dipped the end in some hot wax to seal it off, made her a present of this, this power-dildo. When she came down for the mating. Ah, yes, she took it up into herself, in and out it went, a gasp on her face, coming lightly and frequently to my handle, the gift was season made light and there was no reason for it, absolutely no reason at all, and it seemed, she said, later, "I think we were getting somewhere. . . ."

I mean, when I took the table down from the wall, there was a stripe left across the distance itself where no paint had been laid on, and the bare wood itself showed up like, like a forethought, not after, at all. The camera in the shop for a month, who shall I take pictures of, you know, as the symphony comes quickly onto the radio, the Japanese genius giving himself totally, skillfully to this, uh, white European tone poem of the last century expounding in my room, the wall next door. . . .

No, it is more the atmosphere of the silence that one recalls in the time before he, uh, comes into the rest of it. Perhaps there is no warning at all. Perhaps the clues the celebrities give are fair warning, then, the loss of silence, of solace, of the longer days which no one wants to remember anyway. And what do you say to him, ah, you've escaped this irony by being a writer, then, at least you have some-thing to do now, and so much money, what'll you do with all that money, don't you want anything at all, are you completely mad after all, not to want something at least, how long have you been poor, how long since you've read a book through entirely I am still trying to remember, yes, the soul yearns for love and for little else, the white food for the soul the mind the eye all bearing down within these more specific hollows, it is really just a matter of following it out, you know, and of getting there at last to the place where the words come off even, flat, one after the other. And listen, listening to her breathing, come on, baby, make some noises for me, I like to hear you sigh and sing, the white pole rising, driving. . . .

But the calm undercurrent scores the rest a waltz, and not the last one, either, you made the difference once or twice, more than once, really, how many were there offered themselves in some new way, it is time to collect, to hold to what is sentient beyond the mountains where the poles have been drying for the past three months, you'll have to go to town while they're drying-out, find a house to paint for Striz or Wally, get some boards and go back in there to get started around July fifteenth perhaps the floor up by August first, a month on the roof and walls, no, you won't want to leave that soon, and you should (should!) get some cinderblock down for the fireplace, a place out there in the mountains, a little food in the other room, just a quiet place to get down on top of her, slipping into something nice, they say, holding her by her shoulders, piled up, hot breath, explosions of light. It is best to hold one's breath, let her blow up into your mouth, the hot air from inside blows the fire in your own heart, "Sometimes he is a butterfly and sometimes he is an elephant. . . ."

"Though the work is continuous there are four clearly defined sections containing all that has will to feel or to move. . ." is rather, uh, inclusive. Even the fantasy itself is satisfying, and the crowd at the bar, there, as the guy guffawing and shouting laughing down at the end, he had moved to get closer to the tube, so when the rats came in to eat Ernest Borgnine, though, really, he asked for it, overdone as it was. But next to him, the two old guys, one totally wired the other drunk, talking about literature and their dreams and about symbolism, the one old guy down to here in his Cuantro and beer, the other old guy couldn't believe in such an eclecticism, but they were dinosaurs, really, I haven't heard anyone talk about literature with the critical jargon of educated men in a bar, for six or eight years, they are all of us mesmerized by the tube, into rote obedient silence, and our craving for words and for speech has permitted and encouraged the slow drift to the obsessive and the violent, a gradual intensifying of sensation trying to take the place of the satisfactions of discourse.

But love, ah, but love, largely a matter for a man and a woman the third time around, Sunday morning. . . .

The reefs, the shoals; across uncharted lessons of the passionate discourse he pauses dynamic overthrow the loose course of the chart itself the map, the diagram of passage through distant islands, coastal waterways, mountainous regions. "I wrote of only half of what I saw," Marco Polo reports. The mountains themselves, massive and undisturbed, collected platforms, overturned looming categories, reflected diaphanous monumental shattering gigantic columnar sentences and paragraphs, overturned legions, the portentous symmetry of sacrificial acts, blood beating patterning life flow designations of ascent, popular and massive explorations of dark unknown substantial increase and produce, flux at energy flow and flight, witness of explosions chasms canyons colors of, red and green the primary elemental path-ways of bush and tree and thorn-bird abyss and waterway and platform and forgotten systems of aerial flight-forms, feathers raining fortunes forward scans the way ahead is really the way ahead and not a metaphor for something else there is no "something else", and as things stand in relation they are never less than the things they are. . . .

Passages through zones of indifference passion rage ecstasy joy anger loss and the equations of love's beginnings, the body's refuge and leaning, the foreign sailings,

170

strangers and familiar faces, wives and lovers and strangers and others, enemies and angry followers, devotees and slaves and pioneers, strange habits and costumes, the flux and mask and drum, the child and the mystery, catechism and defeat the holy orgasm, squirt and plasm and force the face the smile the loose patter, the mastery of the one the shadow the familiar the demon in the laundry, the master in the hand, the lazy waste the polemical disgrace, over magnificence, tool and post and score, the looser wraps around the post, cautious and cylindrical, silly canyons, roofs, caves of assertion, the beloved smiling, calling, leaning through the air, low-flying, sentient, the beast in retreat, man and motion, the clamoring tide, the flow the monster and the angel, the treasure sigh and evocation, dark tunnel of muscle, the button, the gasp, and over all, the light.

. . . he is not a robber; he will woo at the right time. . . .

There is the dream. Compelling and absolute, shifting shore the moon alive between her hands, decision and impulse, he comes forward through the mists along the shore, slow figure of the mists arriving, perhaps, from beyond the reef, the silver surfer gliding soundlessly through time itself, an erect figure on the surface of the waters, erect and soundless gliding the front edge of the absolute event, the light glinting from his surfaces, new and known like a sign along the way is a newer rhythm forged at the sharper lines of the focal plane, her laughter soundless waves of light playing back and forth are also newer younger smiles, the mountain in retreat is the call and the sign, on top of the mountain strangers flying forward leave the air another solemn message turned to light, beached-out, he comes up through the mists, light glinting from all his surfaces, lays the long board down in the sand at the edge of the fire, the breeze blowing in softly off the water, the last big wave subsided, he turns to her seated by the fire, at the edge of the day's light, he stoops and strokes her and speaks...

"I came across the top of the big wave, the water swelled and burst in huge cliffs up-rising, speeding forward, I hung my light arms flying the perfect posture kneeling, standing turning the power of the big wave breaking across the whole of time itself, space the plasm of the sky's energies slowing forward forced the poet surfer spinning shouting speeding the voice itself, calling for you all the way down the never-ending front edge of the big wave, I shot the whole world, all history from the height of the great light itself down deep within the densest canyon of the darkest space, I rode that wave for twelve years standing arms outstretched in perfect form I shot that longest run along the whole shore of the entire planet, swept past islands and cities in the dark of the night, speeding soundlessly across entire continents calling your name, Beloved, leaning forward into the wind I felt the final lunging surge of the power bring me onto this beach on some forgotten, once familiar shore now unchanged by return, I find you waiting at the end of solitude, deep within the song of the earth sings, you have tended this fire at the edge of the sea; you are the sea itself...."

171

The light is fading at the edge of the sea, and on along the shore the light is slowly falling forward through the edges of the dream itself, breaking open lines across the floor the light is red orange yellow blue indigo violet spread across the sky-bolts sewn up, the sign of fire at the edge of the sea, flowing softly forward, she tosses her hair and smoothes the sand beside the fire, her smooth eyes blue and green and smoky brown and lighted from within the fires of her body, speaking low forceful voice the energy of meeting coming down through the soft light ebbing away into the mists themselves, the creatures of the mist along the shore of some familiar half forgotten continent, they sit in the twilight mist of the air around them, by the fire, she speaks the name of the tune of the melody of the rhythm of the song itself calling across the years and motives, love's answering line lingering outer shells, the heart's mind toning the body forward after all, after silence, after isolation and silence, after the long run, she speaks, like the water among the ranks in pools of light and froth, speaks the heart of the song long remembered passion in the shadows of the mist....

" I have seen you flying shining power down these infinite waves light I welcome you home returning warrior in the battles of the spirit ghost-wars, leaning down throughout the centuries I have given myself to you, adventurer, I hold you close within the center of the dream itself I call you back and down among the very creatures of your being down throughout the softness of the light you inhabited the world, the white light growing deep within the center of the dream, I give myself to your vastness and follow myself into you giving my passionate embrace the call and the return, I am the light between your eyes, a spot and marker sharp along the shore, I give you this dream and this magnificence, the meeting on the shore is full of love's beginnings in the heart," she smoothed the air along the waves, "as truth resembling these tears falling light and stay along the world, beginning as men do to be mortal within the sphere of action deep inside my being opened to you, damp and fragrant, the flower by the sea, light streaming from my hair, this song among treasure, you are, surfer, returned and welcome, it is joy...."

And they fell backward, cosmic trance of being pairing the surfer and the beloved, the high dancer on the table slowly turning through the day at form and sign the same in one and two and three, they call the world a healing place, as mating and being call the air around them perfect light, the cities and other of the world perceiving distances eased around the smoother laps are easing out, she dances this slow dance in among his power, mating sign and time the same power driving light between their sighs a perfect meeting at the edges of the sea signing the hours with deeper strokes he enters tight behind her gasps are perfect quick shots release her charge in him calling forward forms against the deeper thrusts are arrows of light in the distance of the night arrived at the first consummation of the dream, she calls him upward flying in position, they sail the night sky's moon alert beyond design , the call the stars a map around the reefs of darker space together muted sighs are the falling of the breeze beyond the darker edges of the sea, head-spun and wet, closed beyond time's fusion in the air a motion through these lines receding down throughout the moon....

And deep within the elemental fusing of their mating energy vibrates back and forth in a humming expansion of air between them the waters roll back and forth as entire continents push upward into the nearer distance between them pulsing light waves scattering islands and fountains of passionate release as he dives deeper within the opening up of her, finds the source of the great light deep within her, finds the great silence broken outward into the absolute music from all around them the universal motive springing into the differentiation of their sameness, and as she gives to him, he thrives on this giving and returns threefold into her deeper than the root and the source, he drives through beginning and ending to the very return, they are on the sacred wheel and it is light itself as they are spinning and turning and generating the faces in the light beyond the perfect union of opposites, as they become one and different, the same, in union, surrounding themselves with themselves, they become who they are turning forever in the music in their slow dance, spacing out beyond the vaster reaches into the totality and celebration of their meeting....

And slow they fall apart in their deeper sleep released, the fire on the shore is glowing the purple light glowing from the surface of the foam of the backwater, and where they call across the dark in in slow whispers say "You are redeemed," "You are redeemed," and the silver surfer rides his beloved into the darkness of the stars, they fold backwards and around each other, the rose and the shell, the silent music....

And the dream is also the song of light itself, there is the path and the way and the beloved intervening, offering perfection; and the way forward is by way of the opposites themselves, always moving on, removing the essence itself into other, deeper spheres of action; they call the moon around the big wave scattering them all along the continent, they build new cities, they call the ground to life, then, and make the earth green with the atmosphere long since shattered, becalmed, they dream the world between them into perfection, they call along the seasons one on one, and between the days are longer nights made new, arrived, completed, it is the man and the lady drawn from within the collective drama of the world. It is re-enacted.... '

So it was not so much watching Elizabeth and Gianni fall in love, walking together along the beach at Santa Claus Lane the day he and Michael threw the frisbee at least an hour; the photograph there on the bookcase, he is bending over the burgers, Pall Mall in mouth, Michelob on the bench, a column of smoke uprising, blue shorts, visor, turtleneck. No, it was really a matter of seeing history together, even to the point of feeling pleasure at the writing; no, it was more a matter of being history in one's self, of seeing the children hastening into size, then of believing that, really, the thoughts were really, there, and that rather proved the cosmic to him, he had said as much to Mudhen the other day, obliquely, to the girl, "Gotta give voice to all that's there"; and they had drifted soon across the cool Montana plateau, the land high up among the rocky peaks, "Somewhere else." The boys at work, Chuck and Bryan had gone "Gee wha," in a sort of laughter at his story of drifting down on the Greyhound from Montana through Bend, Oregon, whacked out on mescaline, vibrating light at the dinner counter, down through the dark highway and into California, talking all night to the lady next to him....

There! It was really the ground one had covered. No divisions! Sassoon had put into a poem in sixty-nine, into the magazine they went, pearled sure shots, the even capsizing of doubt into a journal drawn from the idea of *The Insect Trust Gazette* of Bob Bassara. Really, history and the ground one had covered and falling in love, that was whole shot, he thought, pictures here and there around the room, the rain pelting the sidewalk, gushing down the gutters, "You couldn't see the street," Lila had said this afternoon, pointing out the '58 Chevy with half its chrome gone, for sale sign luminous dayglow red in the dirty window. "It's been for sale since we moved here a year ago," she said, as they were buttoning up to go out in the rain to get some cheese at Quality. Michael slipped out the back gate with Gertrude-dog on the long green plastic rope for a Saturday walk in the rainy weather.

As. The rest driving down against the foreign tides, at least the same water beating on all those shores, she spoke along the waves, what did she have in mind, the Sea?

Reluctantly, we leave the past in order to become history, the present...

Inverse creatures of light and dark, noiseless, immense, powerful reasoning beasts, disintegrating and reforming at will, manifest, concrete, lunging through the air clumsily and profound, adverse and contemplative....

The simplest lines begin along with all the rest, coming from somewhere, that is; he comes from somewhere, that much is clear enough, and the following, then, is not so much a mob of people as what one does, one follows the rest; and the music is more than mere sensation, it is a celebration of some sort, they pull furtively or feverishly and make the feelings more like what there is between us, favor fevers light, and the voice on the radio is sounds alone, even the words are gone with all the rest, they go by too swiftly to be believed; "the style," Bob said about that old short story, not what it was about, "The style," and when he had started to say something, he had stopped him a third time, "the style;" and even the closer ones were, well, almost mysterious about it, it was a new thing, and the radio went along with the photographs, when it came, it came all the way out, and they all kept on singing....

CHAPTER 12   THE MATTER

There have been whole days, go down like this one. Anyway, the sun's out, cool light-day after yesterday's splash and nail, a rush of cleansing water a boom or flash rum-rumble once or twice on the plains, and I wrapped the fleece slippers for Yar's birthday present, next month, really planned Alex's party for next weekend. It is the denouement, of course, and certainly not of life itself, but of the work at hand, this. I told Lila in the car and Georgia just as she was going out with the boys to see Cheech and Chong (really!), that I thought that I would finish this, or rather, that it would finish itself out of circumstance, but since that's not happening, that I'll have to finish it out of thought itself; which is not to say, fantasy, in the ordinary sense of, uh, unreality, this is of non-existence, or the suspicious, or, uh, invalidity, actually, of the information presented, or invented, or exposed. I'd say, found in the process of unraveling thought, "to discover whether there is any mind there at all," Olson puts it. No, it is no more Monsieur Teste, old testicle-head, we used to call this, uh, excessively intellectual intellectual; no it is more precise than that!

You see, even the handwriting picks up speed; but the actual denouement is marked by this mornings' depression over no-lady and the book's rather pointed comment on excessive asceticism. The actual beginning of the decline of the act itself is slow but quick, a pipe and half of the last dysoxin from Bert last summer, the slow pull into black scratch on yellow paper the actual formulation of the decline itself is, then, really slow, not however, a reflection of of the end of life, not that....

Lila said she never gave Gravity's Rainbow a try; me either. It is too obtuse or too acid or too false to command interest? Is this, too, too intelligent or self indulgent to be worth reflection, or is that too vain, ah, the meditation on the present is like that, articles in today's Times about self publishing books on green-houses and solar panels for thirteen grand borrowed from friends, really. No help from the real world anyway.

No, it was about nine yesterday morning it actually started, going down for breakfast at MacDuff's.

Flat gray light along the street, I'm just stepping out at 9 AM for breakfast, a little hangover from last night's opening, late home but slept all night, waking up at five as usual and wired, tired at the same time and going down Milpas with this box under my arm of clothes Yar left behind this summer, he's probably out-grown them already, and the wool fleece lined slippers from this summer, a lot of winter feelings wrapped up in that box, bopping down for food, I come up toward the bus-stop bench down where they gas up the taxis, they have their own, uh, station and I can see this guy half a block away, a crazy on the park-bench, tapping his feet, white plastic running shoes with their black stripes, blue denim pants a plastic jacket light brown unshaved short uneven length brown hair he holds his cigarette between the middle and ring finger head tilts back stiffly goes the hand quick puff and straight out, no inhaling or quick short hyperventilated rush, whew, and the feet going tap-tap two Michelob light cans beside him, when I go by he is saying quick low monotone to no-one (like the voice on Haight, but less focused, they went "acid, acid,acid...") but saying very clearly and distinctly, "Worble-yes, warble, worbel-worbells, a warbl," and so on; I pick up step a bit....

When I was on the street in Palo Alto, I soon saw the master sergeant here and there, he was also a compulsive statue of cosmic disarray, about fifty five years old wearing characteristically a light tan suit which appeared to be pinkish, three buttons tight across his swelling belly a short brush-cut flat top from the San Diego forties his one hand tight behind the small of his back, the other carrying a briefcase, not an attache case but an old briefcase that pleated out at the bottom and held, presumably, rocks and bunched out newspapers, he was standing at attention, usually, like that for hours, motionless and insane, staring straight ahead, his eyes sharply gazing at a surface or plane somewhere about eighteen feet in front of him, though he would swivel his head from time to time in no particular sequence of movements, to give the appearance of attending, his short pants rising perhaps half an inch above the shoetops, revealing thin black sox through which one could see his pale skin, he was usually guarding a parking meter in fronting a quick-print, along the main streets of Palo Alto, stiff attending member of the audience, watching the reruns of his private movie, the Stanford psuedo-student, lapsed, fervored static silence....

You moved too soon, perhaps, the thin high gray clouds are alternately covering and revealing the sun. The poem in its moments is a continuing motive of discovery, the shadow fitfully lines the page with forms or disappears deep within the confines of memory, it was there a moment ago, tapped in to the visual surface, Michael even outlined one on the wall of his in Berkeley and painted it black, the surface of the form is also somewhat new, again, repeating....

The thin high air of the upper slopes catching, reflecting the light around your body, her arms and sighs waving clearer than you can imagine, the color of the headache clears and falls, it is provision, at last, for the forgotten friends, it is nourishment or persistence, and the flatter waves are really quiet days, where you hold across thought into what there is before thought, the cooler impulses to sensation are words, then, calling from the depths of their powers, it is the aleph of word that makes you see inside the sentence, uh, something imagined, imaginative, stoned, the latent sighs have said this or that, and you move them quick and sudden, a flair for station is newer than yr sighs, flowing down again....

It is my prerogative, I suppose, to say anything I want, "giving voice to what there is there," I said to her, obliquely to Mudhen. Seeley actually came over and put his arm around me, "You're looking better," what could I say? I was, as he put it, hanging around his back yard six years ago with my wife ("strange lady") at the time and my three kids, both of us wondering what the hell I was up to, but it looked good, even then, a guy who kept his job, and the old flash-flood of recall, lost in thought and very drunk, very drunk indeed, coming down the alley sloping down the parking lot, I had left Danny over at Joe Hudson's party and gone back to Luke's to see if I could move on a lady who's smiled and said hello as I walked by earlier on my way to the bathroom. But she was gone, of course, she was she, and I went down the sloping driveway toward my car, lost lost lost in thought about, wha, my she and her and wha, where why is this, uh, going this way and what, really is it coming slightly into consciousness as a half familiar voice was saying to its companion, the tail end of my name reminding me to pay attention, "Really, he's wasted..." and I came to enough to go back to the party, dancing, dancing until she turned to her lame boyfriend to say, see. That's how it's done.

Or hours calling back and forth together, you have a classical name, anyway, and really, what did she have in mind, this, sea of forgetfulness, it was definitely a re-run of memory, the day before the day before love said your name again against the air is quick repeating the boys fixed the lawn mower and it looks like we'll get the grass cut after all, the two healthiest plants out on the round table in front of me for their Sunday feeding, another passionate passage deep into the heart of the mountains, Powers of Mind for me to take to work and read while the boys are next door at their ping pong game, my shop-job paint-crew, all day scraping the windows up and down the six foot ladder, bucket of paint and varnish remover in hand, Ira on one side ("When break?"), Ray on the other singing Sixteen Ton, the days go by in sudden shapes, the cadaver through the window, girls giggling and talking about yesterdays's or last night's or tomorrow's, the janitors in the morning talking about his cock, "It's so big I was thinking about a graft," but you'd have no feeling, I said, "Yeah, but it'd always be stiff," he said, limping out of the door, another quick shot at eight AM, done for the say, when's four thirty?

Really, it was the way thought moved across the plane of recall, not so much a matter of circumstance as of just seeing what there is in remembrance, the cool clinging networks of sense and image, there was, in that intense retreat, another newer mode of being, how you are the thing and the thought, no less a matter of what is real and what is not, not so much a matter of power and control, but the clean evocation of the way, a sense of arrival and mystery, another story lodged in the back of yr throat.

There is, just what's there. "Just sharpening pencils at the desk," she said, itching to get back to work, the baby kept her up til six in the morning, "How can it all be work, all the time, I mean taking care of your body and getting the coffee made, the dishes done, going to work, and finally getting down to what you want to do, really the writing," it was rainy and we were both bummed out, "I haven't called because

I'm sure he'll reject it and then I don't know what I'll do," but at least I had the spontaneous caring intensity to pop that out' "Well, that's bullshit, you should just, get it back and we'll start rewriting it, I don't do very well unless I have a deadline," I wanted to be done by the first of the year.

Well, that's novel enough, or new, I suppose that's what it means. "It means what it says." It was only two hundred pages, whew, at nine ninety-five, well maybe he's a one liner, this famous local macho, well he's got his radio programs coming up soon, "When I was a famous writer," and so forth, what is the point, after all, about seeing it through and, uh, the carrot at the end of the stick, ah, the carrot....

Rather, it is the labor and the meditation on the field is supposed to make the difference, somehow doing the work and making it perfect because it's there to be done, calling cool across the ages makes the difference, or the character of the afternoon laid back against the plants out on the table urging sun into them, the boys still laboring over the lawn mower, perhaps it's calm patience that makes the difference days going down across the pages again, I don't remember, I don't remember why I'm doing this anymore I'm just, uh, doing it, really, like the mountain climbers; because it's there, well, no, more even that's a little self-conscious, one is doing, and the hours are rotating disks of blood along yr eye is seeing soon enough the quick hours, rotating disks....

Half a day, half way, already, it's another new ball game you mentioned soon enough to call me back, I spoke the hours quick doubt is a long meditation on silence, you get soon enough to the point where it can't be fixed at all, either it's so far off key as to be unrecognizable or so unique as to withstand correction. The whole character of a paragraph could be, just in another realm, or pure voice waggling out against the sea's forgetfulness, you are these lounging passions smooth along the sky, the day you got out of the car in the financial district, "All right, see ya later," false bravado, yr heart breaking open and not really any idea what the hell was going on at all, I suppose it's dedication or concentration or a cool mixture of both of them....

You marked out new waves, voices called along the shore, the water left no marks on the world, events went, then, more or less invisible distances moved them back and forth the drinkers in the realm of hazardous duty, one of the first men on the moon just cut his finger off and they stitched it back on, "but it'll be later in the week before the doctors know if the surgery was successful." The pause before forgetfulness, she sleeps, repose.

It is nothing on the one hand and voice or action or position on the other. One could be smart or right and still be helpless, there aren't really any assurances, the calm distinction of opposites, a flat run at the target, or a burst of energy in the right direction has him flattened out against ambition leading edges speak the hours a perfect reign of light is motive, or charge. Private lingo subsides at flatter moods, she says nothing more than this: you are the pole and center, but who is she? The rooms are barely drawn, he sneaks around love's edges toward the center of the diagram, phone calls late at night remind you nothing has changed, even the Dylan inter-view came off a little strident today, he's lost the edge himself, uh, too much exposure is dangerous; indeed, it is that permissive air of danger that dogs your throat tighter than the day before, the imagery from the routine life is more exhausting than sudden; perhaps this atmosphere of wisdom is little more than organized gossip. You waited much too long to be believed, and fantasy carries the day forward, at large and looming huge against memory, the doorway moving slowly back and forth. Yes, it is what is seen. A style is also a behavior.

They left the days too far apart, I think they'll fit better closer in-that the night's own spoken lines repeated by friends, your child speaking sweetly, boys around the world are fathers leaning left and right, the colors off the wall and smoothing; of course, they say, it's all right, you know, it's poetic, and that means you don't need to understand it, what the fuck is going on anyway, but the program is there, after all, and the unfamiliar voice speaking in your ear is no floating sense of propriety or accusation, it is, uh, just another voice winding down, I'd settle for that, and the indications from the book clearer here than some-thing less abstruse, a telephone call at lunch, did you find the pipe? Sitting on the book of poems, I said that, all right, snapping back and forth across the room, reins in the words, pulling on the reins to give them size, or distance, the cooler structures are much more easily put off than that, a lingering atmosphere in which, into which one leaps full grown and sudden, the hours calm repeating distance speaking over lunch, you's think a gin fizz at the Buena Vista last Easter meant, uh, a shared atmosphere, or was it just another sense of being used, for what?

As substitutes for the real thing go, I could get into the whole advertising scheme for myself, the picture in the paper is the one I took on the beach, hand at arm's length holding the old Leica and clocking off the whole roll, and the letter, too, "I'd come up tight behind you in the dark and have you gasp my name. . . ."

"I'd have your eyes. . . ." Well, in the last year I've said hello or goodbye to all of them I ever knew which means at best that one is either done with it or starting out on something new entirely, and that ten pages a day is not so very good, the rambling straightforward headstrong emotion of it is intense enough not to be any kind of game at all, baby, it's the real thing and, uh, walk on by, then, the air is smooth enough here to be, uh, reviving clarity within the field of action, the monuments are drawn flat along these strips of paper lessened, removed, stabilized or overturned, the day you said goodbye, enough, recall the whole thing, detail the specifics of the day before you left, but do something quick, I seem to feel myself drying out, diving down, free-fall of the floating pyramid, the day before you said anything at all.

In the earlier hours of the morning we begin the repetitious solitudes of the work itself, entranced in patterned actions, spacing out between meals; perhaps it is that simple, like waiting to get horny again, do you really believe that someone's waving one hand free against the wanderer's hut, along the open shore reviving and all that

Stuff? The real meatball in the fireplace is just another aptitude resolved from the finer sensations, recalling some other year you had something to say, it's a little bit like that again, and the hours retreating slowness a platform a station, a relegated plane, a smartass punk son of a bitch, a high flying clear headed hero of modern times it all evades the rote sensation of the writing and the reading, oh, yes, he does go on into the earlier morning zeroes, the latent rooms have sentenced something in your heart repealing the older life apart, afar, wide-angled and curious, another hype, the sea stroking cosmic angles, a little loose with slightly too much tooth when she, uh, got down to cases, but that needn't matter, you know, all you do is fit it in, maybe he's too small to get it just right.

But that's the dead end of prose, or getting down to cases, it doesn't matter to me anyway, it's more a case of getting there one way or the other, or, lately, of making choices in the realm of, well, then, what do you want, whew, just another day is calming down the near hysterical voices of solitude and forgiveness, it is something new or lambent or stricken from the air, a smooth light lingering lately fallen across the day, a beginning at least here the sea again has drawn aside or parted, or perhaps withdrawn, there is that element of risk or danger or, perhaps, simply a matter of both of us lying a little bit in the example of older movies, where, for the last hour, you get a shot of him sitting at the desk, writing day after day, not very intriguing, but nonetheless, it's the character of the work, no, it's more like something solid reviewing the sharper lines you said, remember, and left the door open for just a little while. Well, over tea and carrot-cake we asked that question, "What did she have in mind?" The fight on the tube over her shoulder, guys down at the end of the bar chattering, there wasn't really any answer that came to and held.

Surely, life ends and begins again, and that's the vision, but what else, what of this business of media and mysticism and the program itself? Striz would talk about "the program" as if it were an invisible tactical sensation of a forward thrusting energy-- surely one ends up, uh, just living his life, and that's vision enough, but then one has seen something, or one has just seen and the urge to share it comes up against the old stonewall of indifference, and one goes on with it, flash, the hand is quicker than the eye, and there are the details to fill in, then, binocular vision, cycopean vision, the left and the right brain, attending, recall, remembering, abstraction, the whole cosmic aesthetic stretched tight through personal event which is, rather, the proof to the pudding, you fit it all in to not so much a neat package of thought or of experiencing, but one comes to see the mood of what he is in, one comes to understand, then, the qua of the equation, patterning, power, self and situation, and it's all of a sudden, not so much sudden, but the fruits of the slow work growing, and one asks, wha, here, how?

But then, there are the imperatives, I suppose, the old teachers locked and somehow it does not quite jell, it does not quite sit well, one would like to invent the apparatus to challenge those old dudes, but it's not the matter, there is the front edge and it is cosmic and it does come down to this, exactly: they all ask for the experience itself and not the conclusions, Erhard does, especially, and the way to it is not something one could, uh, market, exactly, but we have invented the realm, the cosmic conscience, and there is a system to describe, and they do, from Ornstein to Ichazo to Lilly there is the sphere of action and certainly one wants to get it out there, grass roots and all, that's the program, from proselytes to disciples, but then, really, it hangs on two or three simple statements or facts, from here and there over the last twenty years, and it goes: there are lots of people. They all watch the tube. Poetry, the old realm of esoteric states, is obsolete. The poem is now something like a commercial. The cosmic should invade the commercial. A seven-up ad.

Well, that's one way it comes out; it comes out other places, a friend in the bay area, teaching his TV seminars, a famous dude, "talking about it. . ." and it's the oldest cliche in the history of criticism that if one is steadily presented with effects or conclusions he never has the opportunity to see the workings of the process, he never figures out the illusion, and he doesn't buy the soap. Now it's just too paranoid to talk about mass-cult and the aberrations of manipulation, but literary history indeed, any cultural epochal history tells us that the aesthetic changes with the times, and not the other way around, and we do get to new ground. Still, it has to be shown, this cosmic necessity to make it all inclusive and personal, and again, it comes down to a few possibly radical attitudes, that the work itself must include the states of elevation and approach within the perceptual qualities of the act, it's all there, any time you cut into it, the seed and the egg, the various strata of perception, it's really an absurd extension of the now old-hat phenomenological enterprise, though perhaps it becomes the numenological. . . .

Well, that's all too smart, there are lots of smart guys, we have seen them make their bundles and go off into a retreat or an exercise or a program, but it's still a laying on of hands, and their stories are usually all too brief. And they are not poets. The poetic of the absolute should include the stages of perception, and even the last poets, gathered in Boulder at the feet of the great visitor, have forgotten the locale, the setting of the meatball, the curious observer, the noncommittal barfly, the geek on the street, that's us, folks, that's the simple easy patterning of perceptual modes from within the sphere of attention. And they've all forgotten the erotic. The false kundalini and the fag mystics have eliminated the macho of action, not a cowboy and not a suffering failure, there is the success of the stranger, there is the clatter of the sky opening out into these parallel sensations, look! And the screens back there in Detroit in 1967, it's been around, but the tube is the court of last resort, so let's think about it. . . .

We get simultaneous realities, parallel equations, shadow voices, brother-doubles, we get all the apparatus of any mystical system of painting, perhaps; we do not get the synchronism of a Phipps or the alternating states of being in the sound and of the air, we miss the poetics of language even though the poetry is there; it comes down to this.

181

There is the eye in its quickness, its immediacy is the speed of light, it far outpaces consciousness, even, that's how we get it, we go down at the speed of the spoken word, the distance between the speed of sound and the speed of light, we put those things together and slow down, slow down to the speed of the sensual perception, we do not kick it up to the natural, uh, synaptic levels of perception beyond the artifacts of contemplation. We are ripe for it, really, The intervention of the cosmic aesthetic in painting and in the poem, of course, the video, which is both; they are the whole thing and they are collage itself, not the single conceptual and sterile sense of, uh, the head without the heat.

I'm getting to it. What's called for, then, is the image of the act. You are sitting there watching something, and thought intervenes, and the eye blurs into gray space, a transition, and comes up, out, thrown forward, surprised, a little rush, there, for the forgotten or the accidental rush. . . .

The old art, so rooted in the graces and the forms themselves, or styles, or art-lives, or cornball attitudes of being, or the heavier stuff, the mystic who is right above all, they seem all to have neglected the cautious avenues of approach or else have lodged so deeply into art-history and the fame-game that the modernism of the act is subtracted, elongated, made fresh. No, they are not housepainters at all. Consciousness wants agreement after all, it wants instruction. The eye tingles with good work, it responds even before color or mind, it is there before the sacred categories . Well, then, how do we spread the word, all those cute books on crinkly paper, seeds and weeds impressed into the very ink itself. . . .

Yes, really, there is an aesthetic to the moment, the moment itself can be duplicated, replicated, the poem can become both the numen and event, artifact and facsimile, and it can become blood, too, the quick progress of the passage itself, one can come himself to be regarded as an object of meditation, one can come to the power of the act itself and say, here, it is this, seeing.

But then, really, what is it, more mandalas, pictures with time in them, synchronous lapses, perceptual crossovers between doubles; if there is a field then what of set and stance, where is this cosmic ideal, and if it can be duplicated, that is no heresy, after all, then it can be sold, packaged, we have seen some of that already, and surely there is more, and in that challenge there is this assurance, that the material world hasn't got a chance, it bows before the superior weight of the cosmic even though it uses those, uh, ecstatic frames and arrows, the whole suggestibility of the eye is beyond commerce: good money drives out bad.

That's all double talk. But let's posit two framed compositions, let's adjust words to various speeds, let's play on the conscious elements before they are perceived, let's grapple with the perceptible realms themselves. Surely, I know the shadow and the double. There is this, uh, immense audience, hungry for the real thing and not always getting it, and there are the satellites and the networks, and room for more.

Organizational frameworks of the perceptible realm. Or better, a composition which images the perceptible realm itself, from the initial arousal from boredom into curiosity, the fixating of the attentive, shaped, attracted toward the motive of the statement, the gradual focussing of attention onto a plane of indifference, a theme, perhaps, and the plane of attention, arousal, release, the gift, giving, the

due, the dues and receipt. and the rote hustlers, the cops and the crooks, imitators; there is all that is familiar waiting to be perceived; there is the unusual or the fragment, there is all of it, the cosmic, the included.

So it's a simple realm, really, to get the poem out of the museum where it has died, and to get the commerce out of it, it has been denigrated, and to make loneliness less an exile than a preparation for the mountain, there is retreat and there is also return, a style of action, then, to stay on top of it, down to the final monument, he leaves all lands their solitude, and finds dependence less a curse than the glue which holds all men together, and when she argues against possessive-ness it's not so much a rejection of being a possession or a thing, but of being possessed, of having the fire, it is an argument about cold-ness.

So when we talk loosely about The Ultimate Institute, it is really a place to invent the media of this information, to find within the format of the 35mm rectangle, those angles of usefulness which carry composition itself out beyond the image and directly into conscious-ness, an experience before perception, and since the academic has become popular, we'll just have to do it ourselves, it is happening already, media mysticism.

I mean, really, add it up, take a chance, make your moves, the whole thing is so, uh, repetitious, we are left asleep, droning the fallen schemes of, really, boredom. Once in awhile your eye gets caught on something anomalous, scattered, a translation, a direct charge of pure juice, and the fragments form too quickly into a social style, a cult pattern, slick, new; one would pass that by and opt for direct transmission via old channels, and leave the hip, esoteric few their abandoned outposts, one would go for the whole thing, after all, that's where we are now, in the midst of all of it, and seething, frothing, asking for more than surrealism, lines criss-crossed over emptiness, readings from the far out, imageless states without diagrams, there are patterns of syncopation which speak of the body's energy states, colors protrude through the simpler diagrams of form, yes, there can be no question, the old cultish art-styles are done, they are, just, boring; and the absolute and cosmic specialists are just not interesting they are all hype, or they are all asking, uh, for direct experience, for a good poem, really.

As spoke, the way it went was long enough, what was interesting as always new, and the weight, the tension, perhaps, another strident sentiment, not so much a matter of do-it-yourself, the empty styles an avoidance of the chatter, you said it was long enough to wait, "already, perhaps," beautiful ladies, "but does she exist, after all;" Tom spoke of the excesses of narcissism, "but you have to get your

183

reflection from somewhere." And stepped out, at night, dinner and the rest have waited too long for this meditation to succeed, even these old days are slightly used, the green balls pong over the net at lunch, and the girl-boy reading to all those back I saw last night, all his feminine heat a mere parade, leaving me dizzy and perfumed, I ran from the poetry reading choking on smoke, glad I had not brought my children to that ominous and empty atmosphere, the seedless grapes and the spirit is in the music in the radio, straight time, the word of jah, heaving light out from the center constant, I in I have met, fused, the brother and the sister meeting with the mode of action the woman leaving him, included in his last album. . . .

So much to notice, sudden waves of light, the air itself moving forward speaks suddenly, to, toward the day's work scraping windows all alone down between the bushes in the day's last rays, Tom and Bruce next door static in frozen motion on the plank on top of those two ladders, cadaver in the room below, I suppose, the silence in itself a motive in the darker sayings, the empty drawers have let the key aside you spoke a name or two, and no-one answers the letters are too new, tuned-in or saddled to his sad eyes, brave strokes, and just going on, dissonance as much a substructure of harmony as the form itself, too smart, too long away to hear the old language, an explosion of ignorant orphans by what, mere numbers, the easiest days have left California a mythic substance quite unfolded, after all, land of enchantment, stories across the bar, Bud and Joe Meluskey in Palo Alto, your numbers got all wrong, as, doubling back on history two or three times got left behind to see who was there again, the last time you did it made the time another shore of welcome, well let them have their day, ladies, all, it's been so long, really, I've almost forgotten, the day, the day. . . .

At pass, within the schematic of light, or action; he runs counter to the opening surge, and continues to hold across the waves are scattered, the open doorway has a challenge deep inside these seeds are light throughout, growing out through new cars, but have you ever talked to one? The day is a bird hovering on your mountain, he slips back and forward, the moonlight is this wisp of air you made me wait across the room, blank, steaming honors in the air, a famous voice rumbling forward, and met the day's times bloated, swollen, somewhat, even, famous, his declining years, Rockwroth mutes the divan recklessly lounging against the back wall as the compulsive talker corners a lady, draws her forward and then leaves, too shy or mute for pleasure's drapes and columns, the room empty of light, extra clean, your own magnanimous pressure is more than sentiment, even, and waiting outside, the doorbell, a spasm, perfect registers, the room in calm disguise, her pluperfect aliens marching cold-white passion no one published the effort was as great as the effect itself, and went to bed early, the next night waking, walking, the fantastic omens resting easily.

So intense, the first love poems to Sea, imitations of George Herbert and Lancelot Andrewes sermons, the long Miltonic fantasy for Herbie's class, it was always the rush and the urge, even separated from the flesh, really, the ecstatic rush and push of the words made firm alive beyond the hand; perhaps the false Kundalini kept the man at bay long enough for the contradictions to become lines and forms. Pushing heaviness aloft, the loud boisterous cocky lines spread out smooth pages left behind, the half hour fire out in the alley in Detroit only two months before the great riot, five years' work went up under half a gallon of Kerosene, but then, poetry was a chrysalis state to be left behind, he said, he left the ashes in the alley, drove the car to the airport the old '59 Ford Fairlane he'd driven to Wayne State every day that year, wife and child and two or three suitcases and, changed it there, the ticket for the Virgin Islands for one for Berkeley, what a choice, but then in '66, where was the action, out into the Gurdjieff group, Michael's dramas straight from Fowles and acid psychodrama, the biography. . . .

The moments in a career of poetry are longer thought, remembered, visiting over Olson's grave, never found it, it was not there; Wandering through Dogtown with Quasha, reading the power poem to Vincent, "Charles would've liked it," the white light, small intense light invaded his body, a transfer of power, really, it was the ten year trance, a pursuit of power, weren't they all after it, the macho of mysticism, the being of the poem, well, beyond craft, even, beyond teaching even beyond publication, it was the hermetic mystery made solid seen against the violations of the line, the words going concrete, cosmic, spasmic, going through Quintero's head out there in the El Centro desert, the center of the dream went heavy into song and dance, the thrust of her body in the back seat out by the levee in the summer heat, Kaye in the back seat, wife and kids at home; Linda in the front after class, or instead of class, choking over it, barfing out the window he sent so deep into her throat, "I just love that," after Jim put her up to it, "Will I really get an A. . . ."

And gone into silence, fading through the darkness of the seventies, frigid backlash of frozen moments lasting longer than we thought, the poems grew through the year's correspondence with Harry in New York, from the mountains of Montana, "just like Jackson Pollock," he wrote, a year before he jumped out of his mind, all the poems that erotic flash of words up the back from between his legs, the mind responding flash between the eyes you spoke my name, "Does she even exist?" Sea wrote the last letter he tore it up immediately, crisscrossed with "will he understand me," and then he did, rushing through the night's quick intensity, out, outer, outest and firm the voices went beyond completion, something with seven lines, maybe, measuring the force of the stanza, watching lines grow organically into sentences, poetry engendered into prose and made pronounceable, a literary exercise and grown to power, after all, the mandala in the room is made alone, the mystic's room grown more solitary than you'd care to admit.

It was that sort of career, the first compression, devolving the hot erotic surrealistic line down into the word, into the concrete, into scatter-screens through which the emissions were, like psychic orgasms, planed flat iconic mutations of sequence without the grace of rhythm, synaptic firings from the cerebral cortex, they were that, those 1968 scatter poems a few got printed here and there, as if anybody noticed, he thought, horny for greatness, filled the black notebook with masterpieces of new black light, the days went by, two, three poems at a time, ten, who remembers, and making strange photographs, close, personal snapshots less infused with the cold styles of the present narcissism than with the schizophrenic glow of business, the epic seizures flattened out beyond the rush and flash of pure perception, shamic flow, the hole in the bone she entered into herself and came on it, gave the routine fantasy a moment of being, and then receding into what was knotted until Dean untied it in six cool hours in the windowless office that winter.

But all in all, a language was encoded, invented, as Lily says, to be an expert, invent the territory, except then you're there, all one, all alone beyond the reach of time, coming back, the Silver Surfer in his realm, what attaches to the vocal pulse into perfection, push, rush, go, be, and the poems, day by day, filling box after box, book after book, the intense imageless compendium of devices all of them triggering, firing on the conscious apparatus, making new effects, discovering another newer high each time around; no, the advantage over death was too great, and after six months of writing in Dick's office every day she burst in on him one night, very cool, got him up on his desk, unzipped his pants, got him in her mouth, off they went together, he was too much tied to tradition, the book said, to let go into all the ladies who tried to give him what he wanted, but those are the thoughts that come after three years of being alone, too long to be remembered, the vision in the dusky hours, waiting at the corner.

All that time, the twelve year wave, white water, light reflecting from his shoulders, the steady gain of power, was the recall of those early images the camera had given. Surely, the poem always fell off at the line, but the photograph went criss-cross from corner to corner the diagonal appendices to the whole space left him weakened intense but weakened by the flat iconic vibrations in the corners, look in the corners and find another newer sort of poem, the pictures of windows that went on for three years, only to be printed out, put into an orange box and left with George in Detroit.

I mean, the photographs had presence, where the poems had power. Maybe it was the time in them, on the wall, twenty-five prints in line, sorry, they're not for sale, the retrospective in Swain's basement in Mazola, in Mary Jane's studio upstairs, huge doubles, the binocular of spatial criss-cross, cycopean mental spaces left to right and right on left, they were not the same as poems unwinding flat serial spatial density quick as, as quick as that they went the mind's light distance.

Hot stuff in silence, cool hipsters sliding by, firm technicians, the rote stylists sliding through the grooves, either on the circuit or listing out to drugs, young Michael in Mazola, down at the Top Hat talking to no one, and "Do your thing," dissolving into his own sweat, choking on the juices of the specific ferment clamoring out to tell the rest, there are no riders out there in the darkness, the cool stylists firm up the territory for the new ground, it opens out for the new age inevitably forces its way in, as gentlenesse that line permits occlusion, the ferment and the charge are lines aligned by time the sense the sense that you are within the realm of action.

Hot turns, six or eight cardboard boxes, the long corpse-box from Palo Alto, stuffed hurriedly into Wally's warehouse in Mazola the few weeks before he left he didn't want to think about it, at least this time he didn't burn them, where this goes, into the vault downtown, I left them out for awhile, surely not too long, the book calls it, "After Completion." So the hot career is more than a paragraph unwinding in silence, it is the writer's category, the poems rushed out day after day, year after year, where are you now, sweet lady muse, your cries satisfying every fantasy, Sea said in the last letter, but does she exist? At all? And standing there as you work, at the foot of the ladder Tom said, crying out, "Hurry up. . ." as cool as the diagrams you presuppose in sense, in darkness, the urge and pleasure singing out the day is let alone, arrived, intense and personal from Michigan flats or Greek islands the California desert in the high Montana mountains, stuffed into the warehouse, essay and psalm, uncovered, stashed, stacked, plunged in within the fantasy that poetry should be the realm of action it once was, not this, uh, museum of attitudes, where are Milerepa's hundred thousand voices now? Huya!

The wing and sentence, the television around the corner, the bar in time for the series, the owner comes in and accuses the girl at work of being stoned, she gets real hot and, just walks out, quits, just what he wanted.

Even so, you don't remember, it is just too far away to remember, and the simpler voices of these old, entrenched teachers is a sounding, the crazy voice in the backyard, or up on the ladder, scraping all day, down the side of the building under the shade of the eucalyptus trees, flakes of paint chips flying into his hair, his pockets, up the ladder with the scraper (a new blade at last), the wire brush, puttying windows, getting ready for the other guys, two days behind them. Clear stillness of Montana streams, the water swirling light around the rest of it, up the Jocko in the summer sunshine, trying to get the tent up by the stream, trying with Jody, trying to make it work, he loved her so much, such a lady his craziness in the way, after all, and gone away into this, silence between lives, he waits at black scratch on yellow paper the days go out against the room you left behind all of it or some of it or the rest of it, where are you new, seaside and wet against the air, now, resting, filling your heart, again, she comes around. . . .

The point of all this, after all, a personal learning, the extreme narcissism of the age, a reflection of something, anyway, would apply to what? It is the character of the aesthetic to build on the remnants of the old view, of the past, of what has passed, of what is now obsolete, but still the old corny Keane-eyes stare forth, on twenty three year old faces, or on the street, sixties reruns of old drop-out winos, loser-styles, no, there's more to it than that there's more going on than the safe old return to what was there before, since the old minority thinks it has all gone away, ah, whew, they finally look like they used to, and the bare finality of smooth sentences, no it is no longer the same, and the palpable distance pertains even over the gasps of distance, of something remaining changed. It is a matter of disguise, but the distance remains.

Simply, the subject is consciousness, aware of aware, the same reflective pool of unknowing constancy is still repeated, and these themes of bird or concept are new-drawn against the constancy of what has been defined not so much as history but as the bare perceptual mode, driven forward, intense and personal. . . .

The style of the piece is fitful, extreme. There are plenty of words. It all feels OK; I mean, reels around and stabilizes at this moment, he fools around. There are different voices making the center. The varieties of pace and pitch all imply the flat sameness of conscious behavior, it could be tested, a numerical scan of opposition. Space warps to distance, the rabbits running out into the headlights the midnight Nevada darkness highway, Whump! Whump! they didn't make it through the headlights, all night we drove, Beethoven's Fifth spread them out on the highway, tiny brains, photo tropic.

Everything pulls against the even flow. That is our uniqueness, our specific separation. The male of consciousness at the female of unconsciousness, mind and the dream, and the tension that is between them is art, it is erotic, the flow up the spine is the prostate current, the seed and the egg. The current runs along the line; it is the time of seeing, it is the open image, it is even the Penthouse middle finger lady at rest, a passive sensual outer, the library of distinctions, no ball games. Or is it that simple? Every variation from the absolute is an individual case, and the cosmic attitude is also all inclusive, they shallowed out these rote fathoms still reminding.

So he is empty between the eyes. Concurrent trance states declare the motive not to get high but to perceive the sameness of the moment. She loosens her clothes, then, she pulls it apart, the voice behind your ear is not just another silence made visible, it is the cosmic expression of rhythms mounting into, uh, picture and scene, the room grown bearable, the clown show ending its third week, you spoke too soon, like this, a macho foolishness, the ladies at their labor, the boys failing, or falling short, we come to, we come to this, the schemes we say we still impart are such a wholeness that we call them full, or all inclusive, yet still, there is the center of the dream, or the passion in the woods, or opportunities missed, or mixed, she comes into your world and stays, sure, complete; hot, we say, the words for it are easy enough, so listen.

The whole thing resounds around the Big Picture, what is the Big Picture, they come into it, she shows herself, she lifts up her butt and says, take me, and he does, and they don't know it, they are committed, the blood flows, the heart beats, love.

CHAPTER 13   THE SIGN IS MADE

on location in the Southern Sahara, steel rims flaunting their patience;
and even this handle feels right.

Patience and the divine madness,
love heals some and takes others, and you
say, *"what war?"*

Eagle

Light lines linger. The day before the rest begin, you rise along the seacoast town a larger frame in mind than spoke these layers from the heart's beginnings.

Really, enough of overtones. The directness of the flavor is close at hand, you think, the sign is made, at last, and forced out of you quietly enough to surprise even yourself at last; the desert of pain is no single artifice, cooler laps are made in mid-point shelter the allowable future seen-foreseen the day ahead, even, even and flowery you speak with utter strangers, behind bars, the lady waiting for the piano player, sitting all night at the bar, fending the punks, your own eyes glazed, a little, perhaps, by Metaxa, the conversation with Ralph intervenes, how he gave up a life as a mediocre rock and roll musician complete with fifteen year old honeys to be a failure, he seems happy about it despite the long face. You buy him one.

As if:

the night before littered with kindness, even the essays have turned out all right.

The layers less hesitating than before, or other. You know, the terms turn, baby, voice-mix and pure teaching. Loops around true centers make this movie less exact than perfect, did it. You spoke of the novices in their loosened hours. Fuck it, Jody, I'll write as I please, Ashberry et al, the units drawn from different areas of the cortex, the Beat shit more a matter of Art History than this, this is black scratch on yellow paper, commissions and executions are just around the bend, quick easy shots, the phenom phenomenal is measured on the phenometer, an astounding two point seven from left field off the wall a reading in hand would spell the antecedents right now seem to come alive in not remembering: twice this morning easing off onto the rug beside the bed, fantasms seem a part of the erotic surge to being is not

189

the same as getting laid, anomalous strength of the cute disposition for the cult deciders how they are like that, or some less intense fellowship might be no less unrewarding, but more sentient, fallow, equaled.

Roughed-out, spoke and sentenced, you are like this or that, he said, I am! The roasting hooves of the grammar itself is, a rough sliding of run-on sentence thought and feeling colliding deeper strata of the naming of energies, cooling bacon on the kitchen table speak your own names too quickly to ease your songs along the radio-waves are the noise in the room, tied to the concrete realities eg., sunlight on the wall, descriptions of experience as: meant to say, you are this, you are that, the trance of the moment in reading, for instance, giving out your name to strangers, meetings over ice and snow, the teacher in the realm of observation would, uh, instruct them at the finer cranking terms perhaps twenty five words a minute speeding along the four four of the radio is only operating in terms and rhythms of the population at large, or, rather, instead of really speaking the language there is an, uh, intention to coincide with the rhythms of the bodies of the population at large, at bay, cranked out at last, cranking at brush and roller, two and a half hours getting around a room, a freebie, perhaps, and a promise to Lila to come over for touch-up, said.

But even the fragments collide evenly, the cool flat plane of consciousness exists for, perception is the pleasure of the senses in the act of registration itself, non-stop rush of quotients, or, speed is of the essence, cooling by in evening dress, unitive fictions, the unitive, bursting forward, and good reviews everywhere, as, after two months off, you get off and into the rhythms of the months ahead, mergers in the mountains have cast forlorn dragon-heads deep within the dancing celibate monks deep within the caves of the Ice Hotel, the sculptured walls and pillows on the bed a home to Keester's Prism Man who feeds on light and gives these reproductions freely to the eye, a chrome plated car, all of it glistening and driving down the street, custom music, as, in production you drive ahead for love you spent those years underground streams have loosened the rocks at the top of the hill are meteorites en retard, long along the silent hours waving too, and flow, piss on de la Vina, pass on interruption, the same distance as if to here; in between the days some revelations call pure juice more than the names of others hauling in the lines you wove back and forth, higher than anything. . . .

All right. Yes, it is the sunlight, pure joy, *tui* doubled is where I ended up on two throws, and enough of that. You get the shakes from the closeness of the actual arising, arising from the rock-in-hand, the double Eagle, what comes slowly and gives, your own photographs scattered around the house in more or less abstract definitions, "what cannot be perceived by the senses," as absurd as that, can you believe what my friend said?

Steam on the outside of the window, close at hand the lady dreams her own dream lying on your bed her wings spread apart at the wet center stroke and fold the roses on the line, strong pole center enters up deep within, to say, here, her, the flowers on

190

the line are sage and shallow, as fingertips come close enough to say yes, again, and going off, bouncing centers on the way to heaven, cosmic juices flowing forward, your juices, drinking at the fountain of light, there goes another love song, as if the doors were somehow always opening outward, sing again against the evening's gambits, heard unknown voices singing names as songs unknown fathoms sliding calm disturbance, come on over, baby.

Proper lines, the black ship sailing smooth enough to call the liners down into jazz writing as opposed to rock and roll writing, the difference between solos and the repetitious rhythm more like the sobs the ego makes as it goes down in front of you, she has her shirt unbuttoned, and you hold her hanging breasts like the milkman, pulling on her bags and singing soft noises as her breathing heightens, her eyes glaze, you make her bend her knees back softly lower her onto the bed, her legs apart, as "stroke it, baby," still pulling on her breasts she rubs herself a long time rising and falling through the minutes going off all at once, over and over: is an image of the creative will focused onto the fantasy plane of consciousness, as the pieces intrude, and when you have it, there, before you, is more an image of giving, or of the gift itself, a making of love is no mere reflection, even old Springsteen is singing about it, "All Night," the grove of trees is bending forward in the wind, your red-brown hair is loose around your head, the pillow wet and juicy, or, anyway how do you like them apples, anyway, the machines are still running, I made it to sell. Coiling slow perhaps outer: the craft or the work. Moving slow intense lines are spoke around the day's proper limits, snap, snapshot shorter wailing voices left intact, he gives it out, proves it. . . .

Head. Smooth oars collapse, the words themselves accumulate power, not so much by way of the cabala-power of their true vibration levels, which makes them the words they actually are, one, two, three, zed: nor is it simply usage which makes them fall into their proper relationships, it's the music! As heroes pour forth, mute, perhaps, we don't really see the time of the gods recreated, for they were eloquent and magisterial enterprises of the circuit network, they were the names of the things themselves took or taken; and as the rooms have filled slowly with water, we find ourselves all too human to be other than fallible, and as art has gotten all this, uh, play as a cult-style, mediots all, the preoccupation with flesh-over-love is just as obscured from view as medium over message, no, the message is the message and the medium is the medium, there's more to what's said than what's said, and you always know that, it's simple, you always do.

Just, write, and then forget it, is not just talking to one's self, or not simply, solipsisticly spoke, "endlessly masturbating into each other," one could imagine it going a little deeper, and not phallus-flesh, the scheming windows left ajar, her quick shots a matter of confusion, how close was it, then, really, still a matter of dominance, just, uh, working it out, but give, baby, the cooler lines are spread about as, uh, lesions of space, forever young, the album cover shot a pushover for some good fast color film and the right zoom lens, he thought, as still, the work is all alone, driving down the highway ripped-out, your cord hanging, as it were, into the

191

ether, cool clip-shots, and old Mudhen being shitty to the girl with the nice big tits, oh, well, be personal.

I don't remember, or did you say something, black lines floating calmly by as if, as if intended, or followed, really, it is all, really, only a matter of following as closely as possible, the intentions of attention going fast across events themselves, the radio just went out, came in, went slow across the green-lighted band two and a half inches to the right, as, more, music.

In two, you are the rest receding marks are left along the way and meeting in the center of the air, an un-review of something left apart was empty, really, the heart provides its own heat filling-in the hours which are, which are, uh, unrepossessed, ha, fallen into short lapses of stiff upper lips, her keys rattling, like Mike said, "Are you giving me an ultimatum!" Doors slamming, brother of the fuck-poetess hassling his old lady, extra-macho , "Roosterism," Emil called it, right on, and stories of painting ceilings, stories of Suzy and George, ah, the calm battles of the body, should calm down slowly after awhile you'd speak of southern comfort in the mountains yielding in sports attire, ho-ho, sweatshirts and jogging shoes in a pile in the woods, lying down under a tree on top of her, they are bound together center on center, the oohs and aahs are more than name calling in the darkness of the time you have along the way to clean up your handwriting, for instance, no doubt, there's no doubt about it, the music is the thing, the thing is in the music, you hear and you give, what goes, passes, surpasses, surprises, even, the flood of chance reminders, throwing the coins, names they give to day.

The orders of the day are clear enough for that. Calm recall provides the, uh, push into morning's light a promise to renew these alliances at more than some, uh, indistinct heritage marked out by the dreamer's insistence to parallel existences in the domain of simple utterance, a difference between inhibition and modesty, easily confused in the sense of holding back, the difference being a kind of humility or human-ness which gives love its due, finally, as the heart breaks open, not so much out of ignorance as, of, simple hunger, at the end you take it up, it is real easy to say that life's lights are opening now and welcoming here her deep entry into the spirit's body, legs are lives wrapped around your back and presence, the name a man gives to his lady, as, what's the matter with that, you ask, what is the big deal over giving, is that it doesn't happen, they die of loneliness, not old age, not stress, but that's too simple, as health cultists argue for the essential mystery of the whole thing, making bucks, baby, and not fun, the singular life is easy enough, you suspect, as long as you don't really have anything or want anything either but going slowly forward: looking today, for a watermelon.

It was as much, perhaps, Keester's non-stop monologue on cybernetics and the story of a novel about (three steps away from light) Prism Man, that got him started again, straight push of work through to the end of the end, that's how it, uh, happened.

So he walked over to Lila's party last night, a persian melon shifting from hand to hand, walking around the junior high school, past the Army Reserve cars, desert camouflage trucks lined up in the darkness, behind the Men's Rose Garden, then up the hill past the high school, down dark paths, the persian melon shifting from right to left. If he couldn't find a lady, at least he could take a ripe melon. There's cousin Mike, back at the house with tomorrow's LA Times, tomorrow's news today. . . . "There's nothing in it, "Mike exclaims exasperatedly over the seven inch pile of Sunday's LA Times, "there's nothing in it," he repeats, just a little amazed.

I mean, Haley's job is nowhere near ready for the painter, the roof isn't even on, a fire damage job downtown in two shops with the scaffolding already up, visquine blowing in the wind. He gets out of the car and peeks in, it's all straight walls, a quick airless shot, but the light coming in through the roof tells him that it's a roof, really that's up for bid, fuck, two by tens or two by twelves, driving big spikes, it'd better be more like five hundred a week, at Mike seven dollars an hour, he peers in the little brick arched gateway at the back of the building, down the alley, small iron gate into a bricked walkway, just around the corner from Maggie's. This'll call for weekly draws. A Mexican faced fifty five year old guy, fiftyish lady dog face fierce wandering around on a Sunday morning. Sniff and bark and growl, they talk about the job.

"The fire, you know, it went out once, at three AM and we went home and then it flared and ran across the attic and that's what took out the roof."

The party went like this: he walked up to Michael and Lila's house, a quick frieze of Lila's face taut against the backdrop of the lighted room.

"Did you paint the inside or the outside," someone asked later.   It was dark out. He laughed no answer.

He pushed the door open and rolled the persian melon across the floor.

"Oh, Tom," Lila said, passing a kiss out. Like, out. Cool Michael, silent New York visitor Libby who warmed up later to a conversation about poachers and hunting season, next to Lyndon's warm gesturing hands.

"I want to guinea-pig you on this punch," she said. "Oink-oink," he squeaked aloud, shrimp over in the corner, they started coming in later.

Fresh face glittered from the door, then he recognized the husband. "This is Christy, you remember," Lila sang; he held a hand and gave and eyes and squeezes, she pulled in closer to make sure, and did and they pulled back to strong cool brief shake from John.

As, later, they found some time beside the shrimp talking about kids and vitamins the vibrations or the magic was very warm, her husband right there she reached out and adjusted his collar. He was talking next to her and swung around and touched her felt her push back. "That's nice," he said, holding her elbow. But it was at the door, leaving, that the sign was given. More in the cutting through of the voice, "Goodbye, Tom," and up, low, deep into eyes," You're nice," he said, and saw a love smile floating away and out the door, he held eyes as long as possible. Quick, like that she came and went eighteen hours later, still looking at the snapshot itself, receding into Sunday afternoon compressed fantasies of phone calls and then, a measure of his solitude, alternately throwing the coins and smoking joints and writing black scratch on yellow paper, the radio on and the sun sometimes bringing shadows out on the round table by the window where he sat, drinking a beer and writing. Mike had brought up Bukowski, and not about anything but the style. "Yeah," he said, "I kept wondering why it felt so familiar when what was being said was, uh, not really where we're at," and recall of hot fish blowing through the thick desert wind he found three inches of sand inside the living room the next morning. John told him of finding his house full of snow in Alaska, the doors flapping in and out, really, the empty house rocking back and forth, the ink running dry in the felt pen. . . .

So the sky blows by, in no remonstrances, given or other. No point to sunshine's glow in her hair, stories of jogging to Summerland over a backwoods trail, a surfer, Georgia said, and the dreamlike quality of the light retained some solidness, what is this, he thought, is there really some hurry in all this doing of things no breaks permitted or allowed, might call the day a day away, in the midst of remembering nothing, not calling back, or, I'll get a phone at last, for business, I suppose, the dreamer doubts his outer references, seven weeks, he figured, maybe that's too cheap, but it advanced the program through, into May or something, a winter's winter, doing a roof, on those days when nobody in town worked, in the downpours or, uh, drizzles, what's the difference between drinking and going to a party, all these hustlers roaming around the day, whew, what a party going on all night the roving bands of light playing in and out of her hair turning in the motion of the dance, a motive you allowed out pushed forward in the crucial elements drawn forward like life-like light, you smoothed around fortune's fortress, long slow rider in the night visible shaman, dreamer.

I know these islands are falling. The perfect reasons have all slipped away into obsequious darkness, the spirit at rest, a face on the ceiling, lying there on your back, seeing the face on the ceiling, X-ray projection of a video tape of the baby in there "We saw our child, he did everything but get up and wave," intense young man said, "the doctor said it's too early to tell the sex, it's too early to tell the sex," he repeated, astounded, by, what, the process itself, our ability to eavesdrop.

The coffee water moving around in the bottom of the teapot, slowly coming to a boil. Is it calm reflection or the strokes themselves, makes the day like sunshine, the morning is all promises and silence, waiting around, all these ladies with kids, oh, well, what does it, uh, prove, dumb quack quack of the macho purple roses falling left and right around your hand inside her body, feeling around, oh, ah, going after it, the fantasy images move like the slide projector, prone, somehow, or deflated. Anyway, there are all kinds of silence, and the dominant chord finally intervenes,

194

low hum of cosmic space noise, the final, flatulent haze of white snow on the video screen.

You wandered around a long time, roofs on buildings are probably only part of the situation, and what goes by is really only something to do against these falling walls profound distances make the difference between doing the job and hanging around, like the slightly redneck but very gentle letter on philistinism and the "artist's" tendency to forget that the way was chosen, a nice letter in the News-Press.

Oh, well, it's jokes and soulful silence between what you do and who goes down the trail stepped-out calling out loud "There's nothing in it," and then running on ahead; no, no dragons, nothing at all but the vast primordial silence of the few ant-heads mumbling compulsively about this or that, no vast promises, only the psycho-genic fluttering of thought, and that vast flat unechoing silence, that's the color of it, but the complexities leave you quite breathless and alone, your heart bumping between fear and ecstasy, hype of love's codes unfolding, the words the words vibrating spasms from the deeper reaches of the breath-ing apparatus, low hum-moan whine of the answer to the question, home movies call against the air, flat even tone the dials twisting left and right on the radio waves, filled with recorded music, think of it, recorded music!

Three. And back. No wonder we express this inner tension with reruns, there's nothing but these, uh, loops of constant factions spelling the air forward foreign patterns fill the time between occasions, as, slowly opening, unfolding, the pattern of the light along the table-top, a moire of thought and fancy, a dedication, a song renewed along the fence, faces, children, air, light, the body pulsing forward, you left too soon, the long systolic pace home humming recall as eyes across the light, well, I'm certainly no shingler, but you'd speak of other matters as fast as that, and move out to sail the calm evergreen forests gliding slow flat airs the silent winds unraveling force or postern, claim, the pools push orange flaps folding her arcs weaving warn the day ahead is not the same enterprise hard at work you are these lingering episodes of doubt are leaning back and forth, hard, they live a less than fitful insistence is clearly headed out but cling her legs apart and sing a little psalm to the pleasure moving higher perfect lines across her face, mounted, driven, snowbelt of love rising touched profound clues leak out before you know it, slow moving handles arc the loom of chance, ah, fervor, fever, the absolute measure of relative madness, nails and hammers at bay.

What else? You feel it down around the center of your own being, this, uh, bee-vibration of hours smoking freely the name of love gives this up and down of familiar echoing meetings in the air a hierarchy of joints is a plain reminder that more's to come, or wouldn't she say, even, hello, a flower in your hair, I think was how you put it, and lie on my bed a slow stroke between parted wings, you'd give the slow energy a space of meetings air to calm rubdowns.

No, just, saving time, for wha, against wha, the slow rebound of passion from the silences themselves, but you are these rooms aside from this, as has these loops drawn slowly from dream to act, "mentor," he said, but, really, the free hand leads the way around of here, eating crow or pork or curry even, rice and curry for dinner (again), sweet and sour pork and beef curry, actually an intense overdose of heat or speed or protean energy rush, he's an immediate rush of flame, the day's babblings inchoate mass of, the description falls the shadow falls the aircharges, slope immense fathoms delight more random eagles smooth marks, your hammers lying on the ruined concrete flooring slid aside his floating platforms re-built.

Square and level, or lie. They push past quickly enough to speak smooth airs revolve, you are air or movies, what do you call it, fondling at the phone, can't keep my hands off her, they arced from side to side, no jive on the radio cool hum of Jimmy Buffet, fantasies of going to Paris, why not work on, uh, more current fantasies, then, will ten be enough it's all I got, well, OK, it all helps, the radios are no lonely boxes, stations of attention posted around the village to remind one that the boundaries are there, a book on freaks, really, is that all you got to see in this multifaceted richness of psycho-types, the chemical soup bubbling sharp across the moonlit slopes you just left them high and dry, the rallying forth of feudal lords on an important battle you thought was finished, oscillating alternation of the total framework, driving sixteens in with two or three hits, get cranking and move it out, fifteen dollars an hour straight time, is long enough to crank it out, seven weeks, about forty-two hundred dollars, I imagine them happy at that, anyway, hanging sheetrock on the ceiling, tape and mud, the airless flattering your easy patterns without mercy, passion undisturbed and proper. . . .

Slow changes turning from one side to the other lapses into lunch or the specific color of the light along your hair in fashion perfect lines along the way are hardly wasted into work they call you back in sense or passion, the hours quick receding platforms calm the tides among these, uh, others dreaming loud or sentient beings formed between your hands, the same.

So it was Sunday, and walking, a joint in pocket, over to see Sharon, after writing, he called twice through the back window, "Oh Sharon," and finally she smiled through the air at him, come in, if he was expected he was late but he couldn't be sure he'd been expected, as all afternoon, they negotiated over Viennese roast and the Mendocino homegrown, they danced around her empty house over conversations.

"They all want to dress or undress me," she said, the lady and her suitors; "it's like hot meat," he said, "there was a lady this summer, older than me, grabbing my butt and so on; I went along with it, but really, the impersonal touch was just too much," he paused. "It makes you feel like a whore, that's it, really," she said.

Later on, they stood in the kitchen, licking at each other's mouths, pressing and sliding mouths around and over on top of, their bodies held apart, still afraid below their waists to dance and press. Or then along the floor, a touch before leaving, home across the waves of light the afternoon, evening among the flashing glittering zooming mountains of the cinema, Superman hauling messiah fantasies of, somewhere, the hope that the new world and the rebirth could, somehow, take place.

Down among the village streets, the children playing life along these busy streets they come and go, back and forth the air is slow between them, lingering dancers on their skateboards pressed against the wind, a growth-industry of speed and gear; love's distant preoccupations a miracle underlying the formal spaces left between reflection and demeanor; she sits all day by the phone, one last lingering smile at the doorway fading, a message about acting at the right moment, beyond completion, the other side of the mountain, fox-in-hand, you stir this morning's fantasies into action, or being, and being light, you are the magic in the fountain, spreading light along her body underhand, rising, riding down along this surf and tempo.

The mood of the hours intervening, nothing hesitates beyond the air, as nothing itself gives way to the pressures inside events, the inside gives way to the ongoing passion, hard interrupted by description, even, and going along the side roads, you speak of the hours rotating between distances spoken soft along the running trail, and moments piled up, scattered out shadowed, pretending something specific meant you'd call and make no noises squeaked alert intense or, uh, other, they are still railing still hours risks at even meeting in the distances left along the signaling arms waving, passing time or surf, the cars along the highway cosmic intervention of the hours at bay, you meant to say more, and then said too much, perhaps there is no suspicion, or jealousy or anger, only the on-going preoccupation speaking of the hours spent listening to the dust settle on your furniture, the soft sound of feet padding flop flop along the trail, up between the trees along the highway, the measure of someone's speaking slow lines, the heart's highway angling out today across the road you met her in the bushes past the third road on the left, or the day you said, uh, "Intent," and make a portrait out of light, a mouth that speaks, opens and closes, showers out the finer words are spoken, sung, sighed-out, fished, forward.

Surely, the practical signs develop. Events themselves are ready for surprise in the midst of ordinary activity, even the calm surprise easing into focus, sitting at the table in the telephone office waiting for someone to give him his telephone, she just walks up and asks him something, thinking, no, in retrospect, just talking to him, about painting, the bubbling of, something underneath, long red-brown hair framed framing wideset blue eyes perfect teeth, a small space between the front two, short-like lady, gold chain maroon silk shirt, old blue bibs and a blue denim workshirt jacket, class hip, or sixties modern, a, twenty two, perhaps; this long conversation ensues, and he goes away, having gotten a phone number, a brief history of connectibility and where she's working next Saturday, and later on into the afternoon, sometime in the paper, Omar says something about a chance encounter leading into a meaningful relationship it hits him, about the older man and the girl, the proper initiation of contact was no hustle horny from the hips thrust out, did not happen, but, "deferring to," the book put it, the moment was there, simply out of conversation, in the first place and potential, latent, in the second.

Ah, the residues remain, it is narrative that is missing from story, or is there any story, really, to life at all, it is so convenient to have "story." A cartographer, really, he sees her fine hand fine lines stroke the body perfect between blue denims, flower. The day's signs are all around, maybe that's the missing link in narrative, the synchronous and the energy state, no, there are no images, the energy state comes up first and attaches itself to, uh, a hieroglyph of organization which is pictured, rather, given a structural or dimensional environment, vibrating later into the harmonious song that language is, but spoken, uttered out, the conceptual framework is also erotic and invisible, and that constitutes "a communication," which clears the lowest rungs of the attentive faculty, the design of which evocative history of the fumbling beast, doubled out in conscious reflection, double-bounced from the personal into the cosmic the mundane plane of the invention of, uh, culture itself a manifestation of the glue of psycho-types in the chemical soup and technics really the hobby of the mind attempting to rescue poetry from abstraction or silence, really, technics is poetry made visible, finally.

Spreading across song, you are reminded that the private becomes eloquent, the stretcher-bars lounging, it is really, they are chosen, the mix is spread and jar, thorough liners falling through space, love's union occurs at flex and sign, development, the well is being lined, all who come to it take what they will, as the energy goes into whatever manifestation is declared, spaces spoke you are the words along the shore, there is a calmness in his rooms where the pen slides easily across the pages day by day, black scratch on yellow paper makes the muses linger slowly dance these airwaves slowly showing a wave-form and pressure like the real interstices of space-noise a moire of energies pulsating vibrations from the cosmic radio tubes sense or data, plunging recklessly forward the abyss, the crossing, leap-snag and snowbound he rips them sideways calls the roomers forward into the deeper silences abounding lines they met the teacher in the darkness of something men do around the way and bending over the table, are you back and forth or in and out, baby, on Monday morning I dove into your eyes quite by coincidence, telephones in hand, then, the instrument spoke of hours and sentences unwinding slowly forward spins the hours swift rotating.

Leaned aside. Shot past and firm, I'll bet you're getting tired of all this, this, sunshine always the same, no visitors at all, the ladies in their Volkswagens give an eye a smile and then drive on by.

No, nothing doing today; cool sunlight on the radio voices turning back and forth the hobby of walking, the boring selfish disposition of writers, undertoad and waspish, aha, the original croton, the river speaks not so much in images but in expectations, another day off, he thinks of how to spend it not spending anything at

all, fourteen hours of rare exhausted sleep last night, the signs are all for holding, "staying power" and "hard news", whatever that might be. He holds back, no memories, beans bubbling all day on the stove, ah, give back, return and signify the difficult is not yet spoken; walk out, smell the time between now and tomorrow, or respite comes your way once or twice. Walking out, you see the same houses rolling down-town on two feet, you'd talk to yourself again, moaning at dawn. No, fiction is OK in its place, going downhill into somersaults of speech, loose ends your life a shoal a refuge another bare spot in the surf. . . .

So he finished his fortieth year, at chair and hand, the dream before him visible strength in these day to day meetings. Down the line from Montana not so far from his mind, mountains of George's sculpture, of Emil's huge miniatures, and in her eyes last night love came wet from the sea, slender and nude, in a dream of real proportions. He sat in the chair at the end of his own year, floating in space, perhaps a cool wind from the window was all that mattered, really, and her face a mile away, bent over thought and meeting. "I've been patient with you, you know. . . ." "By your standards, maybe," "Oh, well, fourteen years," red gold hair along her shoulders, foot to foot under the table touching touching at last saying from the heart's voices they sat over Shermans and the last of cousin Mike's white wine, the boys giggling twelve year olds in the other room. "I realized that I had no reason not to come over," she said, hand in hand they sat. "And obviously the boys have a good time together."

He stood up and pulled his chair away.

"Oh, I'm not leaving yet." "I know," he said, slowly drawing her to her feet, stepping into the center of the room, "Evening Concert" made them dance into an embrace, they went into each other touching from lip to knee pressed full the body swaying back and forth, deep and light he felt the energy in his body full charge lightning made them wet together mouths spoke sliding pulling slow gentle touch as back and forth the heart's electric charges smoothed them private airs no sound or music intervening pure sensation her hands on his hot ears the hair ends vibrating his hands pulled her hips slow gentle touching one in one at the center pulling back her boy came through the door they were standing a foot apart breathing slow eye to eye he stood.

"It's a good match," he said to her, how he had gone in deeply and pulled away so easily, it was grace, or the beginning of love between them long, over the hours falling back to life, as her eyes spoke, now, going into him, relaxing.

"I can give you patience," she said.

Strange music on the radio. "It's show music." "It's novels," she said. "I feel like I'm in a movie." "You're in the movie," he said, low. "And," she went on, "I'm saying my lines just right." "You are," he said, "it only happens once, it comes up from the inside, the words are there, the ceremony of the meeting," and they give up to its following their words across the coming together in the quiet of the room, papers on the table, feet and hands intertwining slowly dancing cheek to hand to lips to fingers back and forth leaning forward to kiss. "I'll finish this tomorrow," he said, "and read it to you. Then I can start the next one."

"And you're the heroine," he said, and they gazed long at each other a peaceful silence and touching, he dreamed of touching her, right now, and reached out to touch her breast, he stroked her and she looked at him. It went on forever. They sat there together forever, she wet from the sea and telling him her eyes.

They were falling through space, or rising, or swimming in the dark light of existence, billowing framework of music, seeming-hours called them names or bodies, or energies coalescing at the deeper reaches of the infinite sky, a slow confidence lingering over the details of each touch. The moments called them back, and the boys came in and she got up to leave, finally, reluctantly. "I'd like to stay and make love to you," she said. "We know," he said at the car, and the Volvo burned noisily into motion and went back by the front window, his head spinning inside his head like a gyroscope saying, center, on, she's finally showed up, like has made a move, I give, he thought, to this, I make it stay, this moment, yes, I could recall them all, each one, and I could go into it. Possessed, yes, with love, no boundaries, limitations even possible, feeling expanding out into the cosmic darkness, illuminating it' "the it of it", he said, equal parts of different things the same air spoken back and forth, he called her name in the darkness at night again she felt beneath him real as light the other days. "No, not another winter of discontent," she'd said, "how long has it been, really. . . ."

The storm finished yesterday or the day before. Pools of water drying, evaporating sun-green yard fresh grass moving upward minimal expansion. Calm relaxed silence. The mountains of desire, expressed into something becomes specific, focused, shared; something goes across, connects, roots deep in the being, one on one. It is the personal moment becomes love, it calls the future in, into being whatever it is, there it comes, named, a lady, you are that hour returned, come back revived, the spirit's rush and fervor in the flesh of a specific identification, is making love, really, with her, even as being together, there is that circuit fused them both inside each other a permanent moment, there, in the history between them said, here, and thus, and there was no arguing with that, he saw the storm retreating at the end of his year had gone across a wide gulf leaped the hours in a flash of time, spoken.

He settled back, he breathed, he spoke to himself about wine; his son sat at the table and talked about his cello teacher. "All she ever talks about is her dogs and the vet."

"Well, maybe you have to put the time in by yourself," he said in the bedroom, a little sad for his son, the promise of music still undelivered, and hard work ahead. "It's in there and it's your music and you have to come home and sit and put the hours in to make it. The master has to put in the hours."

"But last year we were all playing together," his son said, from the edge of his bed, "Nobody laughed in orchestra, and we all were doing it together."

"Yeah, I been thinking about that. These schools down here aren't so hot any more."

"My teacher caught a kid writing in a book and started yelling at him 'there's people who'd kill to get a chance to read! You just bought that book!' 'No I didn't,' the kid said, and dropped the book and ran off. The teacher ran out and grabbed him; everybody was real quiet."

The sun left some dark patches from the room, round metal top a time machine, curving metal legs resting on the concrete. Today. Long trail winding unwinding serpent tooth of fate destiny the trail the way the way waving to and fro she sails across the newer movies wiped out framework of the sky's forgiveness, sentient beings at play or outer, the rim of the planet, the thin edge wailing songs and dances seem too smooth to be another looming portrait going out at full speed she leans across the distance, the Silver Surfer in his jeans and pennants, a smooth room leans from inside her pomegranate lips parted smiling going off in her mouth in a dream the green banana names the motives foreign, forward, clear among these natives' ribbons songs on the radio, paintbrushes in a bag and fathomed, pushed clear, calm strolling musicians mark their favor, the road is paved with broken arrows, a call at night, fog between your movies; the frame of the light belonging here and now they sail across the moon's movies clarified, staggering, vitamin-teeth, loop and tangle, the web of cool California skies, swoop-smooth, arising hours, laughter between frames, the cosmic glue, lists of words at the party they stood by the fireplace remembering the sentence that ended down at the bottom of the page, there.

So you walk or gasp or let her run her hair back and forth, no gossip struggling intense the layers of pity drop away, the radio a prophetic collage of coincidental fragments of chance to which to which respond the man among his mountains silent shore the cool Eagle surprises the air a sudden shower turn and pinion, rope and claim, disaster at full power the colony hiding the angles of the eyeline lets them hand off the ball and twining framework of the air's pursuit at tail and feather no lint between your bags a fine celebration in the midst no mounting mares have foaled their dusky fathoms shying forward the reading of the moments tells you not to forget, not to sky off or peel these loops aside before their time with your table sanding hours rotating quick flops along the table he heaves aside these passionate distances with their medium angles spared, spread, shoaled pursuit of the phantom genius, the phantom golfer," explorer mutant," seritonin lapse at specific angles intrepid compression coalescing light she soars the gully broad across the easier shapes are changing quick before the eyes.

The ship and sailing shore to shore she sweeps these islands flat perfume beckons gardening ladies profound desire sitting on it in embrace, perfume, mounting cool plumes her open fires hearthed in foreign pass times, as want to remember not to

walk along the way waving one hand free, he said, two hands flap-flying the moon
across the mountains calling furiously up and down the feathers flying down the
line is one the same as cool lines left across the street loose lines made between
them set or settled, the end of his year like that a man at last his own time come
upon him the history of a movement registered on his own scales the longest
unrecorded movement claims attention for the easier hours they left behind in
sentient beings unexpressed rumors sharp the air with newer rhythms here and this
they sail across the mountain, they hold the clan intense glue fathoms the air a calm
zone, rocks falling into even piles of light, the light, the light bursting from within
the heart frees the spirit's battles sing them one by one the motive printed on your
hand, "elapse."

Linger, then, or hold to term the latent figures spray expressed showers between her
eyes, a spot and center calls you back, a manner into calm distinction, as a man his
columns presses forward in shadows marking forth these sharper faces spent
between moments the inattentive grace of your own perfume, passes to the left the
hot angles latent forces desire the surging eloquent miles return to the day's works
settled out and calling, names, the day's doors sweep you away, she says,
"collapse," the dignified rooms have these sharp platforms left to right the same
colors hooked together into rhythms the heart meanders forward honest speech the
dynamic registration of the body's hot pulses, giant fathoms giving birth in self
control you might ease into another loft at full speed the sharp remembrance of
someone new your own longing for presence less a fantasy than a job, another
newer marker presses on across the page in novel stretches shooting forward foreign
luminaries mark your own moods sharp at night the truck arrives no letters in the
box, sufficient information waiting here you spoke too soon to be believed, against
the tide, remember.

As here, below, the radio falling, the distant heights the cloud and fashion of the
passing, California ghost fly-by marks review, diversion of polar attributes where
even the newspaper challenges more real than that or this or thus, sound association
and the specific resistance a masterful gesture reminding, rescinding   clarity a cool
slide into the air, pushing off, pushing forward, light, held up, thrown wavelength
upward the sharper motive an energy rising in within the flame you gazed at all
night strange voices growling from within as the fire teaches all flying magic the
spirit's fall upward upward falling back-spinning arch and turn the twisting dancing
joyous flow freeing the sign is given, the sign is made, you are, and light among
these strangers the earth's brethren brother and sister at cloud beneath your arms the
blood valve pounding light in rhythmic waves the heart's beginnings to be the same
lines love's angle in the crowded moonlight circled around the room he did and laid
these angles in the heart the true teaching from deep within the center of the
movement from the line along your thighs working hard and hard at work.

You made me clear the higher reaches, left and right sight coinciding in this this
parallel vision of the same thing coming down the road, twice, crossover

forgetfulness, she lisps and laps, she sighs again against your own falling heart deep within this flesh and center, the last year passed like that, and passes again you are these roomers spoken out of forward seems the air again you are these mountains moving down and up in cool waves he soars the air the water shining surfer Eagle in the heart's waves leaning at last is not caught this sharp momentum of families in transition you are the sudden motions in your hand, handily, smoked aside this wooden platform, sheetrock, roller, knife and radio, pale clothing splattered with, combs in pocket, hexagrams of nomenclature, the rising tide another calm insistence speaks of the air's light beginning and ending here within the sharp and fashionable moments, calm inherent gestures, clear hours rotating beyond the markers strewn with passionate embraces, they are they and mood within their clamoring persistent angles, elbows, driving driven forward, the fire within the lake, twice he comes around, singing.

No more the calm insistences of night, pressure facing forward under hours in receipt of new messages, dark time and new meetings in the light you spoke of before nothing the light before nothing arises into form the heart's waves leaving for the coast you met them now and then you made my heart the final hour sea-salt and wet between her sighs a spot and season sailing down along the lighter poles releasing doubt a foreign substance stuck within your eyes another newer day receiving life along the way and soaring poles pale rising tides the specific shores have sent us back to this beginning to be the same we are the tip and fountain deep within the spring a sharper light was shadowed clear and center in the forces of the powers of the day the time the light the season's winter no more discontent, how long, and then the rest resting rescues here and there another marching angle says you are, the same would make these hours ringing in the new year calls some solemn tempos longer rooms have made your bus-fare out of dust and light, her softer signs are light perhaps another movie says begin inside the day you went away only to come back larger than life and soon enough to be believed.

The long line out and back, back to back they lie at night in center sailed this calm again is tidal overflow the hearts warriors say begin again the top is still a line along the higher reaches of the mounting flame within the hands along your sighs have spoken out my own name said, set, settled, a sharp focus sure enough to score or shovel, trouble, the city up in arms, arms waving, the old days have passed us by in their own, peculiar pattern, a shallow season just beginning with one, then there are others, passing in and out of view, one after the other, the new army of the senses calling out, "The same, the same, the same," while passion calls the natives forward their cosmic-trance-dance the end of the year the beginning here the light around the body favors fervor naming one another the sign is given in among these rows of lights small individual humans one by one descending the lighted stairway the crowd below a song and silence makes the air around the planet stiffen, coalesce, gladden.

Anabasis chapbook series 2000
LIVING IN THE DOCUMENT
at amazon.com

Bolt Bleu:Bolt Bleu, Jesse Freeman
Stunning language portraits from
Baton Rouge. Photos By Tom Taylor
Isbn 1930259-06-9 44 pp. 5x8 8.00 1998

War Horses, Leonard Cirino
Prose poem sequence Evoking
the ethos of northern California
Isbn 1-930259-01-8 24 pp. 5x8 7.00

Venus Rising, Heidi Andrea Rhodes
Spiritually accurate love poems
From young So Cal woman
Isbn 1-930259-02-6 44 pp. 5x8 8.00

Cling, Lewis LaCook
Post dysjunkt lyrical
Personal narrative voice
Isbn 1-930259- 40 pp 8-1/2x11 10.00

Journey, Francis Raven
Memoir in the present tense. Illus.
Isbn 1-930259-03-4 40 pp 8-1/2x7
10.00

Sometime Around Midnight,
David Campiche
Crisis, memory, and redemption
For a man in a boat with his 2 sons
Isbn 1-930259-10-7 38 pp 5x8 8.00

anabasis
Oysterville wa 98641-0216